Fortune Building in the 70's

with

Common Stock Warrants

and

Low-Price Stocks

by Sidney Fried

RHM PRESS
a division of RHM Associates of Delaware, Inc.
220 Fifth Avenue, New York, N.Y. 10001

Other Books By The Author

Stock Market Profits With Convertibles
Successful Speculation With Put & Call Options

To Dennis and Mark

RHM PRESS
a division of RHM Associates of Delaware, Inc.
220 Fifth Avenue, New York, N.Y. 10001

ISBN 0-89058-600-4

Library of Congress Catalog Card No: 74-16986

Printed in the United States of America

An Author's Foreword

Dear Reader:

Why, in the pages ahead, will you find two-thirds Economics and only one-third stock market? We can answer this by saying that this was about the same space-division in the past few years in an investment service of which we are the Editor. Throughout 1971-1972 we became increasingly concerned about the accelerating build-up in private debt in the economy, both personal and corporate, the staggering increase in federal deficits approaching $100 billions back-to-back in just a few years, and other distinctively negative economic developments.
Our overall analysis led us to the conviction that a raging Inflation and a stock market full of dangers lay directly ahead, and we then proceeded to explain in detail for our subscribers in 1971-1972 exactly what *had* been taking place, what *was* taking place, and what *was likely* to take place in the near future, very much along the lines of the economic analysis you will shortly be reading.

As we write these words, the crushing blows to the stock market inflicted during the truly savage declines of 1973-1974 finds the stock market floor littered with profit opportunities. But, just as economic analysis helped our subscribers avoid the *sliding* stock markets, so will economic analysis, in our opinion, be indispensable for you, the reader, in preparing for what we call *"The Greatest Stock Market Opportunities in Forty Years."*

The mid-1970's will truly be a period for "Fortune Building" but only those firmly based in an understanding of the complex events which will be taking place will, as we see it, be able to take best advantage of the most highly-leveraged profit opportunities. Those "complex events" will be completely grounded in Economics and that is why so much of the book which follows focuses on concepts in Economics which deserve, *and can greatly reward,* your full attention.

We do, of course, understand that a reader seeing a market upturn developing might wish to quickly inform himself about what we consider to be valuable approaches to stock market opportunities as fully described in the pages ahead. There is no harm whatever in first reading the purely stock market sections of the book, contained in our discussion of Warrants, pages 21 through 52, our discussion of "The Four-Step Trading Technique" for profiting with low-price stocks, pages 101 through 195, and our final stock market summary in the last chapter. But the reader should then give very *full* attention to the economic concepts in the balance of the book, because that, in our opinion, will be an equal partner in the success that the reader can achieve with the stock market concepts we describe relating to "Opportunities in Warrants" and "Opportunities in Low-Price Stocks."

A Most Important Point

After reading this book you will quite naturally wish to know:

(a) What *Warrants* are trading in today's market; what are their applicable terms and relevant statistical data; and how does the author rate these 350 Warrants in terms of leverage potential and relative reward and risk.

(b) Regarding *Low-Price Stocks,* which are the 50 low-price stocks of greatest interest in terms of net assets and recovery potential in a later bull market; which are the most promising *20* in the opinion of the author; and what are the relevant statistics for each of these 20 top choices in line with the criteria explained in this book.

Since you are purchasing this book through a book store, there will naturally be an appreciable time lag between this author's manuscript and the time that you take it off the bookshelf. Since, in the stock market, even *one day's* news and events can bulk large in the fortunes of an individual company and its securities, giving the above information and opinion of this writer in the categories described in the book itself would be of doubtful value, and perhaps even counter-productive, since the reader would be unaware of important changes that might have taken place for some of the Warrants and low-price stocks since the book's publication.

Consequently, the publisher, R.H.M. Press, has agreed to make this writer's current and completely updated analysis and statistical presentation, covering all the points described above, available to each reader on request, and at no additional charge.

To receive this material, giving a full statistical presentation and the writer's current evaluation of Warrants and Low-Price Stocks in today's stock market, you need only send your full name and address (be sure to include zip) to:

R.H.M. Press, Department 95
220 Fifth Avenue
New York, N.Y. 10001

The writer takes this opportunity to thank you for the interest you have shown in this book.

Sidney Fried

A Publisher's Foreword

The author of "Fortune Building in the 70's With Common Stock Warrants and Low-Price Stocks"—Sidney Fried—has a 30-year reputation in the financial community as trader, market analyst and writer, that needs no embellishment from us.

However, as Editor of a widely-followed investment service covering Warrants and Low-Price Stocks, Sidney Fried, in the weekly issues of that service, anticipated the 1973-1974 market catastrophe right from the beginning, and step-by-step as it developed, with such unerring accuracy, that we think it important to present a summary of that superbly-timed advice.

These quotations, taken from the issues of that investment service, as dated, now follow with each numbered excerpt corresponding with the appropriate number and date on the stock market chart of the New York Stock Exchange Composite Index. We urge the reader to absorb each quotation with care. Their sum total gives invaluable insight into *today's* plight of Inflation and monetary turmoil, and provides exceedingly helpful groundwork for the important pages which are to follow.

R.H.M. Press

ALL QUOTATIONS REPRINTED FROM

THE R.H.M. WARRANT & STOCK SURVEY
PLUS
STOCKS under 10

New York Stock Exchange

New York Stock Exchange's Composite Index

WEEK ENDED AUG. 30, 1974

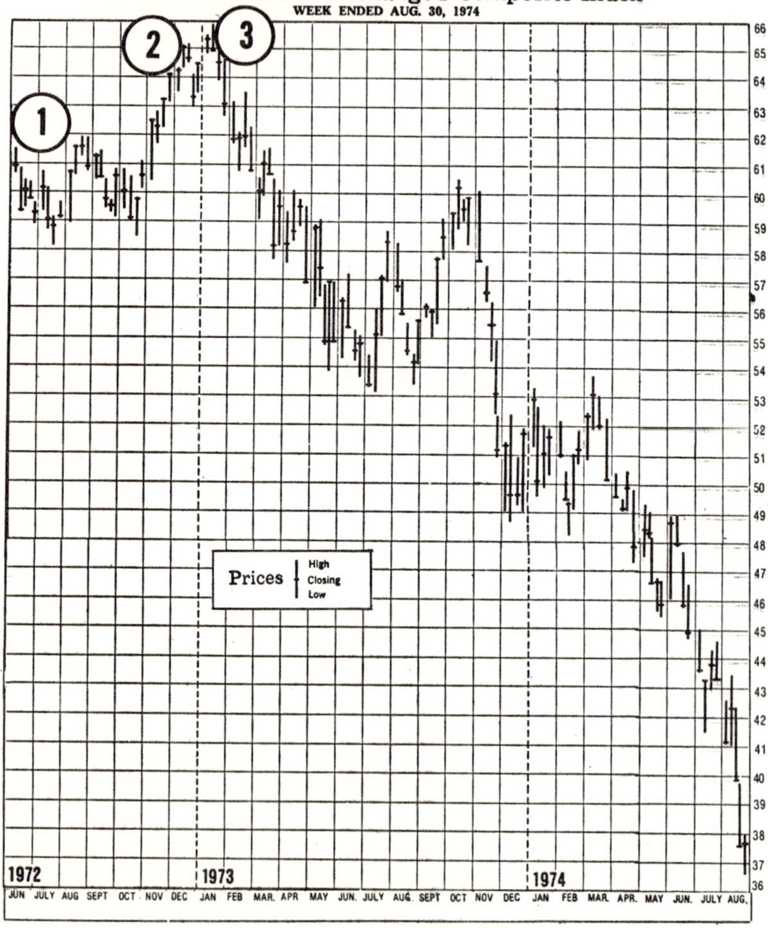

Chart Courtesy of The New York Times

(1) **6-30-72:** "The Number One red flag of danger is unquestionably that the inflation rate is again strongly on the upswing . . . 1971 saw fiscal and monetary stimulation of the economy to a degree unprecedented in our country's history. . . . While all the above made sense *politically,* it really involved a massive closing of one's eyes to monetary realities, and accepted large dangers indeed for political advantage. . . . Subscribers should err on the side of pessimism rather than optimism and reduce their holdings all along the line. . . ."

(2) **11-24-72:** ". . . Mr. Nixon obviously decided he would take no chances and must have leaned heavily on the Federal Reserve Board. At least, those gentlemen proceeded to supervise an expansion of the money supply at such a frenetic pace that it broke some monetary records for the United States. Now we have the summation effect of all these powerful influences and the economy is proceeding to expand rather rapidly. In the euphoria of the past few weeks, with the Dow-Jones Industrials passing the 1000 mark and all that, most observers are now exulting that we will not only have an economic boom and a stock market boom, but with only minor inflation and no hint of 'tight money'. This, we must insist, would border on the miraculous. What has been planted in the past few years are the seeds of a furious inflation, and an expanding economy is to such seeds as a hothouse is to a flower (analysis of monetary statistics at this point). . . . Are we supposed to add all that up and come up with only 'moderate inflation' and quiescent interest rates? Let's enjoy this rising stock market, but let's keep a sharp weather eye for dark clouds which may *very* shortly come up on the now bluish-grey horizon."

(3) **12-29-72:** "We know there are many economic observers who see only sweetness and light for our monetary system, the economy and the stock market in 1973-1974. We couldn't disagree more."

New York Stock Exchange

New York Stock Exchange's Composite Index

WEEK ENDED AUG. 30, 1974

(4) **1-26-73:** " *'CREDIT RATES RISE ON A BROAD FRONT.'* One might call this the death of an illusion, and it was really a three-part illusion which seemed to afflict almost the entire financial community for the past four months or so. The three parts of the illusion were: (1) there would be only negligible increases in interest rates and money would be plentiful in 1973; (2) the rate of inflation would be minor; and (3) labor would settle for modest increases in wages, well within the 5½% guidelines. Of course, with an expanding economy and rising corporate profits, such a scenario could not help but be ringed by rosy clouds—but each and every part was an illusion, and was indeed sheer nonsense. (1) We are going to have not one but several bouts of 'tight money' in the next six to eighteen months, as we see it; (2) the rate of dollar depreciation (let's call inflation by its more informative name) is going to be painfully on the increase; and (3) new labor contracts well in excess of 5½% will be spilling into the financial headlines all through the next six months. . . . What is the most important factor to be kept continually in mind by subscribers? It is that *most* Warrants and low-price stocks enter a more precarious market period at or very near their 1972-1973 lows! This sets up any number of possibilities of truly outstanding profit opportunities on further market retracement. . . ."

(5) **3-2-73:** "Consumer credit is rising to new peaks and net private debt is now more than *$1.6 trillion.* This is a direct outcome of the unprecedented and unwise ballooning of the money supply during all of 1972 which reached 8.2% and which made money nice and easy for business to expand plant, and consumers to go into debt, to build a fire under factory output. We could enumerate a dozen more obvious errors in judgment, but then we have been doing this in almost every issue of the Survey since last July 7th when we had our first 'Money Watch' essay starting with the sentence: 'America is hooked on debt.' . . . Current policy must remain as we have been describing it for all the past months: careful attention paid to remaining quite liquid to take advantage of the large opportunities now forming. . . ."

New York Stock Exchange

New York Stock Exchange's Composite Index

WEEK ENDED AUG. 30, 1974

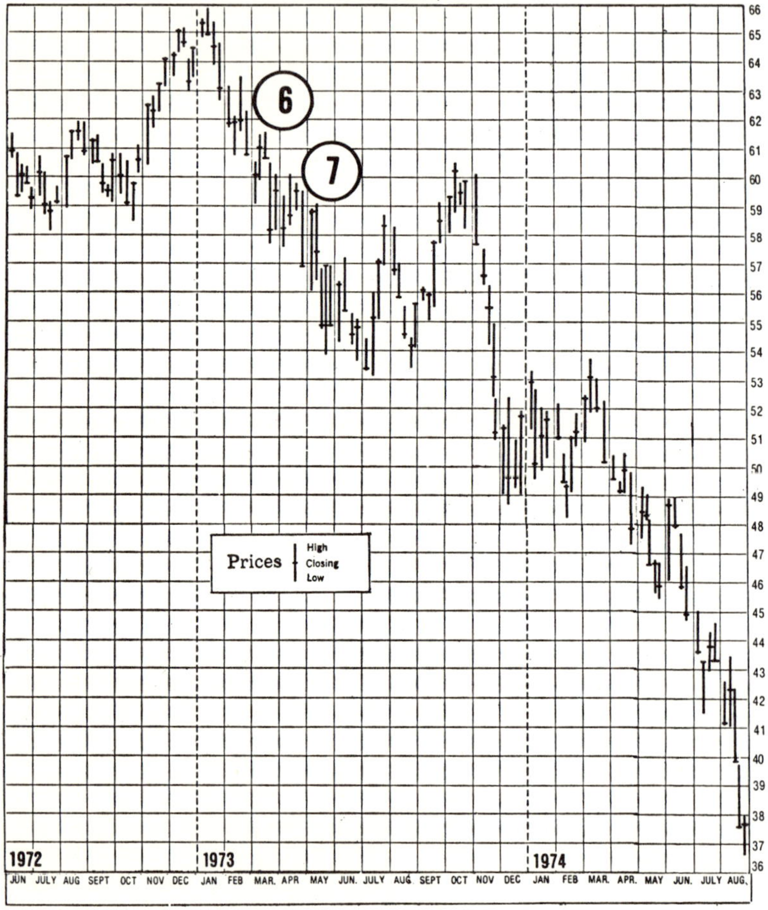

(6) **3-9-73:** ". . . Now, the major factor to keep in mind is that the climbing costs we have just outlined *will be built solidly into the cost structure of American business.* You don't hear much talk about wage *de*creases, and raw material costs are caught up in a worldwide inflation and will not easily come down again. What then about corporate profits when a *third* factor inescapably works its way into the economy—tight money? For the past six months we were expressing our opinion about a replay of the 'tight money' syndrome in these pages, and we were at variance with most financial analysts who were seeing things *we* couldn't see—plenty of money in 1973 and at stable interest levels. Not only are they proved to have been obviously wrong by recent events (short-term interest rates are up from a low of 3% in February 1972 to just under 6% today), but the same analysts are still dragging their feet in recognizing the full scope of what is to come . . . *Conclusion:* Whether at this point, or later this year from a higher level, we are of the opinion that the lower trend line of this latest trend channel is going to be shattered on the downside. When this takes place the stage should be set, we feel, for the creation of the most dynamic Warrant opportunities seen for several decades, and subscribers should be making certain that they are adequately safeguarding their available investment funds so that they can take advantage of the best of those opportunities. . . ."

(7) **5-18-73:** ". . . This writer sees no reason to adopt a bullish stance at this time and takes his position with those subscribers who stand aloof from virtually all Warrants and low-price stocks. . . ."

New York Stock Exchange

New York Stock Exchange's Composite Index

WEEK ENDED AUG. 30, 1974

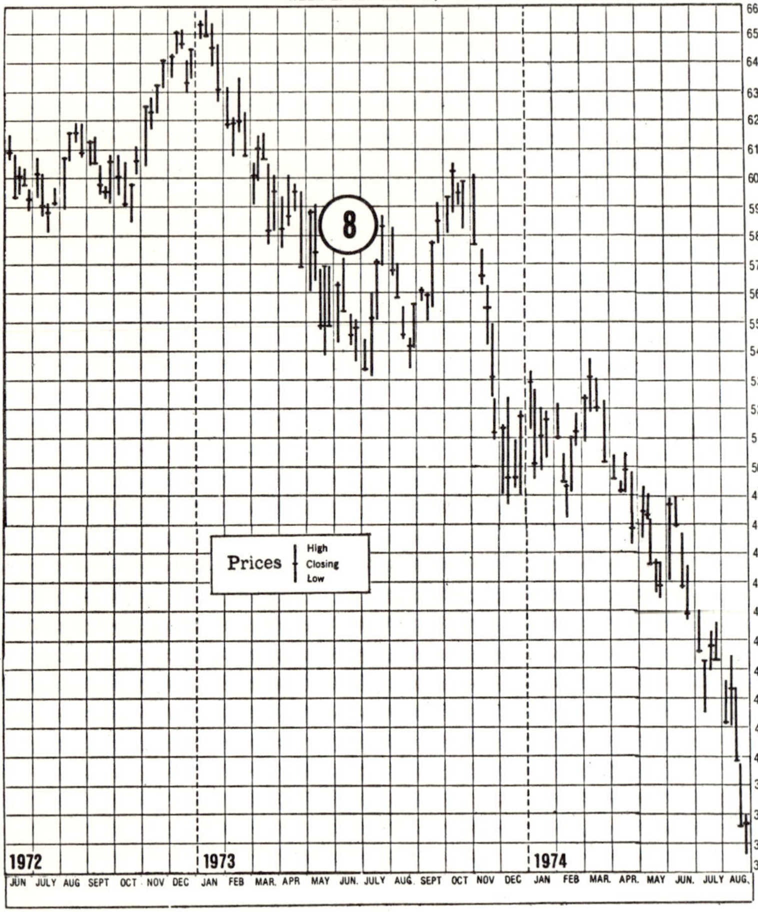

(8) **7-27-73:** ". . . We think it is also time to take subscribers back one full year to the Survey of 7-7-72 when we began our 'Money Watch' essays and opened the first discussion by saying 'America is hooked on debt.' What are our updated statistics? As reported in that first essay, *Mortgage Debt* had soared from \$36.7 billion in 1941 to \$499.9 billion in 1971 — but as of the end of the first 1973 quarter it had reached \$579.9 billion. *Consumer Credit* had ballooned from \$7.2 billion in 1939 to \$137.2 billion in 1971 — but as of April 1973 it had climbed

to a new record of $161.5 billion. Looking at over all figures, we reported that: 'In 1946, the total private and public debt stood at $400 billion. By year-end 1971 this figure exceeded $2,000 billion. Debt had multiplied five-fold in just 25 years.' It is important that you be brought up to date on the galloping rate of new debt. The Department of Commerce estimated that by the end of 1972 total private and public debt had reached *$2,250 billion* and a recent estimate in which we have confidence sees this figure at *$2,500 billion* by the end of 1973. Private debt particularly is rising much faster than the increase in Gross National Product. What does it all add up to? It means that like an addict needing a larger and larger dose of his narcotic to keep going, our frenzied expansion needs a larger and larger dose of credit to keep momentum. The most politically-oriented Federal Reserve Board we have ever observed has done nothing to put a brake on this totally unsound credit expansion but has *abetted the expansion* by continuously expanding the reserves it supplies to banks. Only in the past few weeks has the Fed seemingly become frightened by the genie it has helped to conjure up and tightened up in several directions. *But the natural process of economic laws* had already begun to do the job anyway. Relentlessly, the cost of credit has climbed, month after month. We must say we have been astonished to watch so many highly-placed financial analysts in the past year move from positions of 'It (tight money) isn't going to happen' to 'It won't be so bad' to 'Gosh, it's happening!' But Certificates of Deposit at 10% and Federal funds at 10%, 15% and even momentarily 20% (!) are hard to ignore. . . . Now we come back to that 'summer rally' and we trust we have gotten the point across to subscribers that one's enthusiasm must surely be restrained because of all those dark financial clouds scudding about our economic skies . . . the major error subscribers must guard against is rushing into Warrants and low-price stocks (or any common stocks) with the bulk of their funds only to run into another decline to lower levels and find their capital 'locked in', unable to take advantage of the *far greater opportunities* which would result from renewed decline, or even just testing of previous lows. In the next issue of this Survey we will continue our analysis of why haste is quite uncalled for, and indeed quite dangerous, in the current market."

New York Stock Exchange

New York Stock Exchange's Composite Index

WEEK ENDED AUG. 30, 1974

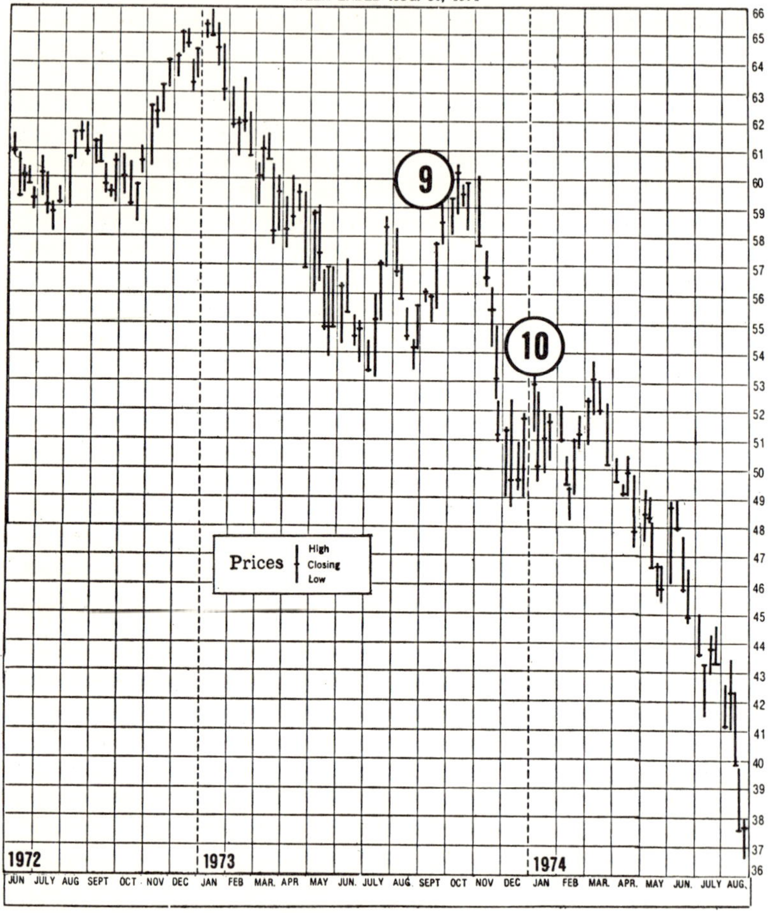

(9) **9-14-73:** ". . . continued inflation has an enormous constituency while those who opt for allowing the business cycle to take its course in order that our free enterprise system may not be irreparably harmed are in a tiny minority. Left to run its course, this inflationary boom would run out of money and an across-the-board correction would take place which would make much more solid our economic underpinning. But there would be some deflation, some unemployment growth, considerable pain in overblown, overextended segments of the economy. Which political

doctor is going to put his name on *that* economic prescription? Nevertheless, that downturn is going to take place, and the longer we avert it by frantic scrambling to find money to keep the boom alive, the more painful that downturn is going to be. That is why we continue to emphasize to subscribers that *the greatest Warrant opportunities still lie ahead.*"

(10) **11-30-73:** ". . . Now the question as to whether there can be a quick reversal of current problems and, therefore, an early market bottom to be followed by an immediate strong and continuing recovery. Such a hope springs from the mistaken idea that the market's problems, the economy's problems stem solely from the cut-off Middle East oil, and the consequent hope that if oil shipments were restored that would solve everything. Nothing could be further from the truth. We have a file three inches thick marked 'Energy' and we pull out an article headed: 'No Let-Up in Energy Crisis.' It was from the Money Manager and it wasn't last week's issue or last month's: the issue was dated *April 3, 1972*. Remember the frightening run-up in commodity prices early in 1973? They are still way up there and companions to the high prices are *shortages.* What has happened is that the vaunted 'growth' of Gross National Product is running out of everything all at one time. Running out of money as evidenced by high interest rates, running out of energy, running out of paper, metals, lumber, and we could append a very long list here. All through 1972 we were saying in these pages that the business boom fostered by easy money—*oceans* of easy money—was going to see a bill presented for this politically-engineered orgy of 'prosperity'. We are getting that bill today and no one likes it, but we don't have any choice but to pay that bill in terms of enforced economic slowdown with high potential of even worse to come because once the cycle turns down *no one* can predict how far it will go, whatever comforting articles you are reading about how minor the downturn will be. . . . For more than a year now we have been liberally sprinkling throughout these pages the words: 'Watch and wait.' We are now very much closer to what we were watching and waiting for: potentially historic opportunities in low-price stocks and low-price Warrants. We ask subscribers to continue to exercise patience. The rewards are now much closer!"

ALL QUOTATIONS REPRINTED FROM

THE R.H.M. WARRANT & STOCK SURVEY
PLUS
STOCKS under 10

New York Stock Exchange

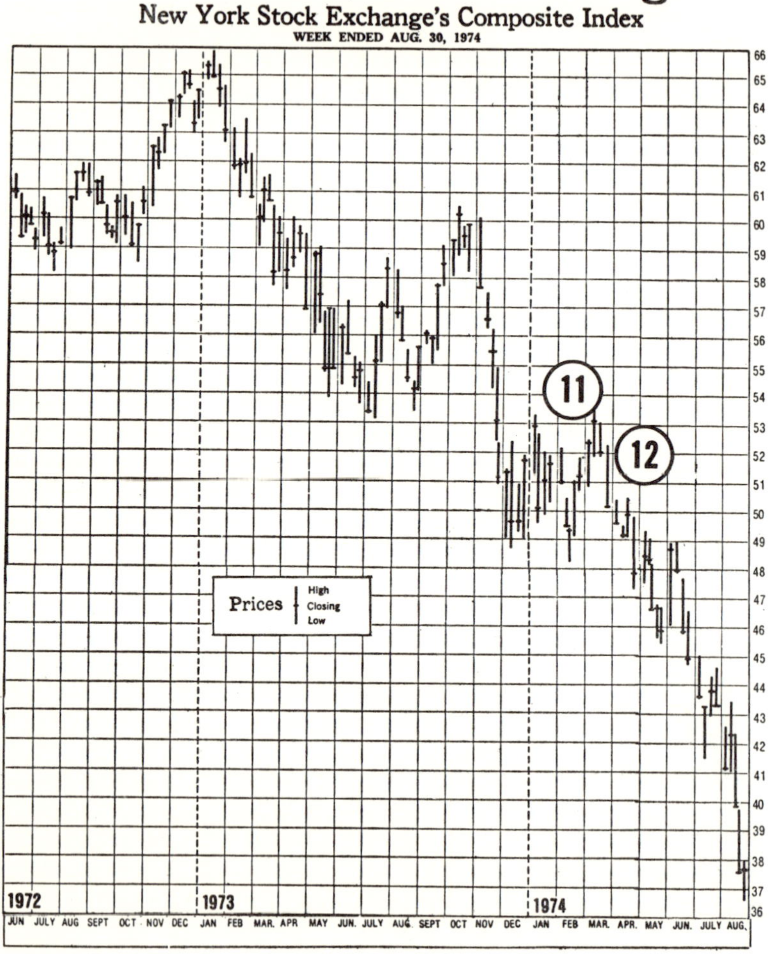

(11) **3-1-74:** "... 1973 was a banner year for corporate profits. The frantic shoveling of more money into the economic furnace through 1971-1972 had produced its desired effect of an economic boom. But now we are paying the price for this in runaway costs at the same time that the boom has run out of steam in many important sectors. A lowered pace of advance in sales and still rising costs are going to make it very difficult for most companies to top 1973 profits in 1974, and many will be reporting lower profits. Should this be taking place when additional dark economic clouds are scudding across the horizon (a distinct possibility for the balance of 1974) there could be quite a bit more blood on the market floor. . . . Flags of caution and, yes, danger, remain flying."

(12) **4-26-74:** "Looking a bit farther ahead, subscribers should be completely aware of the fact that the scale of opportunities for both low-price Warrants and low-price stocks is approaching a '1942' level. It does not matter that the 'Averages' are much higher than they were in that year. Thousands of stocks and hundreds of Warrants have simply been destroyed in price and *already* if we were convinced that a true stopping place had been reached on the downside, we would be pointing out the brightest 'pearls' to be found amidst the market wreckage. But we aren't convinced, and the destruction will probably go on while our technical studies go on too, with the aim of discerning where the real floor might be. If we then go into a period of market lethargy and deepening discouragement, the R.K.O.-type Warrant opportunity ($500 to $104,000 in 4 years, remember) should not only become available—it might become less than rare. And among low-price stocks, we will find ourselves choosing from a Christmas grab-bag of rich opportunities. We have to repeat: it has been a long haul since June 30, 1972 when we first advised subscribers to '. . . err on the side of pessimism rather than optimism, and reduce their holdings all along the line . . .' and we don't enjoy remaining negative for such a long period of time. But the road is nearing its end, and at the end of that road are the greatest profit opportunities we have seen in 30 years. The only ingredient subscribers need—a bit more patience."

New York Stock Exchange

New York Stock Exchange's Composite Index
WEEK ENDED AUG. 30, 1974

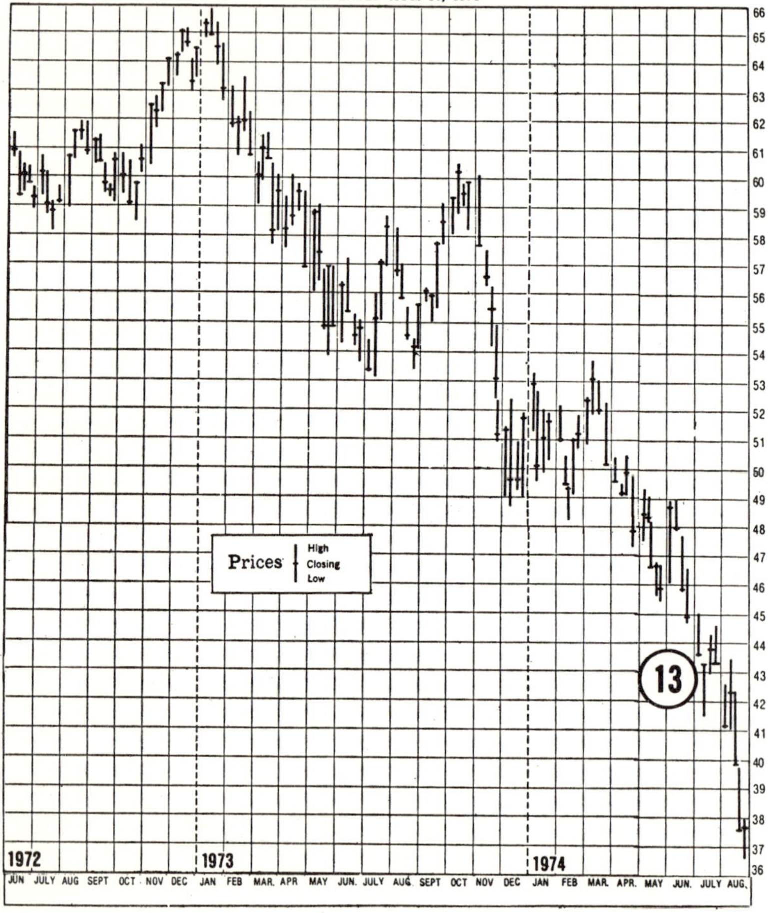

ALL QUOTATIONS REPRINTED FROM

THE R.H.M. WARRANT & STOCK SURVEY
PLUS
STOCKS under 10

13 **6-21-74:** ". . . we repeat an obvious fact: *Hundreds* of excellent situations in low-price stocks and low-price Warrants are reaching lower and lower and still lower prices—far out of line with intrinsic value and present and potential earning power. Superb trading programs are shaping up which will be producing 50% to 100% profits on successive market rallies and declines when a true bottom is reached and a necessarily long period of sideways base-building begins. But to begin too soon could tie up cash at higher levels and we stress with all the emphasis at our command that subscribers need not run these risks of impatience. The trading opportunities—and the later long-term holdings for leveraged recovery profits in high-leverage low-price stocks and Warrants—will be with us for a *long* time once the turn comes. We keep studying the relevant aspects of the worldwide economy, our domestic situation, and the stock market itself, and the evidence just continues to point to more trouble. So why recommend a change in policy? *Much* better things are ahead. Let's make sure we remain financially whole to enable us to enjoy them when they arrive."

The Profit Potential of WARRANTS

$500 to $104,000 in 4 years.

That was the record of an investment in one common stock Warrant — the R.K.O. Warrant — between 1942-1946.

It seemed at the time, and even for quite a number of years following, a rare occurrence, not to be easily duplicated.

Yet, events 25 to 30 years later have, in this writer's opinion made almost certain that there are "R.K.O. Warrant" opportunities with the same large profit potential being born in today's market. And not only one or two such opportunities, but very possibly many more. It is a time to know:

What Warrants are;

How they are issued and start trading;

Why Warrants can plummet like stones, and soar like rockets; and

Why it was exactly such characteristics that produced the wide gain in R.K.O. Warrants, and can with more likelihood than in the past 30 years produce such profit moves again in today's markets.

What happened in the past few years to bring about this potential?

First: There were only about 10 Warrants of real interest trading in 1942, itself ensuring that such a high profit opportunity as R.K.O. Warrants would not be easily duplicated.

But the number of active Warrants commenced a steady growth in the 1950's and 1960's, so that there were about

50 Warrants by 1955
100 Warrants by 1965
200 Warrants by 1970

And then, in a literal Warrant explosion (giant American Telephone & Telegraph itself coming out with a very important issue of *31 million* Warrants in 1970) the number of actively traded Warrants climbed by 75% in the years 1970-1974— from 200 Warrants at the start of 1970 to about *350* Warrants by the end of 1973, with the Warrant list still expanding steadily, as we write.

We will shortly explain how and why the number of Warrants expanded so dramatically.

Second: The *best* Warrant opportunities, the ones promising greatest percentage profits, such as the $500 to $104,000 R.K.O. Warrant move, develop and mature during falling markets, and develop their magnified profits during subsequent market recoveries. Market pessimism typically has a catastrophic effect on Warrant prices (you will soon understand why this is so) making them sink and then sink some more, and intensify downside momentum as general market pessimism deepens, until Warrants which were only recently selling for $30 and $20 and $10 are selling, respectively, at $10 and $5 and $1, with a goodly number sinking into the highly-leveraged "pennies" area. We will soon give many examples of exactly this process taking place in current years.

Then, when the market turns around to recovery and pessimism slowly gives way to hope, further to optimism, and then to a "boom" psychology, a strange (and wonderful to their holder!) thing happens to the Warrants. They find themselves *inescapably tied to their common stocks,* automatically magnifying their advance, moving 5 times, 10 times, even 20 times faster than those common stocks. We will shortly explain *exactly* how this happens, how it *must* happen, once a very low-price Warrant begins "tailgating" its recovering common stock.

But first let's go back and detail the move in the R.K.O. Warrant, since this one example can sharply outline the form which developing Warrant opportunities can take in today's market, and fix in the reader's understanding all the most important concepts which can specifically produce such large-scale profit opportunities.

A Beginning Definition — What IS a Warrant?

A Warrant is a certificate issued by the individual company itself, representing the right to buy a specific amount of the company's common stock, at a specific price, for a specific period of time. Whereas "Rights" or "Call Options" typically have a life of only a few months, a *Warrant* just as typically has a life of 5 years, 10 years, and many times even 15 and 20 years. Thus, the Textron Warrant does not expire until 1984, and the APL Corp. Warrants until 1988. A few Warrants are perpetual and never expire.

The R.K.O. Warrant

In 1940 the Radio-Keith-Orpheum Company (R.K.O.) reorganized after some years of bad fortune which left it unable to meet maturing debt. As is necessary in such cases, debtors of the company received most of the assets in the reorganization in the form of a new R.K.O. common stock and a new R.K.O. Preferred Stock, while holders of the old common stock received only 1/6th share of the new common stock for each full share of the old stock they formerly held.

To soften this blow, however, and probably to appease any possible anger of the original holders of the old R.K.O. common stock (which might have provoked annoying lawsuits) the planners of the reorganization decided to "sweeten" the meager offering. According to the plan finally adopted, in addition to their 1/6th share of the new R.K.O. common stock, the former stockholders would also receive *one full Warrant,* which would be good to buy one share of the new R.K.O. common stock from the company itself at $15 per share, the privilege to last until 1947 when the Warrants would expire.

In this way it was recognized that while nothing much could be done for the old stockholders on an immediate basis, if the company did prosper, the new common stock would advance, and the Warrant would develop value, providing additional compensation. Readers will soon find out in these pages that hundreds of Warrants currently trading came about in a similar "sweetening," to encourage acceptance by stockholders of merger or acquisition terms; or to facilitate sale of new issues of stocks and bonds by adding long-term Warrants as extra incentives.

But 1940, 1941 and 1942 were bad years for the stock market as hundreds of stocks broke, drifted to new lows, and then broke again to further new lows. Apathy set in, producing dull markets among a series of renewed slides, and pessimism settled ever more deeply over the stock market.

As we will later demonstrate in the context of today's stock market, the above description being quite applicable as these words are written, such markets are deadly for Warrants because Warrants pay no dividends, and represent no ownership of any kind in the company. They derive their market value *only* in two ways:

(1) If a common stock is selling *above* the exercise price of the Warrant, the difference between the current market value of the common stock and the exercise price of the Warrant is the intrinsic value of the Warrant, below which it cannot sell. *Example:* A Warrant is the right to buy XYZ common stock at 10 and XYZ common is selling on the market for 20. The intrinsic, *minimum* value of the Warrant is 20 minus 10, or $10, and it cannot sell for less since the holder, at the prices just mentioned, could exercise the Warrant, receive one common share from the company for $10 and sell it immediately in the open market for $20, pocketing the $10 difference. The Warrant can sell *above* its intrinsic value, at a *premium,* but it cannot sell for less. If bullishness is rampant and many investors expect the common stock to move higher, the premium above exercise value can become quite substantial.

(2) If a common stock is selling *below* the exercise price of the Warrant, that Warrant has 0 intrinsic value. *Example:* The same XYZ Warrant is still the right to buy common at 10. If XYZ common is selling at, say, 5, whatever the Warrant is selling for is *all* premium. No holder would exercise his Warrant, which means giving $10 to the company for one share of common stock, since he can buy that same share of common stock in the open market for *$5* without the Warrant. Real value can come to the Warrant only if and when the common stock moves above 10.

In these latter circumstances, the Warrant price will reflect *only* the emotions of investors — their feelings as to whether XYZ common will be moving up or down. If optimism is prevalent, the price of the Warrant could be substantial in relation to the $5 market price of the common stock, say 1½ or even 2½. If pessimism holds sway, the Warrant is likely to be marked down to the $1 mark, and even to the "pennies" level in sliding, panicky markets.

Back now to gloomy 1940, 1941, 1942 with continuously falling markets and ever-deepening pessimism and we find the new R.K.O. common slipping ever lower until it touched a 1942 bottom at 2½.

The R.K.O. Warrant was simultaneously sliding on the then New York Curb Exchange (now the American Stock Exchange) and while it managed to retain a market value of ⅜ (37½¢) earlier in 1942 when R.K.O. common was at 3⅞, the drop in the common to 2½ seemed to decimate the ranks of those investors who had any hope that R.K.O. common would ever see $15 again, where the Warrants would have some actual value. The R.K.O. Warrants sank drearily to a low of 1/16th (6¼¢).

How the picture changed in the next few years! Not only did the general market begin a slow recovery in late-1942, picking up speed in 1943 and 1944, beginning to race in 1945 and then coming to a typical bull market climax in 1946, as can be seen on the chart below, but R.K.O. earnings also recovered from a 4¢ deficit in 1942 to a booming \$2.16 per share in 1943, followed by smaller, but still appreciable, earnings of \$1.57 per share in 1944 and \$1.80 per share in 1945. Up went R.K.O. common stock to about the 10 level, which approximate high persisted in 1943, 1944 and most of 1945, followed by an almost perpendicular additional rise to a 1946 top of *\$28 per share* on the New York Stock Exchange.

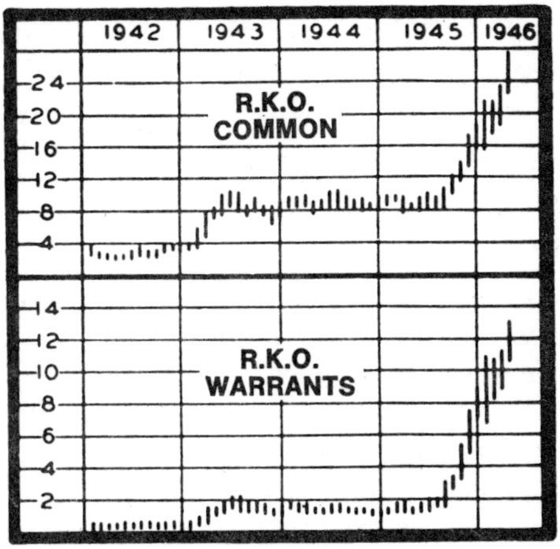

R.K.O. common stock had performed very well indeed. Had one made a \$500 investment in 200 shares at the 2½ low in 1942, by the 1946 top of 28, the \$500 investment would have appreciated to \$5,600.

What of the R.K.O. Warrant at the simultaneous low of 6¼¢ in 1942? Here \$500 would have purchased *8,000 Warrants,* instead of 200 shares of common.

And now comes that all-important point we mentioned at the beginning of this explanation: ". . . a strange (and wonderful to their holder!) thing happens to the Warrants. They find themselves *inescapably tied to their common stocks,* automatically magnifying their advance . . ." The move in the R.K.O. Warrants demonstrated the truth of this statement quite clearly.

Remember that each R.K.O. Warrant was the right to buy one share of R.K.O. common for *$15 per share.*

When R.K.O. common ran up to $28 in 1946, the Warrant had a minimum exercise value of 28 minus 15, or $13, and that is exactly where the R.K.O. Warrant sold on the New York Curb Exchange.

8,000 Warrants are worth $104,000 when those Warrants are selling at $13.

Thus, where R.K.O. common stock had gone from $2.50 to $28, a $500 investment appreciating to ...... $ 5,600

The R.K.O. Warrants had gone from 6¼¢ to $13, a $500 investment appreciating to $104,000

The R.K.O. Warrant had appreciated *20 times* faster than R.K.O. common.

The ability of a Warrant to produce a far greater percentage profit per dollar invested than the same dollar invested in its respective common stock is known as its *leverage* potential. We can already make the point here that the lower in price a Warrant is driven, relative to its common share price, the higher that leverage is likely to become for any subsequent recovery in its common.

Thus, it becomes highly important that in 1970-1974, with the general market showing large declines and most Warrants showing even greater percentage declines (the two-edged sword of the Warrant, remember), the following price slides in Warrants could be noted, among many more that could be listed:

Avco Warrants	18 to 1
Carrier Corp. Warrants	13 to 1¼
Cott Corp. Warrants	4 to 37¢
Continental Ill. & Rlty. Warrants	14 to 37¢
Holiday Inns Warrants	31 to 2
Instrument Systems Warrants	3⅛ to 10¢
International Tel. & Tel. Warrants	12 to 75¢
Jones & Laughlin Warrants	3 to 37¢

LCA Warrants	18 to 81¢
LTV "$115" Warrants	82 to 1.87
Loews Warrants	39 to 3¾
National Industries Warrants	16⅜ to 62¢
Ozark Airlines Warrants	7 to 63¢
Rollins International Warrants	6¾ to 30¢
Starr Broadcasting Warrants	20 to 1
Triangle Pacific Warrants	8 to 25¢
United Brands Warrants	56 to 1
Zayre Warrants	12 to 62¢

The number of Warrants trading were the greatest in market history;

The scale of price declines in many Warrants were the greatest seen since the 1940's;

And, thus, the opinion of this writer that the stage had been set for more R.K.O. Warrant-type moves, with exactly the same "leverage" principles applying in the 1970's as they had applied in the 1940's.

A Broad Range of Warrant Opportunities on MANY Levels

At any time that the general market goes through serious declines, the potential for more R.K.O. Warrant-type moves becomes greater, and will embrace a greater number of Warrants. This is true, as we write, and could be true at any subsequent time.

But we wish also now to demonstrate the large utility of the common stock Warrant in *any* phase of the stock market cycle, and also the wide range of opportunities on many levels, which may be less spectacular than what can emerge from an R.K.O. Warrant, but should be in the awareness of all investors because of their rewarding potential on their own scale. Indeed, the scale of potential can mount from the moderate level of a *Tenneco Warrant,* which we shall next describe, to the higher leverage of a *General Tire & Rubber Warrant,* whose description will follow, and to a number of other Warrants with which we shall demonstrate varying levels of Warrant profit potential in different types of markets, at different stages of a typical market cycle.

With about 350 Warrants now actually trading, the greatest number by far in market history, the type and scale of profit opportunities will obviously be large in number. In addition, we need hardly emphasize after the previous list we presented of devastated Warrants in the 1973-1974 market declines that *so will the opportunities for loss.*

We wish to stress that the example of Tenneco Warrants, and the other Warrants we shall discuss, are purely for the purpose of explaining the *logic* of a well-selected Warrant. It should be further recognized that there are material differences among the 350 Warrants currently trading, and there is no assurance that the past performance of examples cited would be repeated by any specific Warrant.

We will continue to reinforce proper perspective regarding common stock Warrants — it is a most necessary precaution — and let us now proceed to a description of the Tenneco Warrant as an important example, which will also accomplish something undoubtedly surprising to most readers.

That "something" will be, without possibility of contradiction, to demonstrate that a well-situated Warrant, in addition to offering much greater upside percentage profits than its common stock, *can also be less speculative than that common stock where downside danger is concerned.* Follow our analysis carefully and see if you do not fully agree with our conclusion. At the end of the explanation you will have a much greater appreciation of the many varieties of profit opportunities which the large number of Warrants currently trading can represent.

November 1970 — Tenneco Corp. Issues A Warrant

1970 was a "credit crunch" year. Inflationary forces were beginning to run too fast and the Administration decided to apply the "brakes" by choking off to some extent the steady increase in the money supply which had been propelling the inflation to new heights. When a corporation requires money for expansion or other corporate needs, it can get that money in one of several ways. It can sell more common stock, or sell "senior" securities, that is, Bonds or Preferred Stocks. Or it can borrow the needed funds from the banks, or from institutional investors, such as an insurance company.

But late-1970 was a very difficult time for any of these routes (money was "tight" and interest rates up) and possibly dimmest of all were the chances of getting the huge sum Tenneco had in mind ($133 million) from institutions or bank sources. Senior securities were a doubtful avenue and could have been utilized only at onerous interest or dividend rates. Tenneco Corp. management decided that common stock would have to be sold, but with the addition of a substantial "sweetener" to ensure success of the sale.

Six million shares of additional common stock were thus sold and the $133 million *was* raised, but the necessary sweetener was impressively large — *6 million Warrants* — each share of new common stock sold carrying the bonus of one Warrant. Each Warrant was good to buy an additional share of Tenneco common stock for $24.25 (from the company itself) until November 1, 1975 when the Warrant would expire.

The new Tenneco Warrant came out at a time of deep discouragement for the general market, and for Tenneco common itself which had sold as high as 32¾ year-end 1968, but was now selling at a lowly 19⅜. Little wonder then that the Warrants, trading over-the-counter before commencing trading on the New York Stock Exchange, sold around the *3* level.

We Commence Our Warrant "Arithmetic"

Here we have Tenneco common selling at 19⅜ and the Tenneco Warrants selling at 3, and the first very natural question would be:

If the Tenneco Warrant gives one the right to buy a share of Tenneco common stock for *24¼,* and one can buy a share of that same Tenneco common stock right now in the open market for only *19⅜,* why is that Warrant worth *anything?*

It is quite amazing how so many investors consider this a reasonable question and follow up by dismissing the idea of buying such a Warrant, particularly when the entire market is filled with pessimism. This is precisely why Warrants can fall to very low levels during general market declines, but observe how the most elementary Warrant "arithmetic" demonstrates the fallacy of this approach — and points up a potential profit opportunity for those who do understand.

It is certainly true that with Tenneco common stock at 19⅜, a Warrant giving you the right to buy that stock for 24¼ has no immediate value. Thus, even if the Warrant sold for one cent (!), buying the Warrant for purpose of immediate exercise would only result in a serious loss because with the Warrant you had to pay Tenneco Corp. $24.25 for one share of common stock, while you could buy that same share of Tenneco common in the open market for $19.37. On 100 shares obtained with Warrants, you would be throwing almost $500 out the window, without considering the cost of the Warrants themselves.

However, the Tenneco Warrant had a five-year life, and the whole point of such a Warrant was to buy it and hold it for a hoped-for recovery in the common stock. Consider, for example, how different a picture evolved when one envisaged a doubling in the price of Tenneco common from the existing market level of 19⅜ to 38¾.

At such a time, the holder of the Tenneco Warrant could deliver that Warrant to Tenneco Corp., pay $24.25 for one share of common stock, and immediately sell that share of stock in the open market for $38.75. The profit of $14.50 must give the Warrant a minimum value in the marketplace of 14½ (A Warrant can sell for *more* than its straight exercise value, but it cannot sell for *less* than its straight exercise value, because that is its direct and immediately obtainable market value).

When we now go back to our original November 1970 figures of 19⅜ for Tenneco common and 3 for the Tenneco Warrant, and translate them into the 100% advance for Tenneco common to 38¾, we will know exactly why you might pay $3 for a Warrant giving you the right to buy a share of stock for 24¼ even though that stock is selling for 19⅜, and the Warrant has less-than-zero exercise value at that moment.

Under the hypothesized doubling in price:

Tenneco common had advanced from 19⅜ to 38¾, or 100%.

But Tenneco Warrants, in exactly the same period of time, would have had to advance from 3 to a minimum value of 14½, or 383%

Had Tenneco common doubled in price, the Tenneco Warrants, by simple arithmetic, would have *had* to advance 3.83 times faster than Tenneco common, with no "ifs, ands or buts."

Tenneco Common Versus Tenneco Warrants on the DOWNside

In November 1970, with Tenneco common at 19⅜ and Tenneco Warrants at 3, there is no question that the Warrants would outstrip the common in any advancing market, per dollar invested. In a later paragraph when we describe the *actual* advance for Tenneco common in the months that followed, it will be seen that the Warrants advanced *much* faster than the common on a percentage basis.

But what about a *downside* move for Tenneco common? Would the Warrants show a greater percentage decline than the common, such an unfavorable expectation balancing out its favorable *upside* potential?

Not at all. We will demonstrate this on two levels, the second level pinning down this assertion with unquestionable mathematical logic, declaring the Tenneco Warrant in November 1970 to have been less speculative than Tenneco common!

Level I

Assume Tenneco common did not *double* in price from 19⅜ to 38¾, but was *halved* in price from 19⅜ to 9⅝ ($9.625).

The common stock would have fallen 50% and the Tenneco Warrant could then also have declined 50% from 3 to 1½ without showing a greater percentage decline.

Since Tenneco has never dropped anywhere near 9⅝ since November 1970 we cannot point to market actuality and must fall back (initially) on this writer's opinion, and the evidence of many similar Warrant-common price relationships. Where this writer's opinion is concerned, it is backed by more than 25 years of daily observation of Warrant price movements, with more than 20 years as Editor of a weekly investment service intensively covering the Warrant field.

That experience tells us that a 5-year Warrant on a popular stock such as Tenneco would not have fallen under 1½ with the common at 9⅝. Indeed, it probably would have sold higher in most markets, where panic or truly deep pessimism was lacking.

Further buttressing this view, let's look at a few Warrant-common price relationships in 1973. Here is an A-T-O Warrant with 5 years of life to 1978, paralleling Tenneco in 1970 in that regard. The Warrant is the right to buy A-T-O common at 30 to 10-15-73 and then at 35 to 10-15-78. A-T-O common is selling at 7¼ as these words are written, and the A-T-O Warrant is selling at a robust (overpriced) 2¼.

Here, also, is a Greyhound Warrant, representing the right to buy at 23.50 to 5-14-80. Greyhound common is selling at 13¾, not much more than ½ the exercise price, and the Warrant is selling at 2⅞. Many more examples could be cited from past markets to reinforce our view that in November 1970 and the months thereafter, if Tenneco common *had* dropped to 9⅝, the Tenneco Warrant would *not* have sold lower than 1½, and probably would have sold somewhat higher.

If the reader accepts the opinion and evidence offered, then the Tenneco Warrant at 3 in November 1970, with the common at 19⅜, had the ability to rise much faster than the common if that common moved *up,* but would have done no worse than the common, if *down* was the direction the common took.

Level II

But let's now leave opinion and evidence behind and nail down our point with mathematical exactness, using quite simple arithmetic.

At those November 1970 prices of 19⅜ for Tenneco common and 3 for the Tenneco Warrant, let us consider two alternative investments:

(1) You buy 100 Tenneco common at 19⅜, costing $1,937

or

(2) You buy 300 Tenneco Warrants at 3, costing .... $ 900

Let us introduce that all-important *actuality* here, where Tenneco common did, in fact, move up to 28½ in February 1971, just three months later.

At this level, the 100 shares purchased at 19⅜ (for

sake of clarity we are ignoring commissions throughout) for $1,937 would be worth $2,850, a gain of .... $ 913

But the Tenneco Warrant had, in actuality, in the same time period exactly, appreciated from 3 to 10¼, developing an expected *premium*. The $900 investment in 300 Warrants at 3, with those Warrants at 10¼, was now worth $3,075, a gain of $2,175

Consider carefully. Only $900 invested in the Tenneco *Warrants* had produced more than double the profit accomplished by the $1,937 invested in Tenneco *common*. More than twice the investment in the common had produced less than half the profit shown by the Warrants.

Now consider the downside: *Had* Tenneco common declined 50% from 19⅜ to 9⅝ (let's use *9.68* to get the decimals exact),

The $1,937 investment in the common would be worth $968, showing a loss of .... $ 968

But where the Tenneco *Warrants* were concerned, even if they had gone to 0 (!), the total investment of $900 in the 300 Warrants at 3 could not possibly have shown a greater loss than .... $ 900

The Inescapable Conclusion

When "Investment A" *must* do better than "Investment B" on the upside in the profit column, and *must* show less loss on any downside move, there is no other way to describe this situation in the stock market than by saying that "A" is less speculative than "B". And in November 1970, with Tenneco common at 19⅜ and the new Tenneco Warrant at 3, there can be no question that the Warrant was less speculative than the common.

The advantage of the Warrant was much greater than indicated above because we could not conceive of it going to 0 with the common at 9⅝. If we take a price of 1½ for the Warrants, the original $900 investment in 300 Warrants would still be worth $450, and the "more than twice the gain on the upside" for the Warrants, for less than half the investment needed for the common, would also have been "less than half the loss on the downside" as well.

The "way-out-in-front" superiority of the Tenneco Warrant is a good definition of what we mean by a "well-selected" Warrant (in November 1970, of course) and begins to tell readers the opportunities that are possible in the list of 350 Warrants trading, *particularly* during periods of market decline when one believes that a turn to the upside is in the making.

Some Further Insight From Tenneco Warrants

When Warrants sink to low levels in relation to the price of their common stocks (the common price at a higher multiple of the Warrant price) they become full of opportunity, usually the lower the relative price of the Warrant, the greater the leverage and the greater the opportunity.

It should work out, then, that at *higher* levels for the Warrant the profit potential (leverage) will be smaller and the risk greater. This is exactly the case and our same Tenneco Warrants will fully demonstrate it.

In 1971, Tenneco common reached a high of 29⅝ while at the same time the Tenneco Warrants were at their high of 11⅛.

How did the opportunity at 29⅝ and 11⅛, respectively, compare with the earlier levels of 19⅜ and 3?

We note first that 29⅝ is *2.66* times 11⅛ (a low multiple) while 19⅜ is *6.45* times 3 (a considerably higher multiple). This is only a rough guide to "leverage" — we ourselves use a more complex formula, modified by experience with individual Warrant performance over a period of time — but this simple fact alone immediately swings the Tenneco Warrant at the higher price from favorable to less favorable.

Taking the 29⅝ and 11⅛ levels for Tenneco common and Warrants at the 1971 high, assume another 50% advance in Tenneco common which would take it from 29.62 to 44.43 (using decimals for accuracy).

At 44.43, the straight exercise value of the Tenneco Warrant would be 44.43 minus 24.25, or 20.18. How much of a premium would be paid for the Warrant? Not as much on a percentage basis as held true at 11.12. All Warrant experience demonstrates that at higher levels, a Warrant premium will shrink. Therefore, we estimate that the Warrant would sell, say, at 22.25, which would be a doubling in price from the 11.12 starting place.

A 50% move in Tenneco common from 29.62 to 44.43 would have produced a 100% advance in Tenneco Warrants.

Note first that where from the 3 level in November 1970, a 53% advance in Tenneco common (19⅜ to 29⅝) had produced a 270% advance in Tenneco Warrants (3 to 11⅛), the Warrant moving ahead 5.1 times faster than the common, an additional 50% advance in the common had now produced only an additional *100%* advance in the Warrant.

The "5.1 times faster" had dropped to only 2.0 times faster.

The picture looks less attractive from the vantage point of downside risk as well. With Tenneco common at 29.62 and the Warrants at 11.12, assume that instead of advancing 50%, Tenneco common began to slide and returned to its low of 19.37. It would be logical to assume that the Tenneco Warrant would also return to its low of 3, and the logic here holds whatever minor variations in prices would be possible.

Tenneco common, in sliding from 29.62 to 19.37 would have declined 35%

But the Tenneco *Warrants,* in declining from 11.12 to 3 would have declined *73%*

At the November 1970 levels of 19.37 for Tenneco common and 3 for Tenneco Warrants, the Warrants promised to advance much faster than the common stock on the upside (from 4 to 5 times faster), while on the downside they would show no greater loss than Tenneco common on a percentage basis, and probably would show a *smaller* percentage loss. At these levels, then, the Warrants were far superior to the common in every way, as we demonstrated with mathematical certainty.

But at the higher levels in 1971 of 29.62 for Tenneco common and 11.12 for Tenneco Warrants, the Warrants promised to advance only moderately faster than the common stock on the upside, and to decline *much* faster than the common stock on the downside.

The Lessons of Tenneco Warrants

We have begun to demonstrate the different levels of Warrant opportunity, from the very high-leveraged R.K.O. Warrant-type of opportunity with its striking "$500 to $104,000 in 4 years" record, to the much more moderate opportunity of a Tenneco Warrant.

Readers should have a better realization at this point of the value of keeping alert to opportunities on *both* such levels, since the many hundreds of important Warrants now trading actively can produce Tenneco Warrant-type opportunities quite frequently in many stages of the market cycle, where such "well-selected" Warrants promise far greater upside gain than their common stocks, along with lessened downside risk.

The reader's understanding should also now be enhanced as to the varying levels of risk and reward as common-Warrant price relationships move up and down the market ladder.

Maintaining Perspective — Atlantic Richfield Warrants 1969-1972

Particularly because so many investors have unfortunate experiences with many Warrants — the habit of buying them at high prices and in buoyant upside markets! — it is necessary to give examples of how much money can be lost by unintelligent Warrant speculation at regular intervals in these pages. We turn then to mid-1969 when Cities Service decided to sell a huge issue of $100,000,000 in bonds.

Desirous of ensuring the success of the sale of this issue, Cities Service turned to 500,000 shares of Atlantic Richfield Oil common stock that it held in its portfolio and decided to give the purchaser of each $1,000 face value of the new Bonds, *5 Warrants,* each good to buy one share of Atlantic Richfield common from Cities Service upon payment of $110, the exercise privilege to expire on September 1, 1972.

After issuance with the Bonds (the new Bond issue was indeed an easy sale with the Warrants attached) the Warrants began trading separately and made some history — good at first, terrible later, as we shall soon see. By August 1969 Atlantic Richfield Oil was boiling up to a 118 top and the Warrants were selling at their emotional and overexcited top of 47¼.

Let's stop for some simple arithmetic to demonstrate how foolish were the purchases of Atlantic Richfield Warrants at 47¼ with the common at 118. If the common would advance 50% from 118 to 177, the Warrants would have an exercise value of 177 minus 110, or 67. Based on many thousands of "leverage" calculations for Warrants which this writer has made over about the past 25 years, we would estimate that the Warrants would then sell at about a 10-point premium at this level, or at about 77.

This would be a 63% advance for the Warrants from their 47.25 level, and little better than the 50% move in the common. Should the common move to the *down*side, the enthusiasm would vanish and the Warrants were likely to drop considerably faster on a percentage basis than the common stock. Furthermore, Cities Service hadn't been very generous in the life it gave its Warrants — only about 3 years — and a decline in the stock stretching over a period of time would truly work havoc on the overextended price of the Warrants.

Which is exactly what happened. Atlantic Richfield Oil plummeted in late-1969-early-1970 to reach a low in the mid-40's, recovered to the high 70's in 1971 and then had another sinking spell in 1972 to the same mid-40's. The common stock never did get anywhere near that 110 level again after the exhilarating move in 1969 and the *Warrants* skidded downhill from their 1969 top at 47¼ and never got near that high again, instead drifting lower and lower until, in September 1972, they expired at — 0!

At the 47¼ pinnacle the 500,000 Warrants were worth $23,625,000 in market value. In about three years this $23 million in value vanished completely.

Warrants are distinctly a two-way street!

The Unchanging Logic of the Common Stock Warrant

We trust that what we have just described with Tenneco Warrants has alerted readers to the large potential profits in Warrants, when well-selected, and with the proper price relationship between common and Warrant. Are these opportunities peculiar to the early-1970's? May they perhaps disappear, or change for the worse, in some future markets?

This is in no way possible. The relationship between common and Warrant price fluctuation is a purely mathematical one and *must* work exactly the same way in the later 1970's as it worked in the earlier 1970's. To fully drive this point home, and to give another example to fix the important concepts firmly in the understanding of the reader, let us go back 20 years to the 1950's and consider the market behavior, and the guidance we can secure from that behavior, of a trio of Warrants of an important company.

General Tire & Rubber Warrants

In September 1956, the General Tire & Rubber Company acquired the A.M. Byers Company, and as part of a "package" given in the acquisition of the company, A.M. Byers stockholders received a *Warrant,* good to buy one share of General Tire & Rubber common at $70 until June 15, 1959, and then at a slightly higher price thereafter until June 15, 1961, when the Warrant would expire. When trading in the Warrants began in the open market in that same September of 1956, General Tire & Rubber common was selling at 53 and the Warrants were selling at — 4½.

Same old question — and we know from experience that this is the way many even fairly knowledgeable investors feel when they suddenly, and not on their own initiative, are in possession of something called a "Warrant", as were the previous stockholders of the A.M. Byers Company. The question they asked themselves in various forms was:

"Is there *any* value to a certificate (the Warrant) which gives you the right to buy a stock at *70* when you can buy that same stock in the open market right now for only *53?*

A good number of these A.M. Byers stockholders holding the new General Tire & Rubber Warrants were happy to get 4½ for their Warrants after asking themselves the above question. Like so many before them, and after them, they did not think of using some elementary arithmetic in this situation — a deficiency we find in *many* areas of the stock market!

We will now re-create that period of time in September 1956, and *use* the elementary arithmetic, and we will again demonstrate that the General Tire & Rubber Warrants were a far superior investment at these prices than was the well-known General Tire & Rubber common stock itself.

With General Tire & Rubber common at 53 and General Tire & Rubber Warrants at 4½ (the right to buy at $70 per share, remember) — what would be the effect on the Warrant if General Tire & Rubber common were to double in price from 53 to 106?

From the discussion of the previous pages we know that the Warrant would not sell below its actual exercise value, which in this case would be 106 minus 70, or 36.

In moving from 4½ to 36, the General Tire & Rubber Warrant would have moved ahead an impressive 700% as against only 100% for the common.

Next question: What would be the effect on the Warrant if General Tire & Rubber common were to lose half its market value, dropping from 53 to 26½?

Here we again leave strict mathematical calculation, for the General Tire Warrant never had to endure the common stock dropping that low and we fall back on the type of experience previously detailed in stating our opinion that if General Tire & Rubber common had declined 50% from 53 to 26½, it was highly unlikely that the Warrant would have dropped more than that same 50%, or from 4½ to *below* 2¼.

This thesis can, in our opinion, be accepted with complete safety, and the conclusion must then be that in September 1956, with General Tire & Rubber common at 53 and the Warrants at 4½, the Warrants were a *far* better buy than the common since they promised to move ahead a minimum of 7 times as fast as the common on the upside, but to show no greater percentage loss, and possibly less loss, than the common on the downside.

Let us go even further now, once more away from any *trace* of opinion and belief (that General Tire & Rubber $70 Warrants would not sell below 2¼ should the common decline 50% to 26½) and once more find complete mathematical certainty in comparing the following two alternative investments as to their potential gains and losses for:

(a) a doubling in price of General Tire & Rubber common from 53 to 106, or

(b) a halving in price of General Tire & Rubber common from 53 to 26½.

We start once more with our prices in September 1956 of 53 for General Tire & Rubber common and 4½ for the General Tire & Rubber $70 Warrants. We ask you to compare two investments, involving one amount in the common stock, and the other involving *one-half that amount* in the Warrants. That would give us two alternative investments as follows:

(a) Buy 100 shares of General Tire & Rubber common at 53, cost $5,300

(b) Buy 588 General Tire & Rubber $70 Warrants at 4½, cost $2,650

Upon the common doubling in price from 53 to 106, a profit develops in (a) of $5,300

But at 106 for the common, the $70 Warrants are worth a minimum of 106 minus 70, or *36*.

588 Warrants at 36 are worth $21,168, a profit of $18,518

A much smaller investment in the Warrants ($2,650) had again produced a much greater profit than the larger investment ($5,300) in the common!

On the downside, upon a halving in price for the common from 53 to 26½, a loss develops in (a) of $2,650

At 26½ for the common, this writer still reminds readers that experience dictates that the 5-year $70 Warrant for General Tire & Rubber common would not sell below 2¼. But we do not need this base here at all, since we can accept the hypothesis that the Warrant could drop to 0!

For while at 0 we have lost our entire $2,650 investment in the Warrants, this is still no greater than the loss in (a) where the common stock *also produced a loss of $2,650.*

Corroborating Conclusion: In September 1956, with General Tire & Rubber common at 53 and the General Tire & Rubber $70 Warrants at 4½, the common stock was *more speculative* than the Warrant on clear mathematical logic.

For just as with Tenneco Warrants in November 1970, if we consider *any* amount invested in the common stock, one-half of that investment made in the General Tire & Rubber Warrants would show far greater profits on the upside, but could not possibly show any greater loss than the General Tire & Rubber common stock on the downside, since at *0* for the Warrant, with the entire investment wiped out, the loss only equals that endured by the common. Since we know that this important 5-year Warrant would never have gone to 0, we also know that the loss in the Warrant investment would have *had* to be less than that suffered by the common stock.

When we place two parallel investments side by side and find that investment (b) *must* show a much greater percentage gain on the upside and a lesser percentage loss on the downside than (a), there can be no doubt that investment (a) is *more* speculative than (b).

The Further History of the General Tire & Rubber $70 Warrants

Since General Tire common had a spectacular run between September 1956 and December 1959, moving from 53 to the equivalent of 280, the $70 Warrants obviously had to have an even more spectacular experience, one completely dictated by *arithmetic*. When the common stock sold at 280, the Warrants *had* to be worth a minimum of 280 minus 70, or 210, and that is where they sold. Thus, the anticipated results of the far superior leverage of the well-selected Warrant:

General Tire & Rubber common had moved from 53 to 280 .... up 428%

General Tire & Rubber $70 *Warrants* had moved from 4½ to 210 .... up 4,566%

Two other General Tire & Rubber Warrants also performed very well for their holders. A $60 Warrant issued at the same time as the $70 Warrant described above, moved from 7¼ in September 1956 to 215 in December 1959.

A $25 Warrant began trading in late-1957 (the Warrants attached initially to a new $12 million issue of General Tire & Rubber bonds), and moved from a low of 5 to a high of 90 by early-1967.

In each of these individual General Tire & Rubber Warrants, the same mathematical logic previously described labeled them as far better buys at their lower levels than the common stock of General Tire, promising much more percentage gain on the upside, and no greater percentage loss, or considerably less loss than that common stock on the downside.

Tenneco Warrants in 1970, General Tire & Rubber Warrants in 1956 — readers see clearly now, we trust, that similar Warrant opportunities developing in coming months and years from the long list of 350 Warrants currently trading, will show exactly the same potential profit results we have described, when the same price relationships have developed for attractive situations. The logic is *mathematical* in nature, has applied to Warrants in *past* markets, applies *presently* to well-situated Warrants in today's market, and will surely apply to selected Warrants in *tomorrow's* markets.

Relative Rewards, Relative Risks — The Guideposts Become Clearer

With Tenneco Warrants we went through some logical arithmetic which outlined potential rewards when the Warrants were at 3 and the common at 19⅜ in November 1970, and the greatly *heightened risk* in the later months of 1971 when the Warrants reached 11⅛ with the common at 29⅝.

At the lower levels, the upside potential of the Tenneco Warrant was *far* greater than downside risk. At the *upper* levels, potential risk began to quite evenly balance further potential gain.

This all points up a guidepost which must always be kept in the forefront in analyzing Warrants. When a Warrant is dropping, leveraged attraction is almost always increasing. When a Warrant is rising, its risk is almost inevitably rising too. The best Warrant opportunities develop during falling markets — the deeper the decline, the greater the potential opportunities. At the higher reaches — particularly during a bull market — risk increases rapidly.

Truism it may be, but "buy low and sell high" is never more applicable than when utilized in analyzing Warrant opportunities. To give this point the emphasis it deserves, let's look at the downfall of one popular Warrant and allow the lesson to sink in *thoroughly!*

Mack Trucks "1956" Warrants

The scope of the disaster for the Mack Trucks "1956" Warrants may be best appreciated when we realize that there were 189,500 "1956" Warrants outstanding on February 16, 1966, so that at the then existing price of 34⅝, these Warrants had a total valuation in the market of $6,561,000.

When the Warrants expired at 0 on September 1, 1966, this $6.56 million had vanished completely for its holders. But suppose those holders had utilized the following logical approach — always the first step in evaluating the merits of a particular Warrant — and invariably starting with the two preliminary questions:

(1) What will be the relative effect on the Warrant if the common stock moves *up,* say 50%; and

(2) What will be the relative effect on the Warrant if the common stock moves *down* by that same 50%?

With Mack Trucks common at 54¾ and the Mack Trucks Warrants at 34⅝ on February 16, 1966, a 50% gain in the common would bring it to 82⅛. Each Warrant was the right to buy 1.47 shares of Mack Trucks common for a total of $50.00. Now, 1.47 shares at 82⅛ are worth 120.72, so that the right to buy this package for $50.00 must be worth 120.72 minus 50, or 70.72, and the Warrant must sell at least at that level. (No "premium" over exercise value would be expected at these elevated prices for the Warrant and the short life remaining.)

A move for the Warrant from 34⅝ to about 70.72 is a move of 104%, as against a 50% move for the common, the Warrant promising to advance more than twice as fast as the common stock on the upside.

When, however, we turn to the *downside* potential, we do not find the favorable characteristics evident with the Tenneco Warrants and the General Tire & Rubber Warrants at their attractive buying levels, where the Warrants were expected to fall no faster than their respective common stocks on a percentage basis, or even at markedly slower rates.

Instead, a 50% decline in Mack Trucks common from 54¾ to 27⅜ would find each Warrant worth — in view of the proximity of the expiration date, September 1, 1966 — somewhere near the "few dollars" level, or even near the 0 mark, depending upon how close the expiration date actually was.

For 1.47 shares at 27⅜ per share are worth 40.24. The right to buy $40.24 worth of stock for $50.00 (the Warrant privilege) has no immediate value at all, and typically mounting pessimism with a falling stock, plus the drastically shrinking life of the Warrant, produces a further "typical" response — the fast melting away of the market price of the Warrant.

In actual fact, Mack Trucks common, in a bearish market, dropped to 33 as the September 1, 1966 expiration date came into view, where the Warrant had no immediate value at all, and that is where the Warrant finished its 10-year journey — at 0.

During most of that 10-year period there had been recurrent periods in up-and-down market cycles when quite profitable opportunities emerged with the "1956" Warrants — for those who were familiar with such opportunities — when the Warrants were at much lower prices and promised much more percentage gain on the upside than possible downside loss.

But in February 1966, the Mack Trucks "1956" Warrants were

(a) too high in price in relation to the common stock; and

(b) too close to their expiration date.

The equation for the Warrants at that unfortunate time was as follows:

A 50% upside move in Mack Trucks common from 54¾ to 82⅛ would have moved the Warrants up a little more than twice as fast as the common stock (so far so good).

But a 50% *downside* move in the Mack Trucks common from 54¾ to 27⅜ guaranteed that the Warrant would be worth 0, the entire Warrant investment worthless.

The odds were heavily against the purchaser.

From the above, it should now be clear that the mathematical logic in pinpointing *undesirable* and *unpromising,* and *dangerous* Warrant investments is just as clear and valid as the mathematical logic which accurately points to highly *promising* Warrant investments.

Far from relying on mere chance, logic asserts itself just as well in spotting dangers as in pinpointing opportunities.

We trust the road to "Opportunities In Warrants" is becoming ever more clear as each facet of these remarkable securities unfolds in these pages.

Short-Term Profit Opportunities With Warrants

Investor awareness of "Opportunities In Warrants" remains very minor, and probably always will be for the great majority. People just like to run in familiar channels!

But for investors willing to be enterprising, to go after larger-than-usual rewards with full acceptance of the many-times larger risks (which often, however, can be kept to minor levels compared with the potential gain, through intelligent analysis, as we have described), the large and growing list of Warrants can present a happy hunting ground.

Here is one example of a Warrant with a short life which could still present an opportunity for highly-leveraged profit because the price of the Warrant was low enough, and the timing appropriate — the opposite, in other words, of what we just described with Mack Trucks Warrants.

Thus, each Ling-Temco Warrant, which began trading in 1961, was the right to buy one share of Ling-Temco common for $40 until August 1, 1966. In September 1965, Ling-Temco common was selling at 22, had been in the doldrums for a lengthy and discouraging period of time, and there was little expectation among investors that the stock would approach the $40 level where the Warrants would begin to have some actual value, in the one year of life left for the Warrant.

Consequently, the looked-down-upon Warrants (usually the case when the stock is down) were selling as low as 1⅛. However, shortly thereafter, a sharp rise commenced in Ling-Temco common stock on the New York Stock Exchange which did not stop until the stock had risen to a 1966 high of 73⅞. At this level each Warrant (the right to buy a share of common stock for $40) had to be worth 73⅞ minus 40, or 33⅞, and the Warrants sold at that price.

Ling-Temco common had advanced from 22 to 73⅞ .... up 235%

Ling-Temco *Warrants,* in exactly the same period of time, had advanced from 1⅛ to 33⅞ ....up 2,911%

The Ling-Temco Warrant had advanced more than 12 times as fast as Ling-Temco common stock in that six month period.

Interrupting Our Discussion of Warrants

Additional and important aspects of drawing profits from high-leverage Warrants appear later in this book, but we now direct the reader's attention to a truly central thesis whose full understanding will alone create the basis for seizing the *best* opportunities in low-price Warrants, low-price stocks.

This central thesis has to do with the "Great Inflation" of the early 1970's; how it developed; how it wrecked the stock market and *created* "The Greatest Stock Market Profit Opportunities In Forty Years"; how we feel the Inflation will soon be transformed into a new and different economic epoch for the United States with some totally new directions which can lay the basis for a much sounder economy and, therefore, a new and powerful bull market in stocks.

We feel sure you have read enough in the past chapters to appreciate the fact that with so many hundreds of important Warrants driven down to such low levels, a new bull market in stocks is bound to produce many historic profit opportunities in low-price Warrants and, as we shall see in a later section, in hundreds of important low-price stocks as well.

The chapters which follow are quite full of many thoughts, and may introduce concepts which are unfamiliar to you. But this writer asks you, the reader, with all the earnestness and force at his command, to read each line *carefully*. The Inflation we have endured just since 1960 — or only the past 14 years or so — has already taken from you almost half of the purchasing power of each dollar you possessed. You can make up for part or all of that loss, in our opinion, and even build capital to a higher level in the next few years, by selecting the right vehicles for market profits from the wreckage now on the stock market floor.

But for the proper *timing,* which is essential for the greatest possible measure of success, you must know all that you possibly can about today's *Economics*. We feel strongly that fully absorbing what now follows will pay you large dividends indeed for the care and attention you invest.

Thus . . . "The Economics of the 1970's . . ."

The Great Inflation of the Early 1970's; Where It Started From — and Where It Will Take Us

Today's virulent Inflation, and its associated severe and threatening problems affecting every facet of our lives, was actually born decades ago in the 1930's when the Great Depression created unemployment, a slide in living standards and a woeful waste of productive resources on a scale never before seen in the western world.

Following the end of World War II, with bitter memories of that experience, various steps were taken by most governments in the non-Communist world to ensure that the unemployment rate was kept low. Varieties of "Keynesianism" were utilized, such policies derived from the economic thinking of John Maynard Keynes, a prominent British economist, who left more of a mark on 20th Century civilization than he had probably ever imagined. Mr. Keynes felt we could "smooth out" the business cycle, thereby obviating "boom-and-bust" unemployment through government adjusting its spending and taxation policies.

Government would operate at a deficit during slack periods — spending more than it took in through taxation — and operate at a surplus during boom periods by raising taxes and reducing expenditures, government thus taking in more than it spent. The effect of this would be (in a manner we shall soon explain) to increase the amount of money available to buy goods during slack periods, "stimulating" the economy, and to effect a decrease during boom periods, "cooling off" the economy.

The desired end was to be the aforementioned "smoothing out" of the business cycle, and the prevention of recession and unemployment typical during the "down" part of a business cycle. But Mr. Keynes overlooked several important factors, as has been emphatically proved by recent history, the effects of which were to make the "cure" worse than the "disease".

One part of the prescription felt good to the entire electorate; that of stimulating the economy during slack periods by increasing the money supply via government deficits. Employment increased, retail sales rose, factories hummed, corporate profits increased. Who could be against this? The other part of the prescription felt bad to the entire electorate; that of cooling off the economy during boom periods by cutting back the money supply through increased taxation and lower government spending, producing budget surpluses. Sales and profits slowed, some inefficient producers went bankrupt, and people lost jobs. Not something to be invited.

Politicians, with the next Election the measure of all things, eagerly embraced the "stimulate the economy" portion of the Keynesian prescription which "felt good" to the electorate and very simply meant votes for the party in power. But when it came time to cool off a boom economy by introducing the measure which "felt bad" and would lose votes, the politicians in power began visibly, and quite understandably, to drag their feet, a process which became progressively more pronounced during the 1960's on a worldwide basis, and came to full flower in the early 1970's.

Toward the end of the 1960's, the beneficent vote-getting effects of "stimulate the economy" policies were so appreciated by politicians in power, and indeed by the entire electorate as we have said, that another means of increasing the money supply to get these desired effects came into active use on a wider scale —policies of "Easy Money" put into effect by the Federal Reserve Board in the United States, and the central banks of various nations in western Europe.

"Easy Money" was fostered by the simple procedure of keeping interest rates as low as possible but, more important, at least keeping money *available,* even at higher rates, so that going into debt was encouraged. The consumer went into debt to buy homes, automobiles, vacations, washing machines, television sets and goods of all types; businesses went into debt to expand inventories and productive facilities. Government on all levels, municipal, state and Federal, went into greater debt to carry on their proliferating activities, with particular emphasis on their "social budget" — "doing things for the people."

Now, there is a process, mysterious to 99% of the Electorate and probably to not much less of a percentage of their elected representatives in government, by which the very act of government, consumer and business *going into debt* creates more and more money, virtually out of thin air, boosting the total money supply at an accelerating rate. (We shall shortly describe this very important process.) When the government increases its debt by operating at a deficit via heightened spending and/or lower taxation, this is called "fiscal policy" which creates more money to spend, aimed at stimulating the economy. When consumer and business go into debt by going to the banks for loans, the fostering of this through "Easy Money" is called "monetary policy" which is also aimed at stimulating the economy through increasing the money supply.

Well before the Presidential Election of November 1972 came on the scene, President Richard M. Nixon was so determined to have business booming and unemployment low at the time the citizens were entering the voting booths, that *both* policies to stimulate the economy, "fiscal" and "monetary", went into high gear several years earlier. Wildly successful, Gross National Product roared past the $1 Trillion mark, a record-breaking amount of all manner of goods cascaded off the assembly lines manned by the greatest number of workers in our history, and corporate profits rose sharply.

In November 1972 the grateful Electorate gave Mr. Nixon

an overwhelming victory and One-Way Keynesianism reached its high-water mark in modern economic history. But the unhappy awakening of Inflation and Shortages were not to lag very far behind at all and in 1973 the inexorable laws of Economics presented its Bill for the wild party of the previous few years. Before we discuss the Great Inflation of 1973 and the corollary stock market bust of 1973-1974, let's ask and answer some very basic questions:

1. What is the specific process by which an increase in the supply of money causes temporary prosperity?

2. Exactly how do you increase the supply of money?

3. And how does the process lead to economic sickness — to inflation, shortages and a bigger bust?

We Start Our inquiry

Imagine a free market economy such as our own, but on an isolated, relatively small Island, so we don't get lost in the complexities of "bigness". On that Island, people are working, factories producing, people buying. As would be normal in any free market system, there is some modest unemployment, factories are working at somewhat less than full productive capacity.

Enter a change. The political party in power and its head, the President of the Island, develop a plan to make things better. Everyone will take their money to the bank and according to the amount of currency they bring and the deposits already credited to their bank accounts, they will be entitled to receive *an additional equal amount* from the government. Everyone will have twice as much money as before with this 100% money bonus.

With these doubled funds, people flock to the stores and showrooms to buy more food, more clothing, more cars. Orders are placed for new homes. Vacation resorts are packed. The entire Island is bustling with activity. As the stores' shelves and dealers' inventories begin to empty, retailers place new orders with wholesalers, and wholesalers place new orders with the producing companies which, consequently, hire more employees and start running extra shifts in the factories. Unemployment vanishes. Profits rise for retailers, wholesalers, manufacturers.

A stroke of genius! People have more goods, unemployment is zero and business profits are up. Could anything be more lovely? (And with a new election due in a few months, the governing political party and the President at the helm are obviously quite happy about these roseate developments.)

Shortly after the election, however, which was a smashing endorsement of the President of the Island and his Party, some discordant notes begin to be heard in our new-found "Garden of Eden". The factories need time to produce more goods, and the store shelves and dealers' inventories are emptying out much faster than new goods can be produced and shipped. Consumers, their pockets still bulging with their expanded funds, begin to bid against one another for goods that *are* available.

Prices begin to rise.

The factories are on 3 shifts but much of the later months' production is already sold in advance even with the higher prices being asked, and consumers clamor to get promised delivery at still higher prices.

New troubles develop. Factories have enough personnel to run 3 shifts, but they begin to run out of the *raw materials* needed to produce their goods. Lumber gets into short supply, steel and all metals, plastics, paper and cartons, and the fuels needed to run everything at full tilt. Now prices really zoom as would-be purchasers, their pockets still bulging, bid for goods where shortages are restricting production. Pretty soon price levels are about double what they were when the process started.

The people of the Island begin to add up the upsetting effects of all the buying sprees on different aspects of their social structure and begin to think that they were *worse* off than before the money supply doubled.

A story or reality? Judge for yourself after you read the following quotations from articles and reports in this writer's files.

Dr. Milton Friedman's (Dr. Friedman is one of America's leading economists) column in Newsweek, August 6, 1973, after discussing a lecture he had given in Sweden in 1954: "I concluded my 1954 lecture by stating: 'Economists have known — at least intermittently — for over a century and a half two propositions: first, that by printing enough money you can produce any desired degree of activity; second, that the ultimate result is destruction of the currency. The American public has learned the first proposition. It once knew, but has now forgotten the second. Only experience is likely to teach it again.' We are paying a high price to acquire that experience."

The glow of prosperity when you blow up the money supply:

John O'Riley in his page 1 column in the Wall Street Journal, January 22, 1973: "The pace of business . . . enters the year booming on all fronts. The unemployment headlines are fading. Consumers are in a spending mood. Retailers have never pushed so much merchandise across their counters. Manufacturers, with order books bulging, are increasingly hard pressed to meet delivery demands . . ."

Dr. Raymond Jallow, senior vice president and chief economist of the United California Bank, as quoted in the Journal of Commerce, August 23, 1973, after a survey trip to Europe: "In the countries I visited I found that consumer spending is at an all-time high, businesses are operating with tremendous backlogs of orders and, in fact, they are at record levels . . ."

And governments know exactly what they are doing:

Business Week, November 28, 1970: ". . . domestic considerations come first for the Fed today (Federal Reserve Board-SF) . . . Fed officials had been aiming for a 5% rate of money supply growth in order to get the economy humming again. Now it apparently wants a 6% or 7% growth rate to keep peace with the expansionist-minded White House . . . So the Fed has been pulling out all stops to get the money supply growing once again . . ."

The Weekly Bond Buyer (now Money Manager), January 31, 1972: The Fed is still at it, with the election only 9 months away: "Federal Reserve policy has pulled out all stops since the turn of the year in pumping out more credit to force interest rates lower in the attempt to create more confidence and to accelerate the faltering economy . . ."

New York Times, November 17, 1969, in a news item from Manila: "The fact that this is an election year has aggravated conditions. Government spending has been prodigal as part of

Mr. Marcos' efforts to win a new term, and the day of reckoning was put off until polling was finished . . ."

Another well-known Wall Street Journal writer, Lindley H. Clark, Jr., in the issue of July 30, 1973: "Government causes inflation by creating and spending too much money, and inflation won't ever stop until government stops doing so."

Shortly after the rush of good business from the money supply expansion comes rising prices:

The Wall Street Journal, August 13, 1973, discussing Europe: "Inflation is happening so much faster lately that single digits such as 5% or 9% no longer suffice to measure the increases in a single year's time in wages and prices. Instead, it is becoming necessary to use double numbers such as 10% . . . Of 19 member countries studied, the OECD (Organization for Economic Cooperation and Development) found seven of them with a seasonally adjusted annual rate of consumer price increases of at least 10% in the three months ended April 30 . . ."

As the inflation proceeds, along come shortages and runaway raw material prices. (and much more about this later.)

Same Wall Street Journal article, August 13, 1973: "The money supplies in dozens of nations are swelling by double digit annual rates these days, the International Monetary Fund's figures show . . . Even triple numbers aren't unheard of in measuring price changes. Such basic commodities as wheat, corn, lard, wool and rubber all show price changes of around 100%, or even much more during the past year . . ."

Then come the really threatening clouds.

New York Times, August 6, 1973: "Business in the United States is operating at a 'very high and perhaps unhealthy pace' according to the National Association of Purchasing Management, Inc., and as a result there are 'frustrating distortions and dislocations.' " Same issue: "Boom Economy in Europe Feared Heading For Crash."

We are going to return to all the above in detail. We have presented these few quick vignettes from the literally thousands of articles in our files to illustrate the fact that what we have just described on our mythical "Island" was not just a "story" at all but corresponding to full reality.

We return to the *starting point* now for the whole dangerous process, which is the expansion of the money supply, and inquire into *just how* money is created and goes into so many pockets to produce its eventually devastating results.

How Government Manufactures Money Out of Thin Air

The two principal routes by which government inflates the Money Supply are deficit spending and encouragement of debt expansion via the commercial banks. Both routes are simple in design and easy to grasp so that it is rather remarkable that few have knowledge of them when they drastically affect not only our economic way of life, but every facet of our society as well — the way we live, raise our families and perpetuate our values.

Our point of departure is to envisage the basic Money Supply. It consists of currency in circulation — the bills you carry in your wallet and the change in your pocket— plus, and far larger, your demand deposits in the bank. A little reflection will show that this covers the money *immediately* available to buy goods. When you pay for any goods or services, from a hamburger at the local drive-in, to a visit to the doctor, to a down payment on a new home, you take bills out of your pocket or you write a check. Anything beyond this is not immediately available.

Thus, you may own 100 shares of American Telephone & Telegraph common stock, or a piece of land near a lake, or some kind of other property which can be sold. But before you are able to spend the money value of that property, you would have *to sell it,* which typically can't be done on an immediate basis. And if you wanted to sell hurriedly, you would probably receive much less than what you could have received if there wasn't such time pressure.

But cash in your pocket or a checking account in the bank *is* immediately available to make a purchase, and that is why it comprises what most economists accept as "The Money Supply". It is easily followed with exactness because the Treasury knows how much currency is in circulation and the banking system regularly reports on the total of demand deposits. Some financial analysts think *Time* Deposits should also be included, comprising money on deposit with banks which cannot be withdrawn before a stipulated time without penalty of some kind — such as Certificates of Deposit, for example — but we see no gain in stopping the general flow of this explanation to discuss such points. Suffice it to say that when you look at any chart of the basic Money Supply, currency and demand deposits (sometimes known as M1), and we will shortly be looking at such charts, you see a marked growth from 1963 through 1970 and then an acceleration of that growth since 1970.

Government Budgetary Deficits — First Route of Ballooning The Money Supply

When government pays its federal employees, buys an aircraft carrier, gives a subsidy payment to a shipbuilder or a pension to a veteran, puts up a federal building, or makes a torrent of other government expenditures, it puts money in the pockets of all who have done this work, or otherwise earned their payment according to our laws. When all the people, as individuals or as businesses, pay income taxes to the Federal government, they have to take money *out* of their pockets.

If government expenditures are equaled by the income it receives in taxes, the budget is in "balance" and all the pockets in America have neither less nor more money than before. A certain sum has gone in — an equal sum has come out. But what if the government spends $300 billion during its fiscal year and takes in only $260 billion in taxes? There will be a $40 billion deficit, with the following effect: the government has put $300 billion into the pockets of Americans as it paid for all the goods and services it bought, and then it has reached into those same pockets for only $260 billion in taxes. *American pockets now have $40 billion more in them than they had before.* $40 billion has been added to the Money Supply, available to purchase goods and services.

Now let's look at a chart of total Federal Spending — and the lower portion of the chart showing whether each fiscal year was in surplus (income greater than expenditures) or deficit (income smaller than expenditures). And remember that a surplus *shrinks* the Money Supply while a deficit *inflates* the Money Supply. As we have seen from quotations in previous paragraphs, the direct aim of the government was to inflate the Money Supply to "stimulate the economy", and budgetary deficits were an important means used by the Nixon Administration to accomplish this end. As we see on the lower part of the chart shown on page 66 (courtesy of M/G Financial Weekly, issue of February 11, 1974), the back-to-back budgetary deficits of President Nixon's Administration, 1971-1973, were the greatest in America's peacetime history.

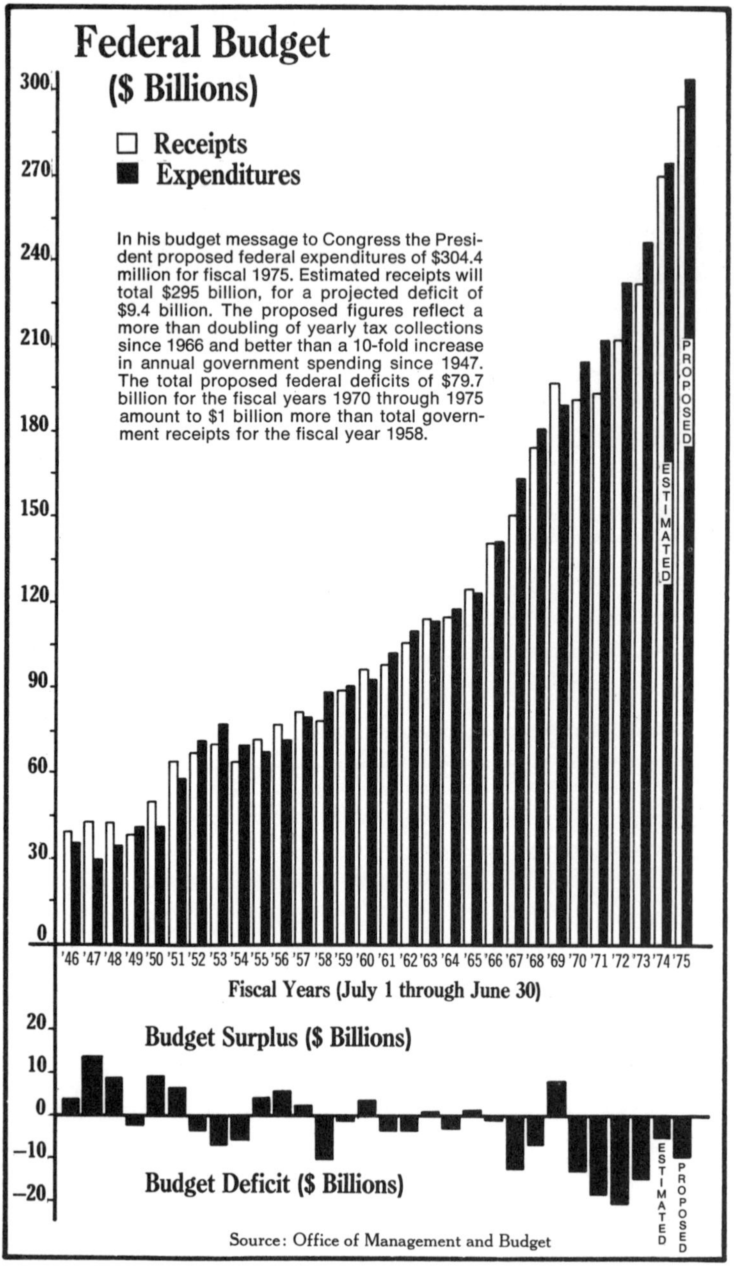

Federal Budget
($ Billions)
Receipts
Expenditures
In his budget message to Congress the President proposed federal expenditures of $304.4 million for fiscal 1975. Estimated receipts will total $295 billion, for a projected deficit of $9.4 billion. The proposed figures reflect a more than doubling of yearly tax collections since 1966 and better than a 10-fold increase in annual government spending since 1947. The total proposed federal deficits of $79.7 billion for the fiscal years 1970 through 1975 amount to $1 billion more than total government receipts for the fiscal year 1958.
300
270
240
210
180
150
120
90
60
30
0
ESTIMATED
PROPOSED
'46 '47 '48 '49 '50 '51 '52 '53 '54 '55 '56 '57 '58 '59 '60 '61 '62 '63 '64 '65 '66 '67 '68 '69 '70 '71 '72 '73 '74 '75
Fiscal Years (July 1 through June 30)
20
10
0
-10
-20
Budget Surplus ($ Billions)
Budget Deficit ($ Billions)
ESTIMATED
PROPOSED
Source: Office of Management and Budget

Encouraging Debt — Second Route of Money Inflation

Banks earn profits by lending out their depositors' funds at a higher interest rate than they are paying to secure those deposits. That's certainly a simple proposition. What many find less simple to understand, but is crucial to this discussion, is that in the act of lending out their depositors' funds, *the banks create more money,* and that this process, aided and encouraged by Government policy, is one of the chief sources of inflation. Here is how it works.

Mr. A wants to buy a new car which costs $3,000, but doesn't have the cash available at the moment. He asks his neighbor, Mr. B, to lend him the $3,000 and Mr. B agrees to do so, writing a check to Mr. A's order, which Mr. A deposits in his checking account preparatory to making his purchase. Mr. A's checking account now shows $3,000 more and Mr. B's checking account shows $3,000 less. Net effect on the money supply? None.

Change of Scenario. Mr. A doesn't go to Mr. B for the loan. *He goes to the bank where Mr. B has his checking account, and gets an auto loan from the bank.* In a sense Mr. B has made that loan possible because if he wasn't a depositor (along with thousands of others) the bank wouldn't have the money to lend. Can the bank lend all its deposits out at one time? That would hardly seem safe because they wouldn't have funds on hand to meet withdrawals. So government regulation decrees that banks must keep a portion of their deposits *in reserve,* and this requirement varies from time to time, and also can vary according to the bank's location. A 20% reserve is close enough for purposes of this discussion, so if Mr. B has, say, a total of $20,000 on deposit in the bank, the bank can lend out 80% of that, or up to $16,000. It is understandable that the bank will want to have all its available funds working to the maximum extent, whether in loans, which are generally high-yielding, or in investments such as government bonds, etc., which are generally lower-yielding. Remember that the bank has to pay interest on its savings accounts and time deposits and must also show a profit for its stockholders. Thus, it has to keep its deposits working.

We are ready now to consider the effect of Mr. B's bank granting a $3,000 auto loan to Mr. A. The bank writes a check to Mr. A's order which Mr. A deposits in his bank. Mr. A's deposit goes up $3,000, against which he can write checks. Does anyone's deposit go *down* $3,000 to counterbalance this? No, not Mr. B's deposit or anyone else's. For Mr. B's *bank* has made the loan, and not Mr. B himself. Mr. B still has his full $20,000 in deposits ready to buy anything he chooses to buy at the writing of a check. And Mr. A now has $3,000 more to his deposit with which he can buy his car. The Money Supply has gone up.

But that is only the beginning of this remarkable accounting. *Mr. A's bank* acquires $3,000 in new money when Mr. A deposits the proceeds of his loan. They put 20% of that, or $600, into reserves as required by law, and find that their lending power has expanded by the remaining $2,400. They grant that $2,400 as a loan to Mr. C who needs it to pay a child's college tuition. When Mr. C deposits the proceeds of the loan in *his* bank, this new bank has acquired $2,400 in new money, sequesters 20% of that as reserves, or $480, and has $1,920 additional to lend to someone else.

Financial experts have the table all worked out to estimate the expansion in the Money Supply caused by $1 initially loaned by a commercial bank, and that estimate is about *$6* by the time the arithmetic we have described makes its rounds. You will soon be looking at a chart of the actual expansion of the Money Supply, not only in the United States, but throughout the non-Communist world. Obviously, the additional money had to come from *somewhere,* and there is no question that the vast majority of it came from the unique ability of each $1 loaned by a commercial bank to not only expand the Money Supply by $1 on an immediate basis, but to expand the available lendable funds by the banking system as a whole by about *$6,* through the multiplier effect we have described. Joining up with deficits in the Federal budget, we have the twin means here for expanding the Money Supply.

The publisher, R.H.M. Press, has agreed to make available to the reader, at no extra charge, a Special Supplement, giving the author's current and completely updated analysis and statistical presentation of the entire list of currently outstanding Warrants, plus a summary of the most promising low-price stocks in today's markets, in accordance with the concepts set forth in this book. A fuller description of the Special Supplement will be found on page 3.

To receive this Special Supplement, important to following developing opportunities, send you name and address—be sure to include zip—to:

R.H.M. Press
Department 95
220 Fifth Avenue
New York, N.Y. 10001

There will be no charge for this Special Supplement.

The "Stimulate-The--Economy" — "Growth" — Craze of the Early 1970's

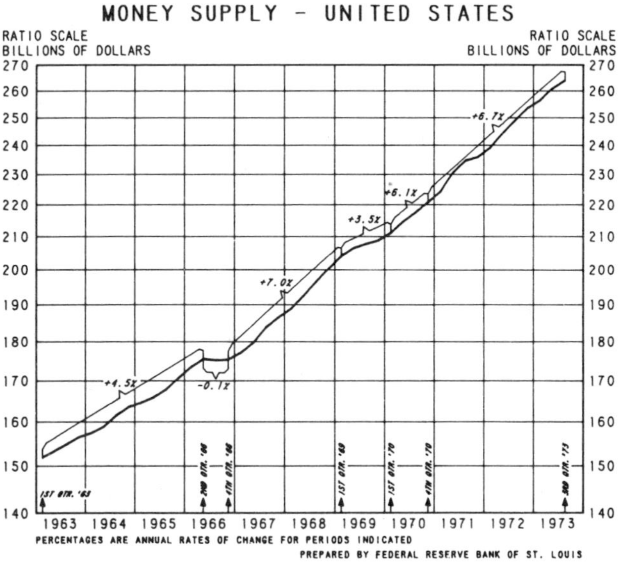

Above we see the palpable evidence of exactly what we have been discussing in the past few pages. Far from our mythical "Island" being an interesting story, but no more than a story, it almost exactly described what actually happened in our country in the years shown on the chart and was precisely accomplished by the very deliberate use of budgetary deficits and encouragement of debt through commercial banks, with the blunt and openly-expressed aim of "stimulating the economy." Government stopped short of saying that the true aim of business acceleration was to gain votes from a grateful electorate, but who did not know that this was the aim?

Indeed, when we enlarge our canvas to include the entire non-Communist world, and observe the same process at work throughout, we shall have no trouble in finding all the evidence we want that the game of "Expand The Money Supply" had purely political ends.

MONEY SUPPLY - BELGIUM

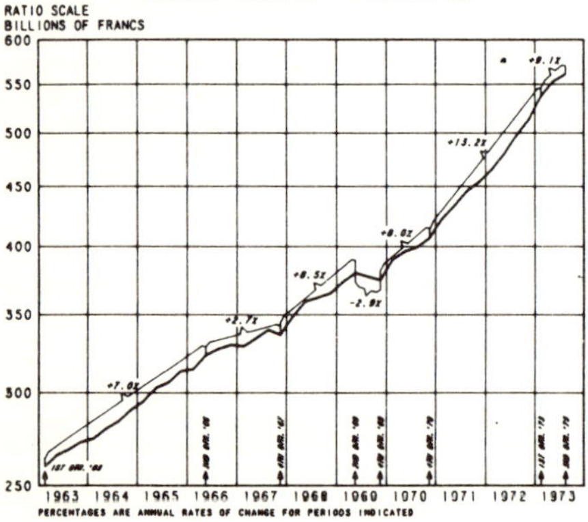

MONEY SUPPLY - CANADA

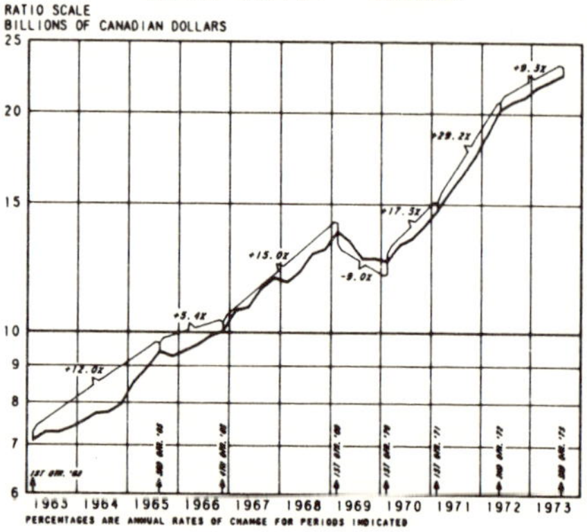

MONEY SUPPLY - GERMANY

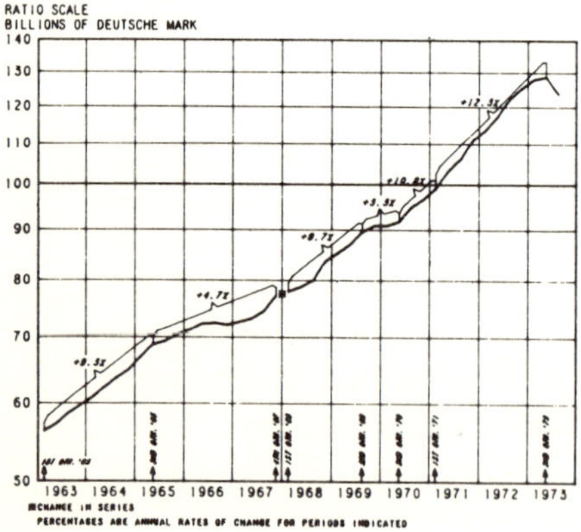

MONEY SUPPLY - FRANCE

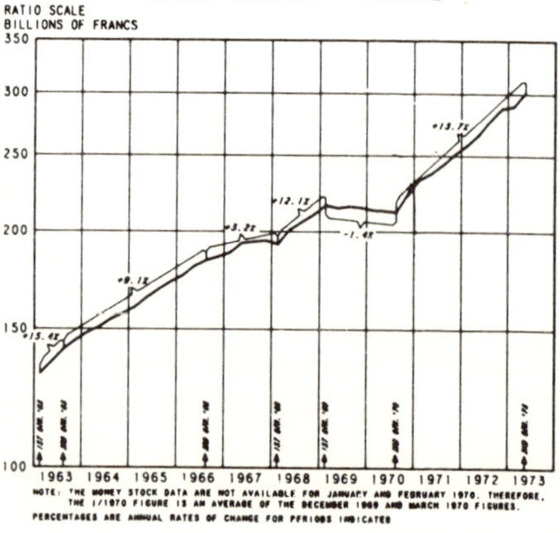

MONEY SUPPLY - ITALY

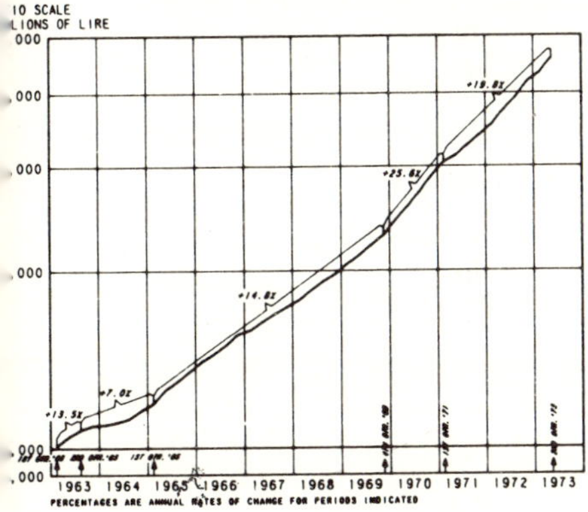

MONEY SUPPLY - JAPAN

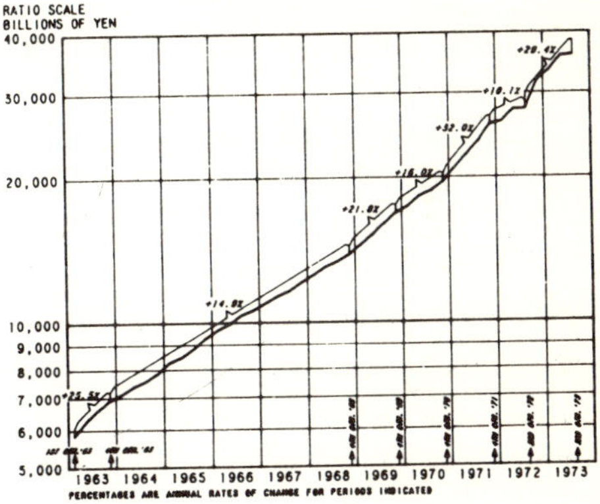

MONEY SUPPLY - SWITZERLAND

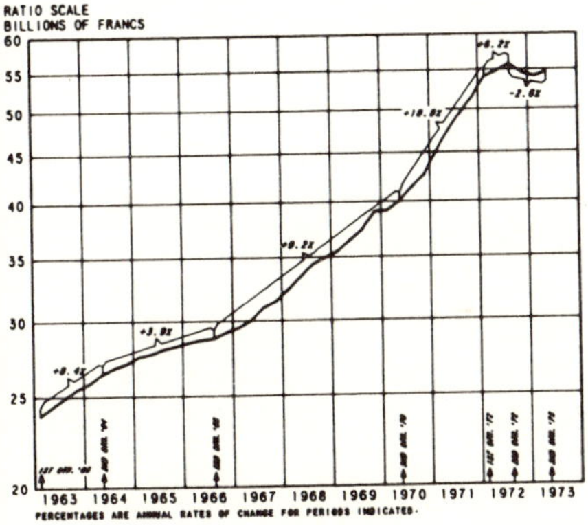

MONEY SUPPLY - UNITED KINGDOM

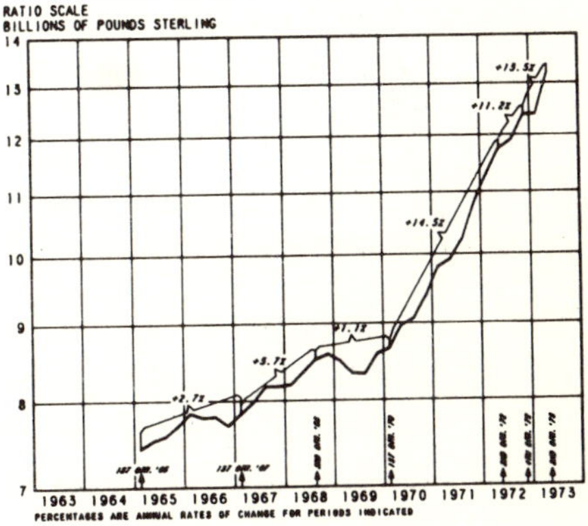

All the charts shown came from the December 28, 1973 issue of "Rates of Change In Economic Data For Ten Industrial Countries," prepared by the Federal Reserve Bank of St. Louis.

We have already noted how well understood were the aims of Money Supply ballooning in the United States. Recall our quotation from Business Week, November 28, 1970, given on a previous page: ". . . domestic considerations come first for the Fed today (Federal Reserve Board-SF) . . . Fed officials had been aiming for a 5% rate of money supply growth in order to get the economy humming again. Now it apparently wants a 6% or 7% growth rate to keep peace with the expansionist-minded White House . . . So the Fed has been pulling out all stops to get the money supply growing again . . ."

Now let's look at other countries to find the political aims spelled out with a similar lack of mystery. (All emphasis is added by us.)

Journal of Commerce, August 2, 1972: "Rome, Aug. 1 — The Italian Government has submitted to Parliament a 1973 budget designed to *stimulate recovery through public spending* that nearly doubles the over-all deficit to a record 4,550,300 million lire ($7,845 million)."

New York Times, July 27, 1972: "Buenos Aires, July 26: Argentina's anti-inflationary forces suffered a sharp setback when the resignation of Carlos S. Brignone as president of the central bank was announced by the military Government here just before midnight yesterday. Mr. Brignone, widely known in international banking circles for his often futile efforts to raise loans, has been Argentina's most outspoken opponent of *inflation-breeding Governmental deficit spending* . . . Argentina's inflation rate reached a record 37 per cent in the first half, compared with 40 per cent for all 1971 . . ."

The Money Manager, October 16, 1972: "Prices Soar as France Opts for Growth: Inflation . . . is accelerating at an alarming rate. Prices mounted 6.5% over the last 12 months, and some predict this year's total to reach 7%. One explanation for this skyrocketing in prices lies in today's liberal monetary policy (read, ballooning of the money supply! SF). The government is conscious of this, and several weeks ago it expressed a desire to limit credit expansion. *Because of the forthcoming elections, however, it cannot dare to make a small gesture.*"

The Money Manager, June 11, 1973: "Italy and France, both currently suffering a 10% annual inflation rate, stress the necessity for growth above all . . ."

U. S. News & World Report, November 20, 1972, from London: "Union belligerency led the Government to discard the idea of curbing inflation through a policy of deflation because of the concern that it would also lead to even higher unemployment. *Deflation was written off as politically intolerable . . .*"

New York Times, August 6, 1973: "Spain, which has one of the highest rates of growth in Europe, is refusing to sacrifice it in the interest of price stability. Both the Government and the Bank of Spain made clear recently that they prefer inflation to the possibility of stagnation even though prices are also rising at one of the highest rates in Europe . . ."

The Journal of Commerce, November 13, 1972: "West Germany, which throughout the 1960's managed to keep price increases to about 2 per cent annually and has earned the 'island of stability' label is suffering today from a potent dose of inflation . . . Helmut Schmidt, Bonn's economic and finance minister . . . has argued that only a concerted Common Market approach can be effective in checking the rising inflationary drift. *To Mr. Schmidt, 5 per cent inflation is more acceptable than 5 per cent unemployment . . .*"

We could go on and on here — our files are bulging. But it isn't necessary to go further than the following excellent and realistic summary of why it was that once the "feeling good" effects of an expanding money supply via budgetary deficit and debt encouragement commenced, it developed its own inevitable momentum. U. S. News & World Report, February 5, 1973: "What is behind the exploding inflation in Europe? . . . Says a Zurich banker: 'The higher the rate of inflation, the more drastic is the action needed to stop it. But Governments everywhere in Europe hesitate to announce unpopular steps that hurt. All put full employment, maximum social welfare and a high rate of growth ahead of price stability. *Governments simply haven't the political courage to fight inflation effectively.'* " (That last statement deserves a *double* emphasis! SF)

Next Step: Reality Shatters The Feverish Political Dream of Expand, Expand, Expand.

A basic fact about the typical individual human is that his wants are insatiable, and limited only by his opportunities to satisfy them. In economic terms, this means any of us would want two or three cars and two or three homes instead of just one, and every appurtenance of expensive living, if we could only afford to buy all of them.

That last phrase, of course, tells us all. Just as on our mythical Island, when each citizen suddenly had twice as much money, he began to buy, buy, buy. The initial result could not be faulted. The individual consumer had more goods; retailers did brisk business; wholesalers rushed to reorder to replenish their vanishing inventories of goods; and factories put on extra shifts.

Profits and wages went higher, while unemployment went down.

A true word picture of the United States in 1972-early-1973! And not only the United States, as running through the news articles of 1971-1973 we find such terms as "Swinging London", the "Miracle of Italy", the "Miracle of West Germany", the "Miracle of Japan". (The word "Miracle" became a little overworked.)

In the United States the average number of automobiles per household climbed and the affluent suburbs became choked with cars so that parking and easy movement became a problem, just as it had been in the central cities.

Per capita consumption of beef in the United States, a hallmark of the "better life", climbed as follows:

Year	*Pounds of Beef Consumed Per Capita*
1962	88.8
1966	104.2
1973	118.0

Overseas, in the lands of all the "Miracles", the following news item was quite typical. Wall Street Journal, October 19, 1973: "As you walk through the streets of central Tokyo, you see well-dressed shoppers snapping up imported luxury goods. They pay $27 for a bottle of Johnny Walker Black Label Scotch and hardly glance at the price tag. For a set of Spalding golf clubs they shell out $760. Chauffeur-driven Toyota and Nissan sedans have supplanted the two cylinder minicars of the 1960's as major contributors to the city's endless traffic jams. Gleaming office buildings go up as fast as old ones are torn down to make room for them."

At about the same time, summarizing the euphoric picture of production and consumption in the United States, late-1973, the U. S. News & World Report said in its issue of October 15, 1973: "With less than three months to go, 1973 is shaping up as the most prosperous year in U. S. history. By almost every measure, business activity after three years of growth and boom is reaching record levels. Total output in the U.S. is moving past the 1.25 trillion mark, a big 11 per cent jump over 1972. Jobs, people's incomes and spending, profits of corporations, sales of new cars — all are setting new highs this year."

Three cheers! Let's hear it for our kindly, wise and far-seeing government!

But didn't someone say that everything pleasurable is illegal, immoral or fattening? This aphorism certainly holds for our current discussion. All the above pleasures of "ballooning the Money Supply" with its welcome political dividends had a fatal flaw — a guaranteed "Waterloo".

Raw Materials, of course; and Energy, of course.

Food, automobiles, houses, boats, appliances, goods of all descriptions, must be produced and manufactured of *real things.* Wheat, corn, cattle, hogs; and iron, copper, rubber, lumber, concrete, aluminum, paper, etc., etc.; all must feed the faster-moving assembly lines, food processing plants and other production machinery; and Energy in the form of oil, coal, natural gas is needed in ever greater quantities to keep all the wheels turning.

The increasing Money Supply had taken the normally limitless demand (who doesn't want more?) and, in part, had made it *effective* demand. But while you can print paper dollars in about as great a volume as you care to, when those bits of paper go rushing out to buy real goods, they find rather quickly that *goods aren't as limitless as money* because there are strict limits on the supply of raw materials and Energy to *produce* the goods.

Just as the clinical thermometer tells us something is wrong with a person when he begins to run a fever, so the wholesale and consumer indices tell us the same thing when the *economy* begins to run a fever — sick from the injection of too much paper money.

Ironically, the same U. S. News & World Report, in its issue of January 14, 1974, just three months after the last article we quoted (October 15, 1973) detailing ". . . the most prosperous year in U. S. history . . ." had now to report the following: "Costs of basic raw materials, the key ingredients of almost everything people buy and use, are shooting skyward. In just two months — from October to December — the prices of a representative group of metals, fibers, rubber, hides and other raw materials increased more than 11 per cent. That is equivalent to an annual rate of 68 per cent."

Putting the picture into a longer-term context, look at the chart of the Futures Price Index of the Commodity Research Bureau (used by permission of the Futures Market Service of that organization).

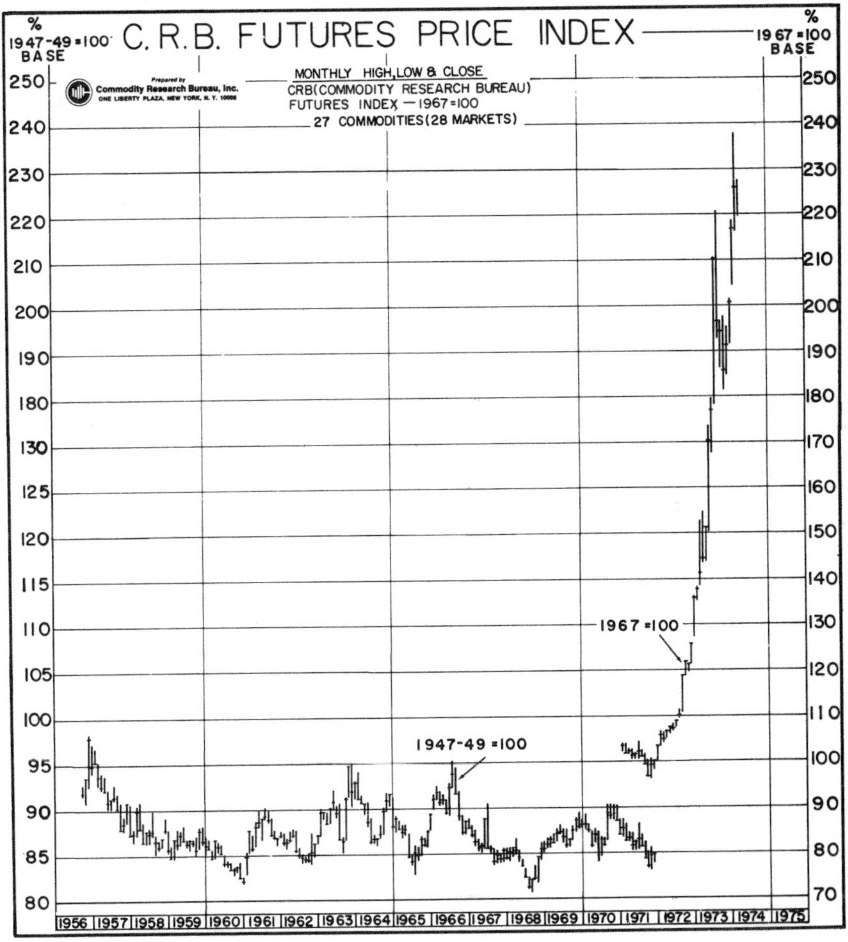

Measuring 27 basic commodities, it shows the veritable explosion in prices as the ballooning Money Supply in all of the industrialized non-Communist nations inspired swelling consumer buying of all manners of goods and services, producing the much-desired "growth" but putting unbearable pressure on the available supplies of almost all raw materials and energy sources with the final result of the greatest and most dangerous wave of inflation ever experienced in the United States and many other nations.

The Path Begins To Lead Back To Low-Price Warrants and Low-Price Stocks

Throughout 1973-early-1974, even as new records were being set throughout the American economy, *including* corporate profits, the stock market declined—first hesitantly, then nervously, then sharply. Leveraged Warrant opportunities began to emerge in the longest list of publicly-traded Warrants ever seen in market history (more than 350 different Warrant issues) as Warrants which had previously been selling at $40 and higher, and at $30 and $20, plummeted to the $10 level, and the $5 level, and $1 level, with many Warrants dropping down to the "pennies" class, in which price area the greatest Warrant leverage has historically developed.

A similar long list of literally thousands of stocks, listed and unlisted, dropped to small fractions of their former highs and many formerly household names, nationally-known companies, became depressed, low-price stocks. More speculative stocks in smaller companies began to drop into the $5 to $1 price range where, historically, the greatest percentage appreciation potential has developed in previous market cycles, during subsequent recovery periods.

There is a direct connection between everything we have described about the inflationary whirl of 1970-1974 and the development of such leveraged market opportunities, with such opportunities having the potential of becoming even greater, *more* highly-leveraged, depending upon economic and stock market events which could be right over the near horizon. It all has to do with one great danger which the American people allowed themselves to be pushed into (and it was also a world-wide phenomenon) because politician and Electorate alike had a very deficient understanding of economics and economic history, and also because (equally important) the "feeling good" part of the "Ballooning The Money Supply" party automatically shunted tomorrow's possible worries into the background.

That great danger is expressed in one word: Debt.

Recall that the chief engine for expanding the Money Supply is the creation of Debt. Federal budgetary deficits increase the Money Supply as government goes more deeply into debt. Commercial banks create more money as individuals and corporations go into greater debt to them through loans of all types; loans to build new plants and expand inventories where businesses are concerned, and loans to buy homes, cars, refrigerators, vacations and a thousand other desired goods and services where individuals are concerned.

As we borrow and borrow and borrow, the Money Supply expands and expands and expands and "prosperity" burgeons.

But the growing Debt, intertwined with all the above, has two unsettling characteristics: (1) Interest charges come due for payment regularly and begin to take a larger and larger share of income, and (2) Debts have maturity dates when they must be repaid or renewed.

While the economic indices are spiraling upward in the earlier stages, with business profits and personal income climbing faster than debt and its interest costs, there isn't generally much trouble about meeting the interest burden or "rolling over" maturing debt. But to keep a money-inflation going, the mountain of debt has to *keep growing too* and as it gets higher and higher, stirrings of anxiety begin to manifest themselves more and more and finally emerge into full consciousness when they reach the stage of "blow-off" price inflation, as raw material shortages hit.

Suddenly there is a more widespread sinking feeling that business may *not* just get better and better and better, that the whole economic machine might slow down because of shortages and "out-of-sight" prices. Deeply troubling questions can no longer be ignored. If personal and corporate incomes decline, can the interest burden be met? And in a more threatening economic climate, will maturing debt so easily be "rolled over" with new debt? It is time to look at the threatening rate of multiplication of debt in the United States in recent history to appreciate the true seriousness of the questions posed above — underlying fears of what the probable answers might be accounting for much of the steep stock market decline of 1973-1974, in our opinion.

Debt — The Ticking Time Bomb

Our country is perched dangerously on a mountain of Debt which has reached such proportions because of the typical inflationary psychology of the past few years that it will threaten the stability of our economy, indeed our very way of life, for at least the next few years, until wiser policies, which we feel are coming, take effective hold. In this writer's opinion, the *best* we can hope for, in the next year at least, is a period of great unsettlement. Several varieties of the "worst" can also happen if we do not find some good answers (they *are* available, and we will later discuss them).

The above being our expectations, we look for a series of very wide swings in the stock market, giving important scope to highly-leveraged, low-price Warrants and low-price stocks to take best advantage of these swings in line with analyses we have already presented and with further guideposts to come in later pages. If a variety of the "worst" develops for the economy and/or the stock market, then profit opportunities will come into view of historic dimensions for hundreds of Warrants and stocks plummeting to severe lows. But let's look first at the actuality of Debt, which ticks away like a giant time bomb in our midst.

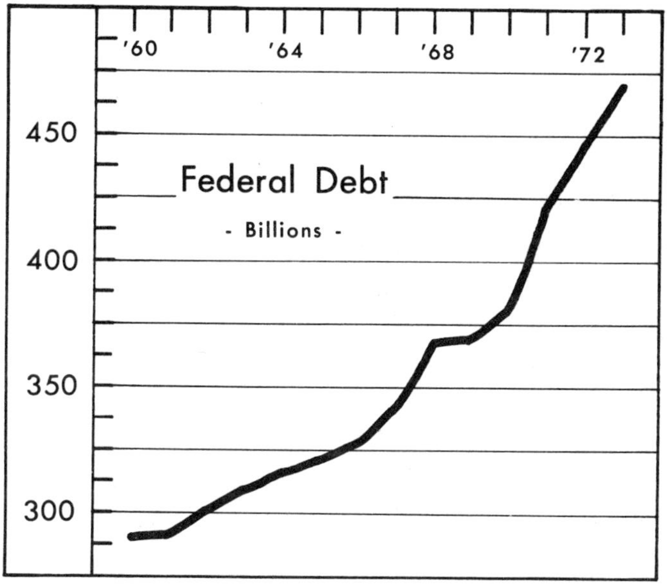

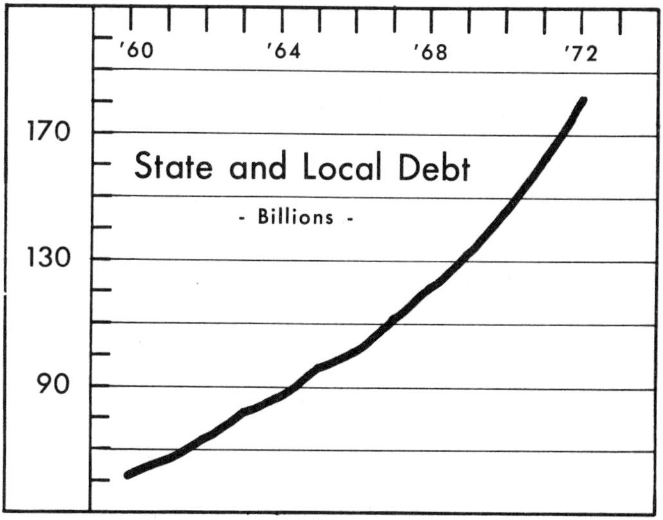

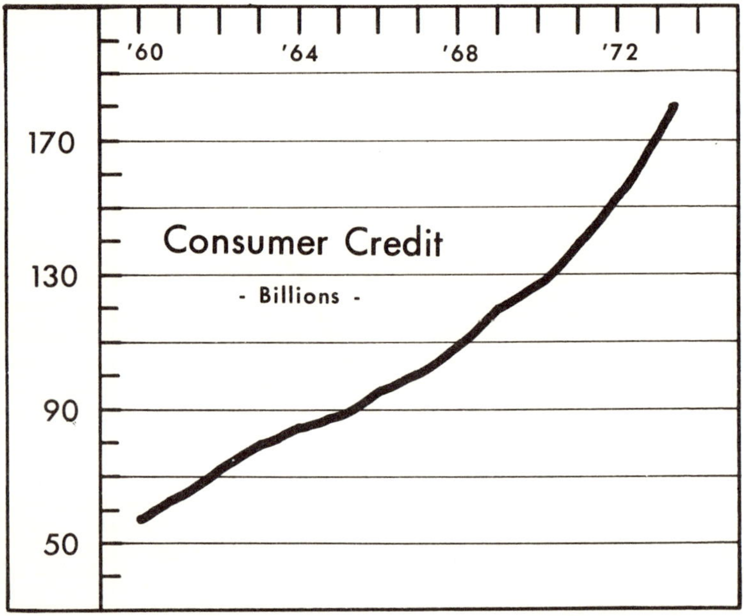
'60
'64
'68
'72
170
130
90
50
Consumer Credit
- Billions -

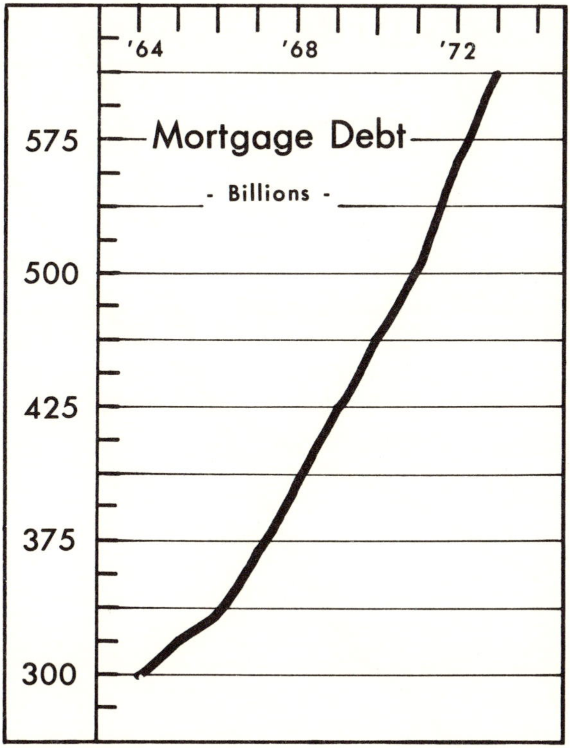
'64
'68
'72
575
500
425
375
300
Mortgage Debt
- Billions -

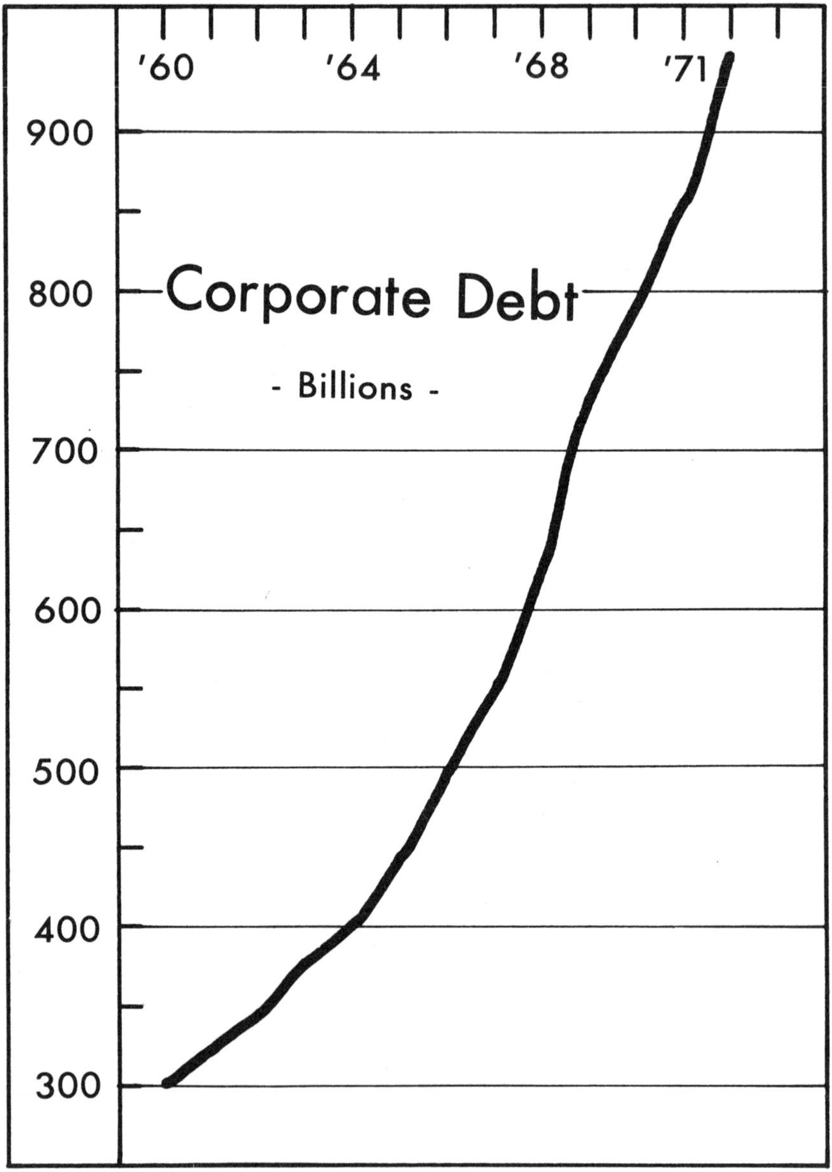
'60
'64
'68
'71
900
800
700
600
500
400
300
Corporate Debt
- Billions -

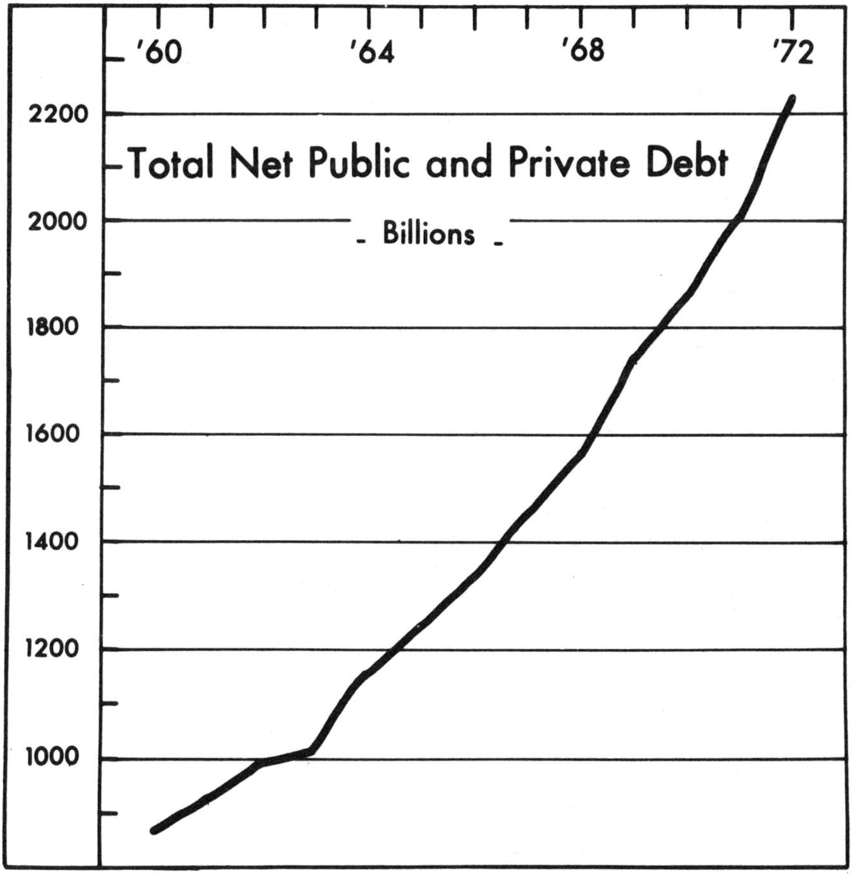
'60
'64
'68
'72
2200
2000
1800
1600
1400
1200
1000
Total Net Public and Private Debt
Billions

There is no precedent in our economic history for the rate of growth of Debt in all sectors, public and private, experienced in the years 1970-1973. The most pernicious factor in allowing the expansion of the Money Supply to get beyond reasonable limits is that it is inevitably accompanied by rising prices which, if this becomes pronounced and prolonged, fosters the belief that one should spend what one has, and then borrow and spend what one does *not* have, because tomorrow the price will be higher. Alongside this belief is the parallel one which states: the Government will never allow a recession but will keep pumping up the balloon with more money, so why be afraid of "over"-spending?

Government, federal, state and local, then borrows more and spends more to have the Electorate smile at them for what they are "doing for the people." The army of American consumers borrows more and spends more with the slogan "Enjoy, enjoy." And American business expands and expands to meet increased demand, building new plants, stocking more inventory and going into greater Debt wherever necessary to accomplish all this, because won't everything cost much more tomorrow, and won't Government prevent any serious economic downturn?

The charts shown represent most of the important components going into the final chart showing "Total Net Public and Private Debt," which has by now probably reached the almost incredible total of 2.5 Trillion Dollars.

It is difficult to say which of those components are the most dangerous. While the Federal government can always print more money (that is, sell more bonds to the banks), this easy road isn't available to anyone else. Many more states and municipalities can be pushed to the brink of insolvency by even a moderate economic decline than is realized by most of today's observers, reared in such a lengthy period of bottomless government cornucopias.

The nation's banks find their liquidity ratio (cash plus government securities in relation to total deposits) at all-time lows when many of their outstanding loans, notably sky-high mortgage credit, could become exceedingly troublesome should recession and heightened unemployment develop.

The hapless Consumer has gone much too far in pursuing the "Good Life" with borrowed money. He now finds *about one-quarter of his income just going toward meeting interest payments,* and if his income declines, what then?

And Corporate Debt (you will be hearing *much* about this category in later pages) would lead to much more wringing of hands if there were not such widespread ignorance concerning the true meaning of the growth of this category of debt.

A few years ago an ecstatic President Nixon announced that Gross National Product of the United States had passed the magic figure of *One Trillion Dollars.* We didn't see a similar expression of satisfaction in early-1974 when another *One Trillion Dollars* figure was reached — for *Corporate Debt!*

Just as is true of the banks, Corporate liquidity ratios are at an all-time low. The ratio of available cash plus cash-equivalents to Short-Term Debt looks like this when charted.

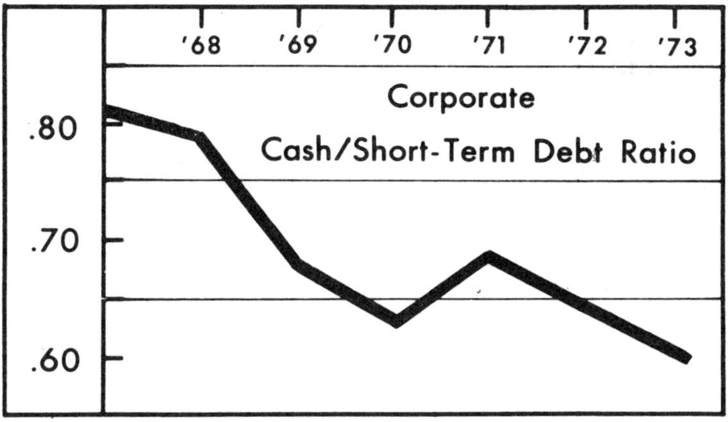

To any financial analyst with experience going back well before the "Balloon The Money Supply" — permanent prosperity epoch, this spells a great deal of potential trouble for many companies. Like the American Consumer who finds one-quarter of his income going to meet interest payments, the American Corporation is in even worse shape, with one-*third* of current earnings earmarked to carry an interest burden now at an awesome level of about *$40 billion.* (That's just the yearly *interest,* keep in mind.)

We find it necessary to report even more dark clouds than those already revealed by the above charts and statistics. With the purchasing power of the American dollar shrinking and shrinking, who is eager to buy long-term bonds? (Lend someone $1 today and be repaid with 50¢ or 25¢ dollars 10 to 20 years hence?) Consequently, short-term credit has of necessity more and more been replacing long-term credit as the feasible mode of financing. Look at the Federal Debt, for example. In 1946, 32.6% of the Debt matured in one year. By 1964, this had risen to *39.4%,* and at the end of 1973, fully *52.3%* of the Federal Debt came due in one year.

Looking at this from another vantage point, in 1946 the average of Federal Debt maturity was about 9 years. By 1964 this had deteriorated to 5 years. And by 1973 it had sunk to a record low of *3 years.* We will discuss the threat to stability involved in this development as soon as we outline comparable figures for the government's companion-in-distress, the American Corporation.

Corporate Debt Moves To Shorter and Shorter Maturities

In 1970 American corporations went to the money markets for $38.8 billion. Of this total (all subsequent figures from the Federal Reserve Board) 76.8% was long-term credit and only 23.2% was short-term, the latter including bank loans, commercial paper, bankers acceptances and government loans.

1971 saw a lessened use of short-term credit instruments, the total of $47.4 billion being comprised of 88.6% long-term credit, 11.4% short-term credit, although one must point out that the *total* borrowed (itself having large consequences) was an all-time record in a really big way, 22% higher than in 1970.

1972 saw a disquieting swing to short-term credit. Of the $54.6 billion total, 15% higher than 1971, only 70% was long-term credit and fully *30%* was now short-term "paper".

It remained for 1973, however, to bring this trend to an ominous stage (why ominous we shall soon see). Firstly, the total of $70 billion in new borrowing was *28% higher* than 1972, which had been 15% higher than 1971, which had been 22% higher than 1970 — an unprecedented rate of acceleration for corporate debt. Secondly, short-term credit actually moved past long-term credit in use, the former comprising *50.3%* of the total new borrowings.

The mounting potential problems are easy to see. When debt matures, you either have to retire it from available cash or "roll it over" — that is, get a new loan to replace the old one. To suggest that government at any level *retire* any debt out of cash is laughable, the reality of the situation with both parties being much more attuned to spending than to saving. And we have already demonstrated the poor cash/short-term debt ratio position of American corporations.

So the possibilities of *retiring* debt can be dubbed negligible for both government and business, and we are left with only one practical direction: replace maturing debt with *new* debt. Can the reader fail to see the *pressure* this puts on the money market? If government, consumer, and business continue to increase their debts and to go to ever-shorter periods of debt maturity, the competition for available new money must of necessity become insistent, and could become frantic. At best, interest rates would rise periodically to a "crunch" stage (the "price" of money is the interest rate, and competition works here just as with any other commodity) making more mountainous the annual interest burden already taking so much of the current income of government, consumer and business.

But there is an "at worst" to consider too — a "money squeeze" developing with new money becoming unavailable to any but the better credit risks and painfully expensive even to the creditworthy. For companies lower down on the creditworthy scale, this would threaten liquidation of inventories and assets, inability to meet maturing debt and/or interest payments and, for an appreciable number, bankruptcy. And once such a trend gets underway it develops its own momentum in a manner we hardly need to describe.

An exaggerated description?

Here are a few recent quotations to underline how the true perils are beginning to emerge into the consciousness of our more knowledgeable observers.

Journal of Commerce, December 19, 1973: "Financing problems of corporations in 1974 have been intensified by the energy crisis, according to a report for institutional investors by the bond market research department of Salomon Brothers. Henry Kaufman, general partner of the firm, points out that financial pressures on corporations would have developed even if there had been no energy crisis. Shortages of fuel and raw materials will cut business revenues and increase expenses, he points out. The report points to the deterioration of the maturity structure of corporate debt, now top-heavy with short-term liabilities. It also mentions the decline in short-term liquidity ratios and the 'eroding ability of corporate cash flow to cover interest payments.' "

U. S. News & World Report, January 7, 1974: "Many companies are facing problems familiar to home-owners — how to lay hands on enough money in coming months to meet expenses . . . Corporations in need of money in 1973 borrowed heavily from banks, commercial-paper markets, and other sources of short-term funds. In doing so, they expanded this type of debt much faster than they built up balances of cash, bank accounts, and other liquid assets. As a result, some companies now have scant ready reserves to bail them out if financial trouble strikes."

Journal of Commerce editorial, December 13, 1973: ". . . the load of consumer and corporate debt has grown to such proportions that any serious recession could produce a drastic shakeout from one end of the economy to the other . . ."

Wall Street Journal front-page headlines, December 11, 1973: "Debt Load, No Trouble Before, Could Deepen An Oil-Caused Recession; Authorities Might Be Unable To Rescue Heavy Borrowers By Usual Stimulative Policy."

Financial World, November 14, 1973, quoting George S. Moore, formerly head of New York's First National City Bank, one of the world's largest and most sophisticated banking organizations: "The credit mountain today is twice as high as in 1929, and *the quality perhaps half as good.*" (*Our* emphasis-SF)

The same awareness is surfacing in other countries where the "Balloon The Money Supply" party took place. Wall Street Journal, January 14, 1974: "Debt Burden Adds to Britain's Woes: Britain's economy, limping already because of union slowdowns and the fuel squeeze, is likely to find its problems intensified by a heavy debt load. The volume of bank loans made in Britain has soared recently, from the equivalent of $1.65 billion made in the 1969-70 fiscal year to $14.6 billion in the fiscal year ended last April. In 1973, consumer borrowing jumped from about 8% of after-tax earnings to 13%. Meanwhile, bankruptcies filed in London courts last year reached a post-World War II high of 1,520. In addition, recent weeks have seen London's financial community coming to the rescue of three so-called fringe banks that were overextended when the London stock market declined and creditors began to fret about hard times ahead." The article then went on to write of ". . . shivers of apprehension running through the financial community."

A Dismal Two-Year Record — And What Is To Come

We have listened to, read and watched many of the leaders of the non-Communist world, including President Nixon, discuss "the problem of inflation" in the past year when it became acute, and have been disheartened (often a stronger word would be needed) at the ducking of the real issues, and at the shrugging off of responsibility by describing the developments as if they were a natural, and therefore unavoidable, phenomenon like an earthquake or a tidal wave. Rather than this being the case, it had all been politically manufactured and clearly visible for some time. Thus, in an investment service of which the writer is editor, the issue of June 30, 1972, we already outlined many of the threatening developments and concluded: ". . . Subscribers should err on the side of pessimism rather than optimism, and reduce their holdings all along the line . . ." The following month, with the issue of July 7, 1972, we summarized much of the information on debt that you have just read, brought up-to-date, and, in fact, we started the write-up with the short sentence: "America is hooked on debt." The following pertinent description was included in that write-up, almost two years ago! "We said before that like the addict, a greater and greater increase in annual net debt is now needed to produce a dollar increase in 'Gross National Product.' In the early 1950's, each $1 increase in net debt produced about $1 increase in GNP. This 1-for-1 ratio quickly disappeared and the ratio crept up, in a quite dangerous manner, so that by 1970, the one-year increase in debt was $117 billion, but GNP was up only $45 billion. It had taken a *$2.60* increase in debt to produce a *$1.00* increase in GNP. In 1971 the floodgates were really opened on 'easy money' to 'stimulate the economy' and since net debt is expected to hit $2,200 billion by the end of 1972, the ratio of a rise in net debt for each advance in GNP could well leap to new highs. The trend is clearly in the direction of ever higher ratios of debt increase to GNP increase. How long can we keep this up?"

In our Survey issue of July 21, 1972 we commenced a series of write-ups entitled "The Money Watch" and much of what you have read in the past pages was carefully outlined then too, with the emphatic warning that a "big bill" was going to be rendered for the wholly unjustified and dangerous policies being followed in deliberately inducing economic expansion for political ends via budgetary deficits, in ensuring that commercial banks could endlessly expand their loans, and in other governmental policies unwisely seeking "growth" without counting the later cost.

So much for the refusal of the Administration, Congress and the leadership of both political parties (they were all equally responsible) to acknowledge the part they played in the towering difficulties in which we find ourselves today.

The Business Cycle Still Lives!

In earlier pages we recounted the efforts of "Keynesianism" to "smooth out" the business cycle through government deficit spending during recession, and government budget surpluses when business began to overheat. Of course, this led directly to hyper-inflation when politician and Electorate alike found out how good it felt to spread more money around to create jobs and profits. We ended up with one-way "Keynesianism".

And quite a number of decades after the doctrine was first embraced, the dangerous caricature the politicians have made of it is getting ready, in our opinion, to produce some threatening upheavals in the cycle it was supposed to moderate. The towering mountain of *Debt* which was used to fuel super-growth is now turning on its creators and we are paying the inevitable bill for our really reckless indiscretions in a measure of economic distress where the "up" part of our cycle of expand, expand, expand has strong chances to be matched by a "down" part characterized by higher unemployment, a very possible *deflation* of the market value of commodities and goods and properties of all types, and bankruptcies and difficulties in an appreciable part of the American business world.

There is an iron logic about the business cycle in our free enterprise system which simply cannot be denied. Distortions arise during a boom when inefficient entrepreneurs prosper right along with efficient producers because the mistakes and poor judgment of the former are covered up by the flush of general prosperity so that the errors and excesses can continue to mount. Unwise expansion, poorly conceived, badly financed and mismanaged, can continue for quite some time, particularly when a boom psychology is being fostered by ever-larger injections of Debt.

But nothing lasts forever. More and more "businessmen" (many not having much talent for such endeavors) find themselves far out on an economic limb, income falling short of mounting liabilities, with heavy debt and interest charges pressing ever more dangerously. Unraveling of the fortunes of the inefficient producers threaten to spill over into the sounder business entities as current bills cannot be met and maturing debt threatens to go unpaid. The call goes out for more money-creation to push the day of reckoning somewhat further ahead. (New York Times, April 22, 1974: "Democrats Spur Move To Cut Tax . . . Humphrey Joins 2 Others In Calling For Reduction 'To Stimulate Economy' ") But the old prescriptions don't necessarily work any more.

Galloping prices frighten the consumer into reducing expenditures on the many frills of the "Age of Affluence", causing even greater pressure on the less well-managed businesses.

The cycle turns down and the extent and duration of the decline becomes quite unpredictable despite the professionally bright and cheerful forecasts of government and banking economists. There is a momentum to consumer retrenchment, and an interaction between weak businesses and other creditors, which can lead to liquidation of inventory, forced sale of assets at distress prices and bankruptcies, the final extent of which cannot be anticipated with accuracy.

The Basic Immorality of Inflation

We will shortly turn to some important guideposts by which we think readers will be able to judge when and where sounder economic policies will halt the inflation and lay the basis for a later strong market resurgence. But we think it fruitful to first pause at this point to dispel the belief of some that you can "learn to live" with perpetual high rates of inflation without doing unacceptable damage to the free enterprise system, under which the United States has flourished beyond the dreams of most other countries, and unacceptable damage also to all the values most of us would agree on as worth cherishing and perpetuating.

Discussions in this area are usually couched in such abstruse economic terms that 99% of our citizens throw up their hands in helplessness, despite the fact that their own lives are being adversely affected by what those economic terms mean ("prime rate", "Federal funds", "M 1", etc.).

Let's now put the whole story on a much smaller stage and we will then grasp how simple it really is to see through the shallowness and indeed the dangerous nonsense of those who seek ways to coexist with an ongoing galloping rate of inflation, and the associated ills of a society wedded to come-what-may "affluence".

A Scenario

You are present when your neighbor's newly-married son is telling his father how tiny his first apartment is. "Why don't you buy a home in this neighborhood?" interrupts the father. The son is taken aback. "On my salary? Where would I get the money?"

"Borrow it, of course. What do you think banks are for?"

"You know we don't have much furniture. What do we do for an entire house?"

"You borrow the money for a house-full of furniture, just as you did for the house."

"We don't have a car. It's alright in the city — we get along — but how do you get around here without a car?"

"Buy a car. As a matter of fact, buy two cars — one for you and one for Mary. The bank will finance it."

"Dad, are you sure I won't be getting into trouble meeting the payments for all that on my salary?"

"Don't worry about it, son. Just borrow all the money you need to get everything you want. And get it today — because tomorrow never comes. Somehow it will all work out."

If *you* were listening to this, what would you think of your neighbor giving this advice to his son? Wouldn't you feel strongly that he *should* be saying: "Be patient, son. Right now it's a small apartment in the city with no car and not much furniture. But work hard, continue your studies at night for a better position, save your money, and you will be able to get the things you want, one at a time, as your savings accumulate. But don't ever go into debt on a scale that would give you financial problems if unlooked for expenses came along, say some unexpected medical bills, or something happened to your job. Buy only what you can afford and learn to wait so you don't mortgage your future to worry and uncertainty."

Putting it as above, on an *individual* basis, on a "smaller stage", we all know which approach is right and proper. But in the past few decades America has been running on a set of values much closer to the "borrow and spend" advice first described. Recall, for example, that whenever consumer borrowing slowed its climb in the past ten years or so, Washington immediately began to worry that business would slow down and began to start talking about steps to "stimulate the economy." Going into debt has been encouraged in every possible way.

Look at another factor — the manner in which inflation singles out some elements of our population to be hardest hit. Those who save their money, for example. "Work hard and save." That used to be the backbone of the American "work ethic" which, in turn, was the backbone of our remarkable productivity. All those who followed this once-honored precept

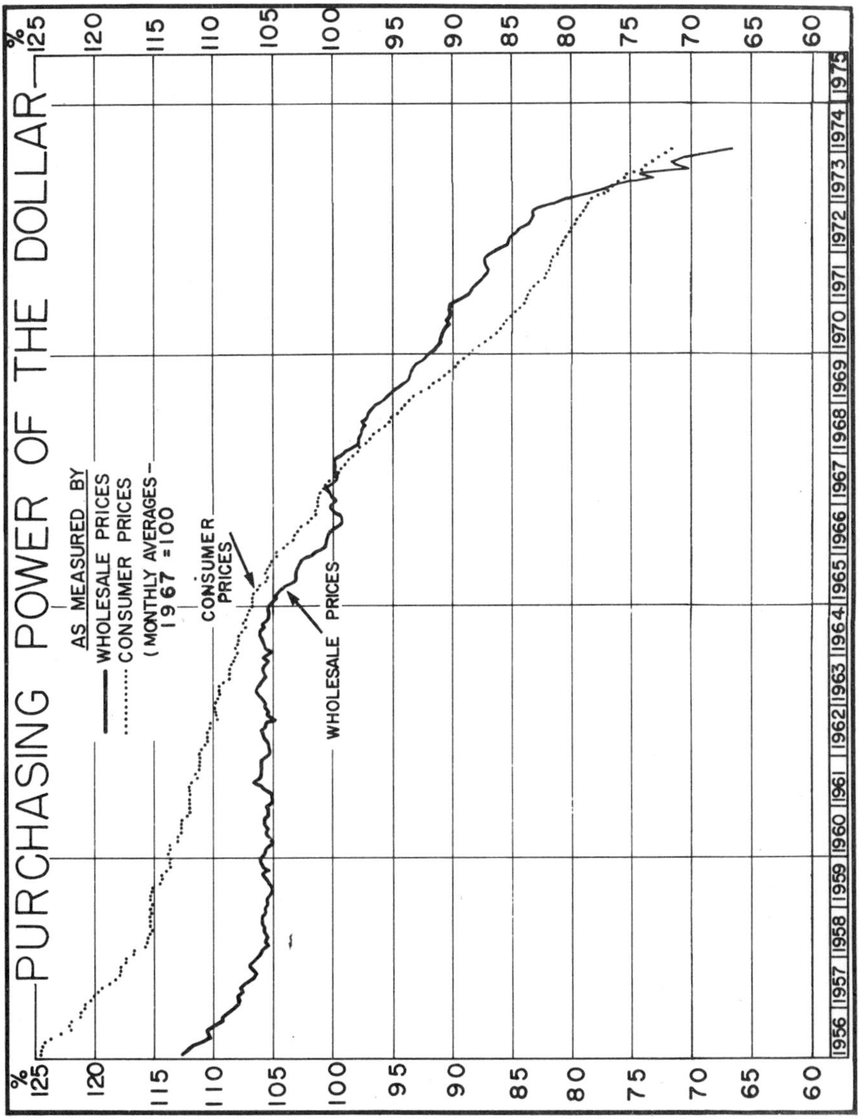
PURCHASING POWER OF THE DOLLAR
AS MEASURED BY
WHOLESALE PRICES
CONSUMER PRICES
(MONTHLY AVERAGES—1967 = 100)
CONSUMER PRICES
WHOLESALE PRICES
%
125
120
115
110
105
100
95
90
85
80
75
70
65
60
1956
1957
1958
1959
1960
1961
1962
1963
1964
1965
1966
1967
1968
1969
1970
1971
1972
1973
1974
1975

have seen the value of their savings more than *40% destroyed* just between 1956-year-end-1973 as shown by the illuminating chart on the preceding page, courtesy of the Commodity Research Bureau.

And, as we write, the inflationary spiral has reached new heights, accelerating at a rate never before even imagined to be possible in our country. The saver is made a fool of — the spender is glorified as the moving force of "an expanding economy."

Cruelest of all has been what the inflaters have inflicted upon the growing numbers of retired Americans, and our elderly in general. No matter how diligently they put aside regular sums in their bank accounts or insurance annuity plans, or pension plans in the past 20, 30 and 40 years, they have been pauperized by the breathtaking inflationary spiral of the last decade.

And as torrents of out-of-thin-air manufactured money sloshes over the economy, what is the effect upon our *political process* of the "sky's the limit," "live for today" atmosphere? Corruption, always present in at least a muted way in every society, springs to life in an inflationary atmosphere like weeds on a hot summer's day. Is this a surprising development? By no means, with historical precedents plentiful. Thus, the Powell Monetary Analyst, December 8, 1973, quoted the following from Andrew Dickson White's "Fiat Money Inflation In France," published first in 1876: "Out of the speculating and gambling of the inflation period grew luxury, and, out of this, corruption . . . It was first felt in business operations, but soon began to be seen in the legislative body. Bribery of legislators followed as a matter of course . . . Even worse than this was the breaking down of the morals of the country at large . . ."

Is there a connection between our problems of crime, drugs, the disaffection of so many young people, with the virus of inflation? Can anyone doubt that there is a very direct and strong connection? The immorality of inflation is self-evident.

"The Greatest Stock Market Opportunities in Forty Years." We Change Course For The Time Being, But Will Soon Return To The Economics of Inflation.

The future course of our Inflation nightmare is not unpredictable, unknowable. To the contrary, we shall be later describing what we consider to be the three most important guideposts which readers must watch intently for guidance as to

(a) whether, and how soon, economic health will replace our inflationary illness; and

(b) whether, as a consequence, we are nearing the true lows for the 1973-197? bear market, or whether there will be only fitful and partial recoveries, to be followed later by still further market declines to still lower levels, before definitive recovery finally sets in.

It is the opinion of this writer that the reader *can profit very handsomely* in low-price Warrants and low-price stocks, *in either or both of the above eventualities,* and we explain in the chapters directly ahead, and in detail, the methods and approaches the reader should use to accomplish these objectives.

We impress upon the reader that there are very important considerations of *timing* involved in the above questions (a) and (b), and without sufficient accuracy in judging that timing, the measure of success in seizing the profit opportunities resulting from the devastating market slide will be less than they could be. Consequently, we shall later be asking the reader to pay particular and close attention to our analysis of the three guideposts which shall help us find the answers to the above all-important questions regarding the Inflation, and its possible duration, intensity and further ravages.

Meanwhile, we turn to another vital area at this point: how to evaluate the worth, risk and appreciation potential of the vast numbers of low-price Warrants and low-price stocks which form the reservoir from which we shall draw the most rewarding of these opportunities.

New York Stock Exchange

New York Stock Exchange's Composite Index

WEEK ENDED AUG. 30, 1974

The above chart reminds us of the market devastation that has been wrought since January 1973, but it fails by a considerable margin to tell us how much *more* badly the securities of many secondary and "light blue-chip" companies have been hurt during that same period, because enough of the securities of the industrial giants have, up to this point, held sufficiently better to give the total picture a less-battered cast than is actually the case.

There have been enough computer studies undertaken recently to demonstrate that thousands of what were a short time ago moderately-priced securities are now low-price stocks and low-price Warrants because of the worst price destruction in the stock market in about forty years. The corollary to that is that the *profit opportunities* for the inevitable rebound are also the greatest in about forty years.

In the pages ahead we demonstrate that the twin pillars of success for the investor in seizing the best of those opportunities, and to their fullest possible profit potential, will be found in two approaches to selection, one being *Analysis of Fudamentals,* and the second being *Technical Analysis*.

Fundamental analysis revolves around the present and potential intrinsic values and earning power of a company and involves understanding of the Balance Sheet and the Income Account. Most investors know little-to-nothing about these areas. When we conclude our quite simple, quite uncomplicated explanation, we feel the reader will realize how severely he had handicapped himself previously by failing to have this basic knowledge.

Technical analysis revolves around the guidance which *the market action of the price of the stock itself can provide.* After about thirty years of daily study of the insights of technical analysis as it strongly influences many aspects of the stock market, and gives continuous and important guidance as to timing, we can only say that the investor who is unaware of these insights has truly self-imposed a blindfold which must severely limit his chances of stock market success.

Analysis of Fundamentals

Balance Sheets Are Easy to Read! And All-Important to Stock Market Profits!

A typical discussion by security analysts of a corporation's financial position is full of so many large figures on such an unfamiliar scale that an investor assumes he must not be able to understand them, and doesn't even try to do so. In some decades of explaining a company's intrinsic value, first to brokerage house clients and then to subscribers to several investment services we edit, projecting our view as to why a particular company's securities are attractive for purchase or, on the other hand, should be avoided or sold, we have always found the key to be to first shrink down the scale of all applicable figures when making our basic explanations. It is remarkable how easily they are then understood by investors with no formal knowledge at all of corporate accounting. And we are certain that the same valuable result will ensue when we now proceed to follow the same path toward understanding a Balance Sheet and an Income Account where readers are concerned.

Forget the billion-dollar company! Imagine that you have a choice of buying two stores in your home town—which happens to be a moderately-sized town. Each is a corporation with 100 shares of common stock as its sole capitalization and each business is offered for sale in its entirety at $50,000. In other words, for $50,000 in each case, you get the entire 100 shares of common stock and therefore own all the assets of the company and are responsible for all its liabilities. Would not a most logical first step be to enumerate and evaluate all the *assets* of the company and then all the *liabilities* of the company, and see what net intrinsic value you are getting for your $50,000, before you even consider earning power?

Of course, this has to be true—it is what you would do if you were considering an actual purchase of such a business. Let's begin this enumeration and evaluation by assuming both stores are in the same business, selling a varied line of moderately-priced men's, women's and children's clothing, and what we shall discuss will be applicable whatever services or products are involved, in any business, large or small.

Analyzing our two store corporations, first on the *Asset* side, we have at the head of the list the most tangible and most precisely measurable item—*Cash on hand.* This would be the balance in the company's bank accounts.

Next would come *Accounts Receivable*—what was owed to the company for goods already sold to customers but not yet paid for. It would be necessary here to make some allowance for "doubtful accounts" based on the store's actual past experience with purchasers who did not pay their bills.

Following this would come the value of the *Inventory.* The store's racks and back room shelves would be holding merchandise ready for sale, plus shipping boxes and other materials. The actual worth of the Inventory would be a matter of judgment in most cases. Original purchase price would be a good guide, but styles change, and some of the Inventory might be salable only at reduced prices. Where the figure for Accounts Receivable would have to be marked down by a modest amount, the figure for Inventory would probably have to be marked down by a considerably larger percentage in arriving at a final figure of value which would be acceptable in our calculations, and individual circumstances would play a large part in such determinations as it affected different industries, different companies.

Cash on hand, Accounts Receivable and Inventory are customarily added together to produce a total figure called "Current Assets" which refers to relatively *liquid* assets. Cash is cash; we expect most outstanding bills owed the company to be paid, producing more cash; and Inventory of goods on hand to be sold, even in part at lower prices where necessary, eventually produces still more cash. "Current Assets" then refer to company assets which are available to meet bills, pay salaries, pay taxes and pay a return to the owner. For all these things you need *cash;*

and those assets which *are* cash or are expected to *become* cash in a reasonable period of time, constitute "Current Assets."

Next we come to "Fixed Assets" which, we can guess, cannot be turned into cash easily or quickly, and normally are not expected to be turned into cash. In the case of our stores, they would be the furniture and fixtures, cash registers, company vehicles, typewriters and similar equipment. Naturally, none of these are expected to be sold and turned into cash because they are all needed to operate the business, and even if the necessity arose to do so, it couldn't be accomplished quickly without, typically, a tremendous markdown in price over original cost.

That concludes the "Asset" side of our Balance Sheet: "Current" Assets made up of Cash, Accounts Receivable and Inventory; plus "Fixed" Assets representing the value of all the equipment and property needed to operate the business.

Turning to the "Liabilities" side of our Balance Sheet, there are "Current Liabilities" just as there are "Current Assets." All outstanding bills, employees' salaries, maturing portions of bank debt or any debt which has to be repaid in the ensuing twelve months, if any, and income tax, if any, coming due. All *must* be paid within a relatively short period of time and, therefore, add up to *"Current* Liabilities."

The first thing this writer does when he looks at a Balance Sheet is to note the figure for Current Assets and then subtract the figure for Current Liabilities. This resulting sum is called "Net Working Capital," a most important figure, representing the net cash available to run the business.

There is no arguing about each item in Current Liabilities—they must all be paid in cash, and in a relatively short period of time. But the only item in Current Assets we accept at face value is *Cash on Hand*. As we have already pointed out, Accounts Receivable may be diminished to the extent that goods sold but not yet paid for may remain that way—not paid, or paid very slowly! And Inventories may stay on racks and shelves—unsold. Thus, when we see a large amount of Cash On Hand in relation to Current Liabilities, we mentally give the company a check mark for a pleasing Balance Sheet. When we see minor amounts of Cash and a necessary dependence on Accounts Receivable and, worse, Inventory, to handle Current Liabilities, we start to worry. And when Current Liabilities *exceed* Current Assets, producing a negative figure for Net Working Capital, we ring the alarm bell. The company is in trouble.

Following Current Liabilities on a Balance Sheet is the *capitalization* of the company. First noted is Long-Term Debt which is debt not maturing in the current year (which category is in Current Liabilities). The size of the debt, whether owed to banks or other institutions or to bondholders of the company, must be carefully noted, including when the debt comes up for repayment in its various segments, and including also the interest burden in carrying the debt.

Next in line would come preferred stock, if any, where we would note the value of the preferred stock as the amount it would receive if the company redeemed it at the specified "Call" price.

And, finally, we would have the common stock, which would have claim to all the remaining assets of the company left *after* Current Liabilities are paid off in full, *after* Long-Term Debt has been fully repaid, and *after* any preferred stockholders have received their stated due.

A Valuable Graphic Presentation of a Balance Sheet

We are ready to take our next step, and toward this end we recall for readers the fact that both companies, which we shall call Company A and Company B, are offered for purchase for $50,000 for the entire issue of 100 shares of common stock in each case.

Let's look at Company A's Balance Sheet first, along with a five-year record of Sales and Net Income, after taxes.

Company A
Balance Sheet

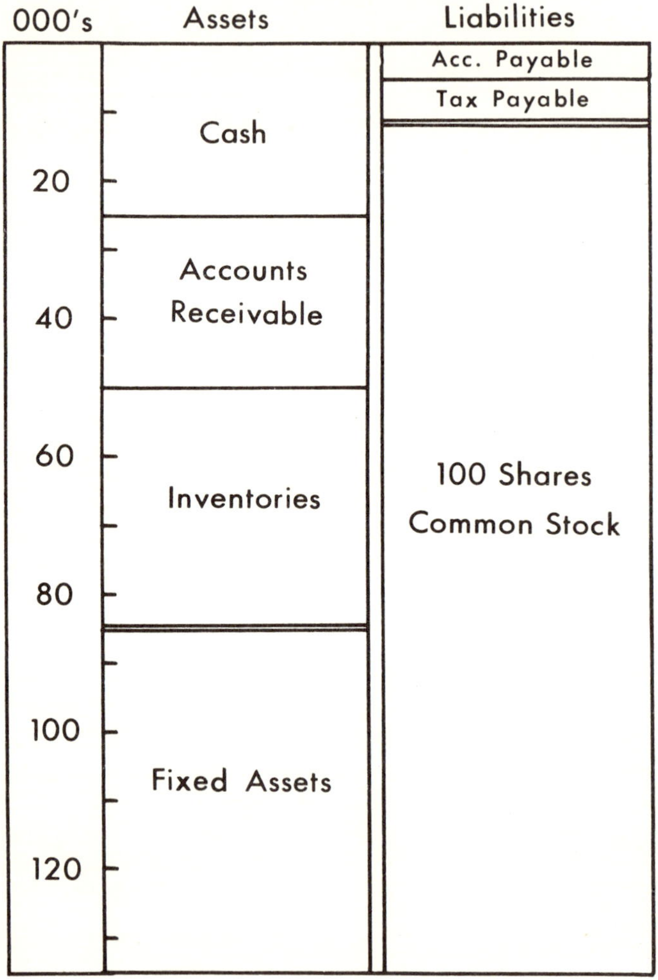

Company A

Assets

Current Assets:	
Cash	$25,000
Accounts Receivable	25,000
Inventories	35,000
	Total $85,000
Fixed Assets	$50,000

Liabilities

Current Liabilities:	
Accounts Payable	$ 5,000
Income Tax Payable	6,000
	Total $11,000

	Sales	*Earnings*
1973	$73,191	$11,242
1972	61,240	10,162
1971	53,095	9,040
1970	50,629	7,163
1969	41,324	6,848

Readers should note that the various elements of the Balance Sheet have been shown in direct scale to their actual value, using the scale shown. Thus, we see at a glance the *relative values* of Current Assets versus Current Liabilities, and the actual asset value remaining for the common stock.

With Company A we note that Cash alone exceeds all Current Liabilities, and that net assets of $124,000 accrue to the common stock.

It's Time to Look at Company B

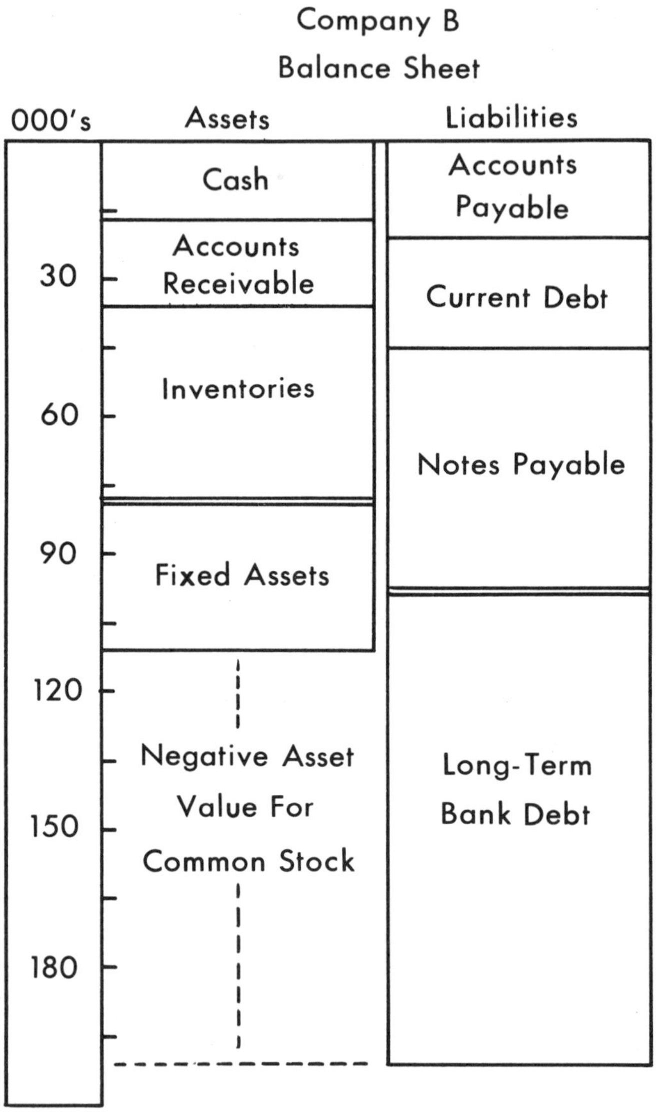
Company B
Balance Sheet
000's
Assets
Liabilities
Cash
Accounts Receivable
Inventories
Fixed Assets
Negative Asset Value For Common Stock
Accounts Payable
Current Debt
Notes Payable
Long-Term Bank Debt
30
60
90
120
150
180

COMPANY B

Assets

Current Assets:		
Cash		$16,970
Accounts Receivable		19,250
Inventories		42,370
	Total....	$78,590
Fixed Assets		$33,400

Liabilities

Current Liabilities:		
Accounts Payable		$21,450
Current bank debt maturing		24,580
Notes Payable		52,480
	Total....	$98,510
Long-Term Debt, owed to banks		$99,230

	Sales	*Earnings*
1973	$38,162	($ 8,299) deficit
1972	40,921	(6,449) deficit
1971	41,258	2,460
1970	50,698	3,977
1969	49,326	(2,369) deficit

Company B's Balance Sheet presents a terrible picture, as does its "Income Account" (Sales and Earnings). Current Liabilities exceed Current Assets, with only negligible Cash. And there is a substantial bank debt to be paid off by the company over the next five years. Current Liabilities plus the bank debt exceed the total of all company Assets, so the common stock of Company B has a *negative* asset value.

Now the very real question is whether, if you were offered the alternative of buying either Company A in its entirety for $50,000, or Company B for $50,000, you would hesitate even a minute in making the obvious choice for Company A.

The whole point of the discussion in the past few pages, however, is that when dealing with the much larger Balance Sheet figures for publicly-traded corporations, the vast majority of investors make no attempt, and in most cases do not have the basic understanding with which to *make* the attempt, to understand what it is that they are buying in terms of intrinsic value when they purchase a common stock or other security. In the pages which follow, we are going to demonstrate exactly how so many investors stepped into a deep hole in the past two years in *not* understanding how to read the simple message of the Balance Sheet—and how the best and most highly-leveraged opportunities in low-price Warrants and low-price stocks in the coming months and years will be best pinpointed by *fully* understanding "how to read the simple message of the Balance Sheet."

Some "Horrible Examples"

Consider now how simple it is to discern a stock with few substantial assets to buttress it on the downside if market circumstances become adverse. Using the method discussed on previous pages of quickly and meaningfully breaking down a Balance Sheet, let's look at one example which comes quickly to hand from the American Stock Exchange. In 1971 the 1,494,129 shares of common stock of Meridian Industries sold at a high of 19⅞ for a market valuation of *$29,695,813*. The March 31, 1972 Balance Sheet shows Current Assets of $8,009,000 but Current Liabilities of $9,122,000. A negative Working Capital figure, immediately putting the common stock "under water" on that account. But there were other heavy liabilities, including $9,350,000 in Long-Term Debt, of which $2,500,000 was coming due for payment on June 30, 1974 and $5,300,000 was being paid off at $30,000 per month, with the balance coming due on May 31, 1978. There was also $2,648,000 in claims of three classes of preferred stock ahead of the common stock.

Let's add up these simple figures another way. When we accept the stated value of $3,797,000 in Accounts Receivable,

$3,087,000 in Inventories, and $8,169,000 as the worth of net Plant and Equipment (none of these ever to be accepted without evaluation) and a few miscellaneous items (Cash was only $598,000), we come up with a total stated value for company assets of *$22,139,000.*

But against this we have $9,122,000 in Current Liabilities, $9,350,000 in Long-Term Debt (breathing heavily down the Treasurer's neck!) and $2,648,000 in claims of preferred stock. This adds up to *$21,120,000,* leaving the pitiful sum of $1,019,000 as Net Equity for the 1,494,129 shares of common stock, or *68¢ per share.* Of course, all the liabilities were very real and unquestionably *there,* but the stated value for the assets could not be accepted without evaluation for *any* company, and certainly not for Meridian Industries, a "fringe" enterprise.

It gets worse when we look at Earnings: A deficit of ($1.26) per share for fiscal 1970, a deficit of ($0.17) per share for fiscal 1971, a minor profit of $0.15 per share in fiscal 1972 followed by a return to red ink.

Negative Working Capital; negligible asset value behind the common stock even if we accept the doubtful figures as stated; a question of where to get money to roll over heavy debt when you have no net working capital and are losing money. And yet at the 19⅞ high in 1971 the 1,494,129 shares of common stock were selling at a market value of $29,695,813!

The more recent result? Meridian Industries has sold down to ⅝ (62.5¢) and the 1,494,129 shares of common stock now have a market value of $933,830, with the 1971 stockholders having lost $28,761,983, almost all of their investment at the 1971 high.

A question: If you, the reader, could have analyzed the Balance Sheet as we did above, would *you* have paid 19⅞ for Meridian Industries common in 1971? Which is exactly the point of these pages.

Another "Horrible Example"—Hallcraft Homes

In late-1971, Hallcraft Homes, ranking among the top ten in production of single-family homes in the United States, with operations basically centered in Colorado, Arizona and Southern California, was selling at a high of 53 in the over-the-counter market, prior to listing on the American Stock Exchange. The 2,033,312 shares of common stock thus had a market valuation of *$107,765,000.* The $2,705,000 to be earned by the company in the year ending April 30, 1972 must have looked very good to the buyers of the stock as the quarterly earnings reports rolled in, but they forgot to look at the Balance Sheet, to anticipate possible trouble. Here is what the significant items were for the Balance Sheet as of April 30, 1972.

Current Assets	
Cash	$ 1,594,000
Receivables	10,085,000
Inventories	71,214,000
Total Current Assets	$82,893,000
Current Liabilities	
Notes Payable	$ 4,225,000
Accounts Payable	11,991,000
Construction & Development Loans	23,409,000
Income Taxes	1,094,000
Land Purchase Contr. & Acquis. Loans	14,967,000
Total Current Liabilities	$55,686,000

If we were content to ignore one major factor (we'll shortly discuss this Achilles heel) the Net Working Capital was $82,893,000 minus $55,686,000, or $27,207,000, or $13.38 per share, and didn't look too bad if you analyzed no further.

Total company Assets were stated at $90,715,000 and from this we deduct the $55,686,000 stated as Current Liabilities and the Long-Term Debt of $17,475,000, and come up with Net Equity per common share of $17,554,000, or $8.63 per share.

A Net Equity per common share of $8.63 for a stock selling at $53 isn't something to throw your hat in the air about, but in any case, *all the above figures foundered on one item*—that of Inventories values at *$71,214,000*. If this figure were to be called into question, all the supposed value behind the common stock would begin to shrink rapidly, since Cash was minute and fixed assets were minor. And that is exactly what happened. Along came high interest rates and operating costs rose. The nine months ended January 31, 1974 saw a net loss of ($1,028,000), compared with a profit of $170,000 for the same period one year earlier and the Chairman of the Company announced early in 1974 that ". . . delays in the completion of routine, recurring interim financing arrangements had been instrumental in creating a negative cash flow." A nice way to say that sales were faltering and the company was running out of money. Down plunged the common stock to reach a low of $1 on the American Stock Exchange. The market value of the stock dropped from *$107,765,000* at its 1971 high to a mere *$2,033,000* at this low.

The lesson for readers: First, examine and evaluate the Balance Sheet very carefully; Secondly, look for lots of *Cash,* and good value in *Plant and Equipment.* If heavy Current Liabilities have to depend upon *Inventories* to develop the cash to meet those obligations, forget the company's securities and run quickly in the other direction. All this will become even clearer as we discuss current opportunities as they are discernible in the wreckage littering the stock market floor after the disastrous 1973-1974 slide.

Some Current Evaluations

We could go on and on with page after page of 1971 and 1972 examples such as Meridian Industries and Hallcraft Homes, detailing the horrendous market losses which took place for company stockholders when weak Balance Sheets couldn't stand the strain of economic adversity. But it is *today* that readers are interested in, not yesterday and, quite logically, exactly the same principles apply. We will shortly be detailing a series of approaches to drawing profits from the mass of low-price stocks littering the market floor and, in making the selections for such approaches, a careful look at the Balance Sheet will come first in all cases because there remains a wide diversity of fortune, good and ill, clearly visible in those Balance Sheets, and why not steer our way to good fortune instead of bad when it takes so little effort?

Here is Whittaker Corp., for example, a conglomerate spanning many interests in metals, chemicals and recreational products with sales in excess of one-half billion dollars. The common stock sold at 45 in 1968, dropped to 19⅜ in 1970, managed to sell as high as 7¾ in 1973, but reached a 1974 low up to this writing of *1⅞*. Having lost almost all of the market value of 1968, is the sharply-depressed common stock the answer to an investor's prayer for a later goodly rise in a reviving stock market? Not without an equal amount of danger when you look at the Balance Sheet! We turn to Standard & Poor's Corporation Records and we find the following disheartening enumeration of debt for Whittaker Corp. as of October 31, 1973.

4½% conv. sub. debentures, due 1988 sub. (S.F.)	$12,757,000
9⅝% debentures, due 1993 sub. (S.F.)	23,338,000
10% debentures, due 1988	21,547,000
5% sub. Notes, due 1984	5,161,000
Term Bank Loan, due 1976-80	60,000,000
Conv. Notes, due 1979-81	15,000,000
Notes, due 1976-80	5,489,000
Non-Int. 13% Notes, to 1997	24,848,000
Notes to 1975	6,120,000
Notes to 1978	9,000,000

"Sub." means subordinated to other debt, and (S.F.) means Sinking Fund where a specified amount of the issue is retired on a regular basis. We did not list a few issues under $5,000,000 and Standard & Poor's comes up with a total long-term debt of $190,675,000 which includes $8,434,000 carried as current.

The first important thing to note is *the annual interest burden,* which, as of late-1973, was running at $16.2 million. Add $1 million for specified dividend payments on two classes of preferred stock, and $17.2 million annually is needed to meet these obligations. We next look at Net Income after taxes and we find the year ended October 31, 1973 produced a deficit of ($2,980,000), October 31, 1972 showed earnings of $8,670,000, and October 31, 1971 earnings of $8,890,000. The $16.2 million in interest payments is a charge against income (the preferred dividend payout of $1 million is not), so what the above figures for net income tells us is that Whittaker Corp. barely managed to pay its interest each year *and* show a modest profit, but how far is the company from a position where it would *not* be able to pay that interest?

The answer to this question is that even a moderate decline in the company's fortunes could prevent it from meeting these heavy interest charges, thereby threatening some form of bankruptcy and the washout of the common stock. The next step this writer automatically takes is to study such a list of classes of debt as we have just presented and consider the maturity dates of the various loans and/or the regular payments to reduce such loans which must be made. Of course, the first one to catch our eye would be the "Term Bank Loan" amounting to $60,000,000, and we would not find our attention misdirected. Repayment is to be spread over the years 1976-1980, annual payments increasing from $8,000,000 to $17,000,000, bearing interest at ¼% above the prime rate in the first three years and increasing to 1¼% above the prime rate in the last two years.

What would Whittaker do with *that* package if red ink started to flow? We trust that the reader appreciates the fact that we would not look much further into Whittaker based on what we have already discussed. The potential for wiping out the common stock in any business downturn is already too visible to consider Whittaker as a vehicle for either trading profits or long-term holding.

A Look at Howard Johnson Company

In little more than one year from early-1973 to mid-1974, Howard Johnson common stock broke from a high of 34⅞ to a low of 6¾, as the "Energy Crisis" and its gasoline shortages cast large shadows over the motel and restaurant business which had earned Howard Johnson large profits. Any similarity between a Whittaker Corp. and a Howard Johnson is immediately dispelled when we look at the Balance Sheet. One can only say for the latter company—What a Balance Sheet! As of December 28, 1973:

Current Assets	
Cash & Marketable Securities	$52,581,000
Accounts Receivable	6,571,000
Inventories	16,179,000
Prepayments	2,835,000
Total Current Assets	$78,166,000

Current Liabilities	
Current Debt Maturing	$ 267,000
Accounts Payable	13,689,000
Income Taxes	4,555,000
Dividends Payable	1,093,000
Total Current Liabilities	$19,604,000

It is to be quickly noted that Howard Johnson's "Cash & Marketable Securities" alone covers all Current Liabilities 2½ times over! And the small amount of Long-Term Debt amounting to $3,924,000 is hardly worth a thought. Net Property of $121,437,000 all becomes assets behind the common stock since *all* Liabilities are covered by Cash alone. This quick look at Howard Johnson's Balance Sheet shows very clearly how far this common stock is from the type of possible financial perils such as we described with Whittaker Corp., and which sank Meridian Corp. and Hallcraft Homes in 1971.

The Vital Contributions of Fundamental Analysis

Thousands of stocks and hundreds of Warrants have been decimated so that they lie prostrate on the market floor, most of them selling at their lowest prices in decades. Our brief rundown in previous pages of the principles of Balance Sheet and Income Account analysis—the "fundamental analysis" approach to market opportunities—should have amply demonstrated that *among* those thousands of low-price stocks and hundreds of low-price Warrants, there are vastly important differences to be discerned—differences which can launch a commitment with much less downside risk and much greater hope of substantial appreciation, as against a commitment with far less attractive attributes. Most of this difference in today's economic world of intense difficulty centers about the two crucial factors of working capital and *Debt*. A poor working capital position and a large interest burden on a substantial debt can act as a heavy anchor does under a boat, preventing the stock from moving ahead.

The prognosis is even more unfortunate when analysis of that debt shows significant portions of it are maturing within relatively short periods of time. Inability to refinance such maturing debt can mean bankruptcy and the wipeout of the common stock and/or Warrants. Or the refinancing may be accomplished at such an elevated rate of interest that earnings growth or recovery becomes that much more difficult. (Thus, it was reported recently that American Ship Building was paying up to *15%* for its new borrowings!)

The whole point of the analysis of "fundamentals" is that so many thousands of choices are available (we have referred to it as a "veritable cornucopia of opportunities") that we can just as easily find a low-price stock or low-price Warrant where the company has a reasonable working capital position and minimal problems with debt, as to saddle ourselves with a situation where Current Liabilities far overshadow Current Assets and where the company Treasurer is wringing his hands, watching the calendar and worrying where the money is going to come from to "roll over" shortly-maturing debt, or to meet large payments of interest when earnings are slim or nonexistent. Furthermore, gravitating toward stocks where a good net working capital position is only part of an over-all treasure trove of intrinsic value, worth far more than the going market price of the stock, obviously facilitates a continuing advance in the stock once it begins to move, whereas stocks with negligible value will begin to labor before too long, in most cases.

The necessity for careful analysis of "fundamentals" is indisputable.

Now for "Technical Analysis"

Bear markets have always, in the past, been succeeded by bull markets. There is no question in this writer's mind that the bear market which holds sway, as we write, will *also* be succeeded by a new bull market. When this change takes place on a definitive basis, a rolling series of recovery moves will commence where many stocks will break out of their bear market lows and commence an upside run to a price more reflective of their intrinsic value and earning power. In all the previous turns to new bull markets that we have watched for about thirty years in professional capacities as trader, financial analyst and editor of two investment services, *low-price stocks* have always scored the greatest percentage gains, so the validity of concentrating on *low-price* stocks and Warrants will be the first point we make in commencing a description of the role of "Technical Analysis." It is a simple matter to grasp why this should be so.

Firstly, low-price stocks have a magnetic attraction for investors in that $2,000, say, buys you 500 shares at 4, whereas the same sum buys only 100 shares at 20, and only 50 shares at 40. *Why* investors feel that "more is better" may be an interesting question in human psychology. Here we content ourselves with assuring readers that long and intensive observation of the investment scene demonstrates that it simply is so, with most investors having a strong tendency to go for the greater number of shares for a given investment which, by simple arithmetic, means going for the lower-priced stocks.

Secondly, and even more important for the record of low-price stocks in producing a greater percentage advance than higher-price stocks in a recovering market, many low-price stocks have a much smaller number of shares outstanding than the typical higher-price stock, so that it takes far less buying power to make the lower-price stock advance in price.

Consider, for example, a company with 1,000,000 shares of stock outstanding, with the stock selling at 3. If enough buyers step up to buy 10% of the outstanding stock at that level, they would need only $300,000 to accomplish that task, buying 100,000 shares at $3 per share. Of course, the stock would begin to shoot up long before they were able to buy up 100,000 shares —*which is precisely the point,* made even clearer when we look at the opposite extreme. Such an extreme would be *General Motors* with *287,000,000* shares of common stock outstanding at the latest report! Trying to buy 10% of *that* company's common stock at a recent price of 44 would take $1,260,000,000 ($1.26 billion) as against $300,000 for the low-price stock. The higher price of the common stock plus the far larger number of shares of common stock outstanding vastly increased the amount of investor money it would take to move the stock a certain distance. Little wonder that a typical low-price stock can move 50% and 100% in the time that a typical higher-price stock is moving 5% and 10%.

About 7 years ago this writer instructed the staff of the investment service he was (and still is) editing to make a direct statistical study of the relative behavior of all stocks in the 1966-1967 recovery, following the sharp 1966 decline. Taking the 4,068 common stocks listed in Standard & Poor's authoritative "Stock Guide" in the October 1967 Edition, which took in just about every common stock with a public market, we found a total of *1,231* of those 4,068 common stocks had at least doubled in price during the first 9 months of 1967, showing a better than 100% appreciation.

Of those 1,231 stocks, fully 1,076, or 87.5%, had started their move in 1967 *under $20* per share.

Narrowing the field down further, we found that 761 of the 1,231, or *61%* of the total, had started their move *under $10* per share.

When we broke down those 1,231 stocks according to the *percentage* of appreciation, we found that the higher the percentage gain, the greater the chance that the stock started from the "Under 10" Group. Thus:

52% of the stocks gaining between *100%* to *199%* started their move under *$10 per share.*

74% of the stocks gaining between *200% to 299%* started their move under *$10 per share.*

83% of the stocks gaining between *300% to 399%* started their move under *$10 per share.*

90% of the stocks gaining *400% and over* started their move under *$10 per share.*

The greater the percentage of appreciation enjoyed, the greater was the chance that the common stock commitment started in the low-price stock group, or under $10 per share.

Thus, when we now turn to a description of the basic tenets of "Technical Analysis" and its role in helping us to select the most profitable vehicles with which to benefit from the eventual turn of a bear market into a new bull market, we know that we shall be dealing with *low-price stocks* and *low-price Warrants* because that is where the greatest profit potential by far is to be found.

What Are Trend Lines?

Stock prices, of individual stocks, of "Averages" of selected representative stocks to picture the over-all market, "Group Averages" to show how a particular group of stocks is behaving, can all be recorded on a simple graph, the price scale on the left hand side, running vertically, and the time scale on either top or bottom, running horizontally. Drawing a simple example, we come up with the following for an imaginary ABC common.

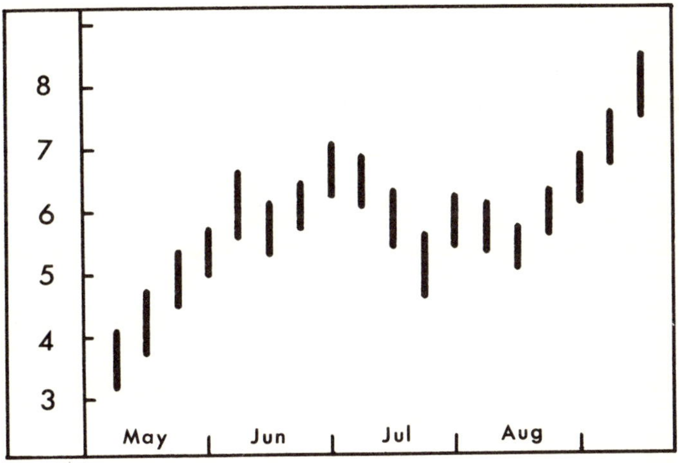

This is a chart of the weekly high and low for ABC common, and after putting down a point for the weekly high and the weekly low, the two points are joined, giving us the trading range for the entire week. The time scale is presented on the bottom of the chart, and the price scale on the left.

Now we have taken a ruler to join the first two lows for the stock which do not cause the line to run *through* any of the price lines (we have marked these two lows with (A) and (B), and we have extended that line to the rest of the chart). The direction of the line indicates the *trend* of the lows the stock is making—hence, a "Trend Line"—and it is a "lower" Trend Line because it was created by connecting two *lows*.

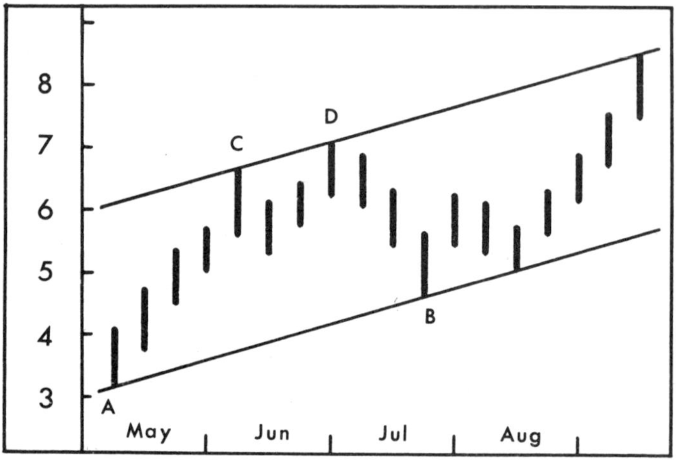

Next we have joined the first two available *highs* for the stock which do not cause the resulting line to run *through* any of the price lines (we have marked these two highs with (C) and (D), and we have extended that line to the rest of the chart). The direction of this line indicates the *trend* of the highs the stock is making—hence, a "Trend Line" once more—and it is an "upper" Trend Line because it was created by connecting two *highs*.

When you observe the two Trend Lines together, you will see that the two Trend Lines are *parallel* to one another, thereby creating what is called a *Trend Channel*. Did we arrive at this merely by artistic license, or are such near-perfect Trend Channels to be found in charts of individual stocks or Averages? The answer is that they are found many, many times and are, therefore, extremely useful in anticipating turning points, as we shall soon see. We shortly deal with the question as to why perfect or near-perfect Trend Lines and Trend Channels form (and we quickly add that one Trend Line by itself is just as useful as a Trend Channel), but first let us look at a few Trend Lines and Trend Channels formed by a well-known top "blue chip" stock —Coca Cola Company common stock—and the guidance we can draw from such Trend Line analysis will become quickly apparent.

Coca Cola Common—Some Enlightening Trend Lines

In 1970, following a relatively moderate reaction, Coca Cola common started a 2½-year upsurge from a low of 63 which was to see a 138% advance to a top of 150. Just as we described with our mythical ABC common, we have drawn in the significant Trend Lines, and they are perfectly illustrative of what we have been discussing. The entire action of the stock is encompassed by the Trend Channel formed by the two Trend Lines from early-1970 to early-1973. Experience has justified, time and time again, the basic tenet that once a Trend Line or Trend Channel (two parallel Trend Lines) comes into being, one can act on the assumption that so long as the price action does not break a Trend Line, *the general direction of that stock will remain the same.*

In that entire rise from 63 to 150, Coca Cola common remained perfectly within its Trend Channel, and an investor with commitments in this stock, and following the tenets of Technical Analysis, could have left his holdings undisturbed. *In February 1973 the trend changed.* This was signaled by the breaking of the lower Trend Line, as is clearly visible on our chart, indicated by an arrow. An immediate sale would have been an intelligent course of action to take, considering the long upside run that had been enjoyed.

But there was another technical "signal" yet to come. Coca Cola common, after breaking through its long-term Trend Channel, commenced a sideways movement clearly shown on the chart, actually extending from mid-1972 to December 1973. We show the lower Trend Line of what was actually a sideways Trend Channel by a broken line. When that well-established lower Trend Line was broken on the downside in December 1973, shown by an arrow, an even more *urgent* "Sell" signal was in order, based on the most elementary criteria of Technical Analysis.

Readers should observe on the chart that *a new Trend Channel* has come into effect, encompassing the entire downward sweep

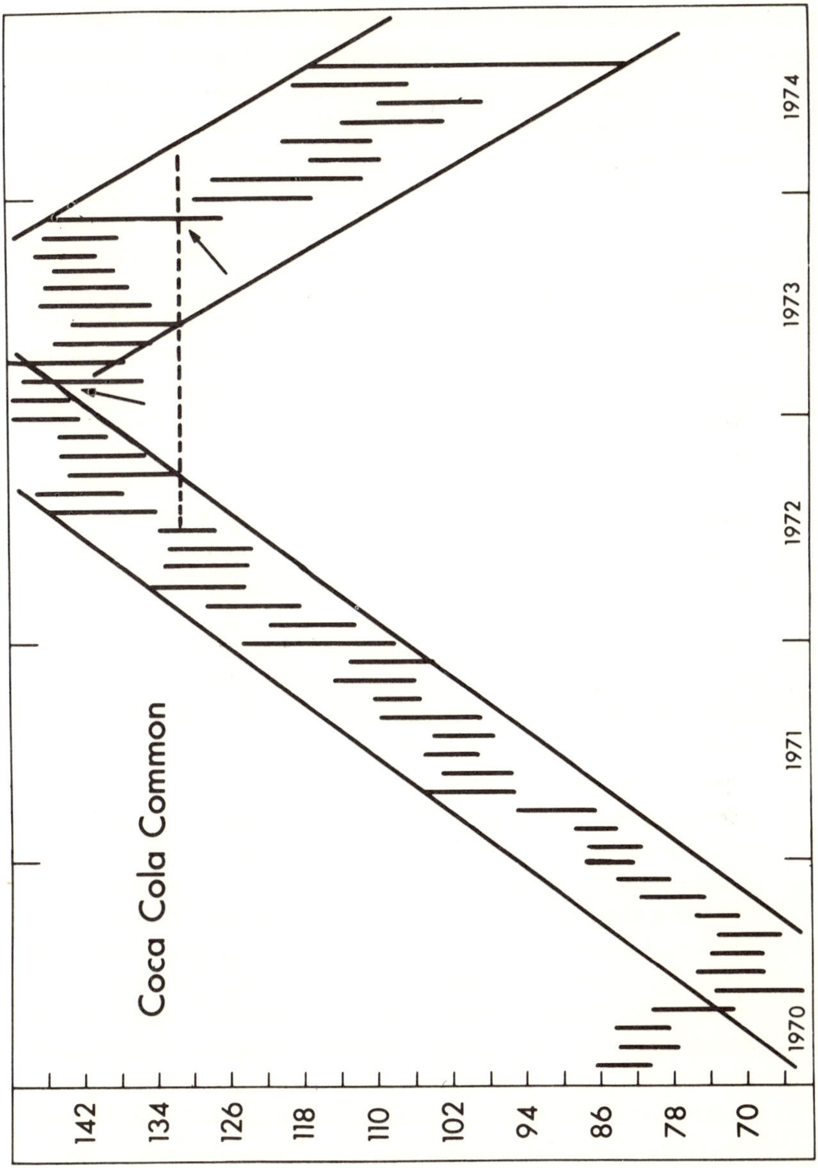
Coca Cola Common
142
134
126
118
110
102
94
86
78
70
1970
1971
1972
1973
1974

of Coca Cola common since early-1973, the entire price action of the stock staying perfectly within the two Trend Lines.

Why Do Trend Lines and Trend Channels Provide Such Excellent Guidance? A Short-Term View and a Long-Term View

For every buyer of a stock there must be a seller, and vice versa. We sometimes lose sight of this unalterable fact when we hear a stock market commentator say: "There was heavy buying on the New York Stock Exchange today, and prices rose sharply." What the commentator should more accurately have said was that there was heavy *trading* on the New York Stock Exchange that day, and there were more investors willing to buy at current prices than there were investors willing to sell. Consequently, the bids of the buyers had to rise until sellers were more willing to sell. But there had to be exactly as many shares bought as there were shares sold.

Almost all share movement, then, is an interplay of the buyer's desire to buy and the seller's desire to sell. We can better understand why a stock will many times show a rather regular series of advances and declines by looking upon it in the following manner, and here we shall put the stock fluctuations into a sideways trading channel, using that particular portion of the Coca Cola chart which had that characteristic. (Weekly chart courtesy of Mansfield Stock Charts.)

When Coca Cola common approached the lower Trend Line, the lower price of the stock would logically induce the following feeling among many prospective sellers: "Too bad. I could have sold at a higher price just a few days ago, and even higher some weeks ago, and now the stock looks pretty low. I think I'll wait for the higher prices to reappear and then maybe I'll sell." Unable to make all the purchases they desired because of the lessened willingness of the potential seller to sell, prospective buyers then raise their bids, transactions are concluded at higher levels, and we see the stock price moving to the upside, away from the lower Trend Line.

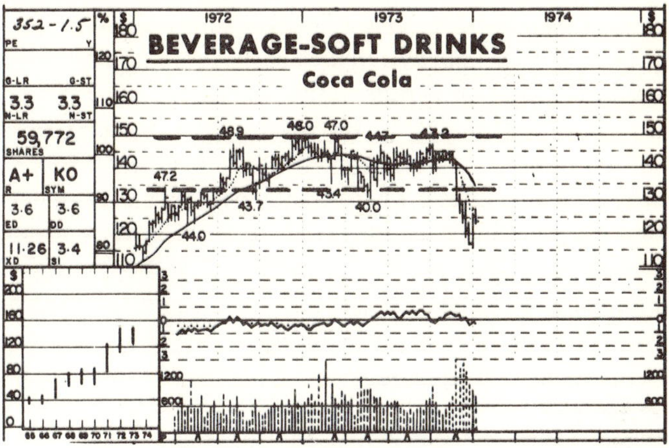

As Coca Cola common approached the *upper* Trend Line, the reverse would take place. Prospective buyers would say: "Too bad. I could have bought at a lower price just a few days ago, and even lower some weeks back, and now the stock looks pretty high. I think I'll wait till it comes down, and then maybe I'll buy." Unable to make all the sales they desire, and with the higher prices making selling more attractive than previously, the sellers lower the prices at which they are offering their stock, transactions are concluded at lower levels, and the stock price moves away to the downside, away from the upper Trend Line. Thus, the movement between the upper and lower Trend Lines of our sideways-moving Trend Channel.

Is it really as simple as we have described, or are there many more factors involved? Of course there are more factors! A good number of investors are aware of the earnings trend and other fundamentals for Coca Cola, and have opinions about the general outlook for the company, the soft-drink industry as a whole, and the direction of the economy and the entire stock market itself. Money may become tight and the need to sell more insistent, while buyers will become more reluctant to buy for the same reason. In the case of a stock such as Coca Cola, *institutional* handling of their portfolios must be taken into account.

All these feelings and opinions, and many more, take various optimistic and pessimistic tacks, and *are averaged out* in the push-pull of sellers and buyers in the marketplace. So long as *new* factors of strength or weakness do not enter the picture, it is perfectly logical to expect what actually does take place much of the time—a shuttling back and forth between upper and lower Trend Lines to reflect the *relative balance* of forces.

Continuing, let us make clear that we are not referring here *only* to a sideways trading range, for the same description would, in our opinion, completely fit a Trend Channel moving *up* and a Trend Channel moving *down.* In the upside Trend Channel, the balance of forces between buyer and seller continues to be resolved by higher prices because the majority of factors are in favor of optimism. In the downside Trend Channel, the balance of forces between buyer and seller has changed, resolving itself into lower prices because the majority of factors are on the side of pessimism. Not only is this *self-evident,* but we can quite logically describe what is taking place, with the more important components being a combination of fundamentals *and* emotion.

Look at fundamentals first, staying with Coca Cola as our example. Let us say that a continuing growth in the proportion of young people in the population and growing disposable personal income is leading to a rising curve of demand for soft drinks. At the same time, costs are well under control for the company and there is no serious over-capacity, demand pressing rather hard on available supply. Sales will doubtless be rising for a company such as Coca Cola, along with net income and, very possibly, common dividends are being increased, or are expected to be increased. Other factors would enter into the picture, such as a liking by institutional investors—trust funds, pension funds, mutual funds, etc.—for a stock such as Coca Cola. Overseas demand for the company's product might be brisk and expanding. Obviously, the number of factors which could go into the *funda-*

mentals of the situation are many, and it is clear when we look at that chart for Coca Cola common once more, the period when the Trend Channel was rising was very likely a period when all these factors resolved themselves out into a decidedly optimistic frame of mind for investors. Buyers were obviously more anxious to buy than sellers to sell throughout the entire rise pictured on the chart. We need not go into a similar description for the sideways portion of the chart, or the downtrend Channel which later eventuated, the balance of forces being relatively of equal strength in the first mentioned, and tilted strongly towards the *seller* in the second mentioned.

Enter—The Psychological Component

Allow us to compress at this point what could easily take an entire book into a few paragraphs! Throughout life we learn what is painful, and we seek to avoid it; and we learn what is pleasurable and we seek to experience it again. A stock going up is very pleasurable—we are making money without any effort on our part at all—and the more it goes up, the greater the pleasure. We begin to associate all kinds of good things with that stock then, and even some "magical" elements begin to appear after a while. Thus, when "oil stocks", for example, have been going up for a long time, more and more investors are likely to whisper confidentially to their friends: "Buy Oils," and soon they no longer even have to explain why, for "Oils" will have developed an aura of "can't miss" about them. We have given this concept a *great* deal of thought in the past thirty years or so and could introduce many supportive thoughts at this point, but we ask the reader to simply accept it as such and turn to a major point vital for this discussion.

All the positive factors we outlined a few paragraphs ago (to consider the rising phase first) are subject to change, with some of the most important factors almost guaranteed to change and *for the worse*. Thus, if the market is expanding and profits are rising, companies do the natural thing—*they expand capacity*. At the same time, new companies come into the business, some of them very well financed, seeking to share in the rising profits, and they build new production lines. Result? The Supply/Demand balance begins to tilt in favor of the buyer, overcapacity begins to develop, profit margins begin to shrink, and the formerly rosy picture begins to turn much less rosy.

While all this deterioration in fundamentals has been developing, the stock has been merrily moving up along its Trend Channel to ever higher levels, speculative interest having now turned to speculative excitement, and "magical elements" carrying the stock along at an even faster rate.

But something is happening which will produce a change. *Reality is being stretched too thin* and the more informed and/or astute holders of the stock will begin to sell. As the balance of forces between buyers and sellers begins to edge more in the direction of the sellers, the upside-tilted Trend Channel can no longer be maintained. *The Lower Trend Line breaks!*

When the upside progress of the stock stops, something else happens. The aura around the stock frays and the former confidence of many buyers is now replaced by doubt. Along with a weakening in the *fundamentals* which formerly contributed so much to the stock's positive action, there is now an additional weakening in the *psychological* component. The stock has lost its magic. Thus do upside Trend Channels come to their conclusion and find themselves replaced by *down*side Trend Channels, often with an interim period of sideways movement, such as we saw so clearly with Coca Cola common. And exactly the same developments occur with downside Trend Channels, with all the above developments taking place in reverse.

We Are Leading Directly to Important Trading Concepts

What we have described up to this point with Coca Cola common is not merely a matter of "interest"—an amusing sidelight on how stocks tend to behave, and how Trend Lines so many times accurately chart that behavior along straight and true paths. Rather do these points possess the utmost force in developing trading techniques to *take best advantage* of ceaselessly repetitive gyrations which have shown themselves operative in stock market charts for as long back as this writer has ever studied them. The interplay of fundamental and emotional factors, with the emotional factors almost always outweighing fundamentals in the latter portions of profound upside and downside moves, are deeply embedded in the structure of the stock market itself and all the millions of investors and institutions that buy and sell stocks. *It is the way the market works,* and there is no reason to ever expect it to change.

What makes it more than ever vital for the reader to follow with care each point we shall now make is that the Great Inflation of the early-1970's has inflicted such indiscriminate slaughter on so many thousands of stocks and hundreds of Warrants that when the turn *does* come (it will, at the proper time), the most profit-promising trading opportunities in 30 or 40 years will, in the opinion of this writer, appear in rotation, one-by-one, for what we believe will be a relatively long period of time, perhaps more than a year, perhaps two or three years. We are shortly going to describe techniques to deal with these opportunities to the reader's best advantage, and before doing this we ask the reader to look at a series of charts so that the points we will make will have the greatest possible meaning and force.

All the charts are courtesy of an excellent series of chart books published by Securities Research Charts (Boston, Massachusetts), and let's take a moment to describe the price scales on these charts. In our Coca Cola chart we used a straight arithmetic scale, the distance, say, between 60 and 80 on the chart, being exactly the same as the distance between 80 and 100, each being 20 points. The Securities Research Chart uses a *semi-log scale,* with equal distances on the chart price scale representing equal *percentage* moves. Thus, to take an example, on an *arithmetic* scale chart, the distance between 40 and 80 (40 points) would be twice that of the distance between 20 and 40 (20 points), but on a *semi-log* scale they would be *equal* because both 20 to 40 and 40 to 80 are *100%* moves. It would be noncontributory to dwell on the statistical niceties of these differences because we want to get on to practical trading techniques, so let the reader merely accept this writer's opinion that Trend Lines and Trend Channels are shown with just as great accuracy and meaning by semi-log charts as they are with arithmetic scale charts. Indeed, this writer, in more complex technical studies (and we study many more factors than we have even mentioned in these pages) uses one type of chart to corroborate the other.

This is an important chart which has additional meanings for

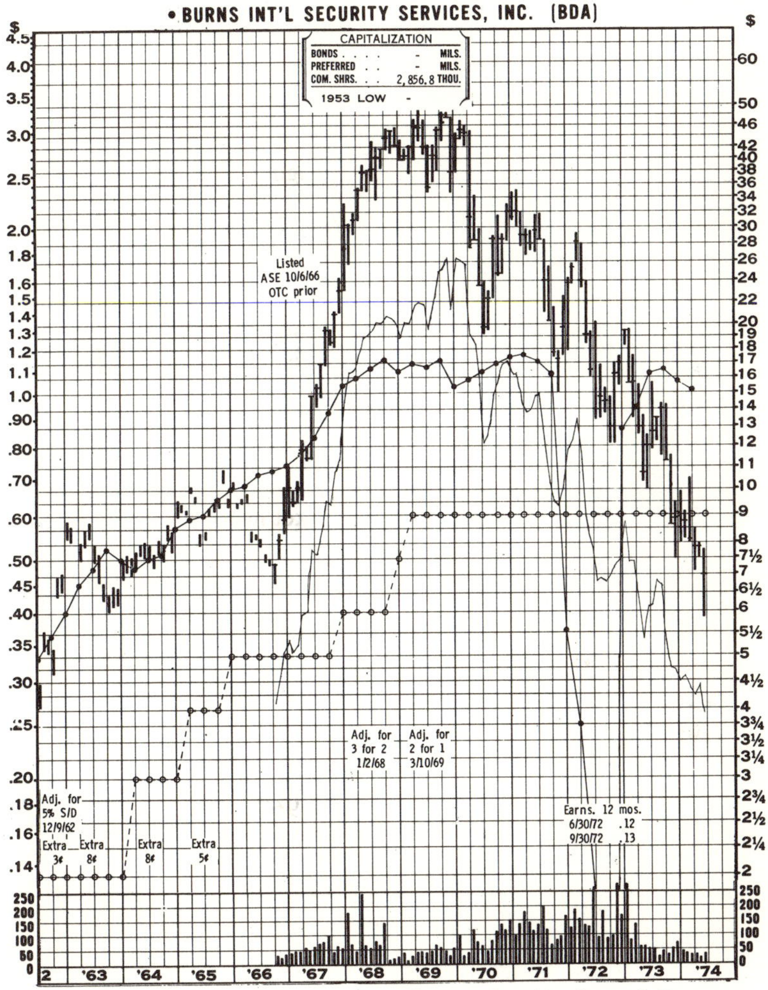

Courtesy Securities Research Company

our trading techniques so we will come back to it on a later page. At this time, however, we ask the reader to note how similar it is to the Coca Cola chart even though this was a low-price, relatively speculative stock when compared to blue-chip Coca Cola. Thus, when the profound move started for Burns International in late-1966, the stock multiplied more than 7 times from about 7 to 50 whereas Coca Cola multiplied only a little more than 2 times during its move. But there is a rising Trend Channel for both charts, followed by a distinct sideways pattern, and followed again by a long downtrend channel in the case of Burns International. As to how long the *present* Coca Cola downtrend Channel will become, future stock market history will tell.

Note the *explosive nature* of the rise in Burns International. It is this point we will be returning to as we later discuss trading techniques.

With California Computer Products we have another price "explosion" in 1966, a minor setback later in that year, then another rapid upside burst, all adding up to a 10-time multiplication in the price of the stock by mid-1967. There then came a sideways movement, followed by a long-range deterioration back to the 1966 starting point near 5½! Once again, we particularly draw the reader's attention to the "explosive" nature of the 1966-1967 rise.

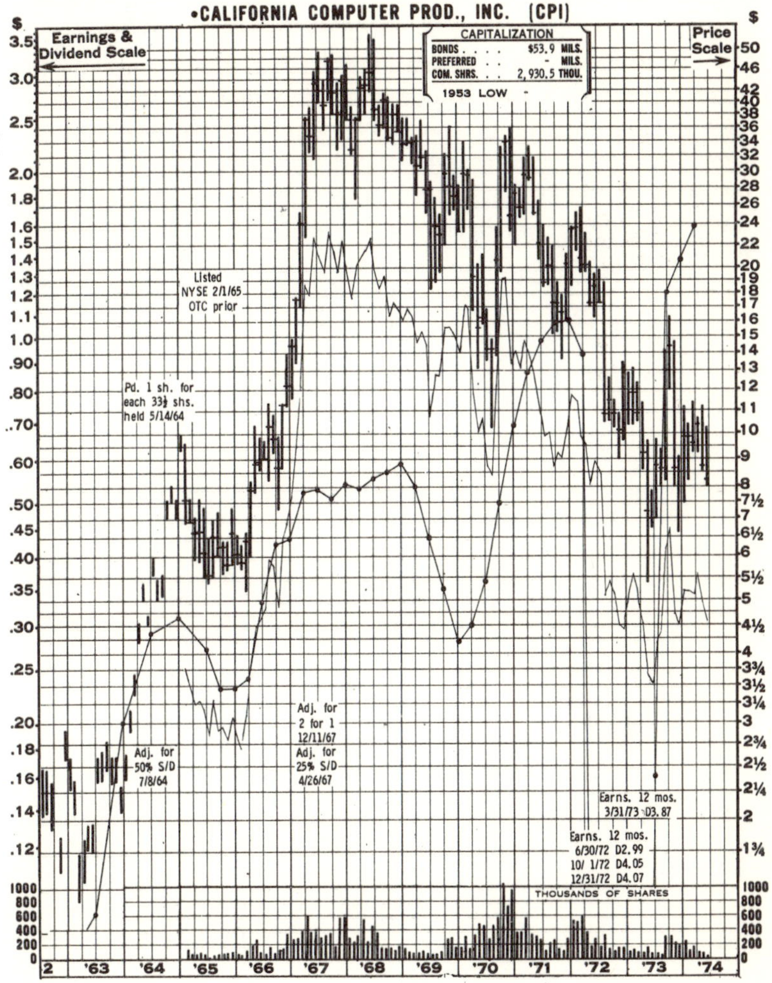

Courtesy Securities Research Company

One does not always have an extended period of sideways movement to inform us relatively painlessly that an upside trend channel has been broken. With CMI Investment Corp. common, a six-fold appreciation from 12 to 75 starting in 1970 broke through the lower Trend Line in mid-1972, had a short run to a further 15-point gain to about 90, and then suffered such a swift collapse that in the space of a year the stock was back to its 1970 starting point near 12. We shall be referring soon to the initial 1970 rise of CMI as giving us valuable insights into the trading techniques which should be best suited to the opportunities now coming into view in a deeply-ravaged stock market.

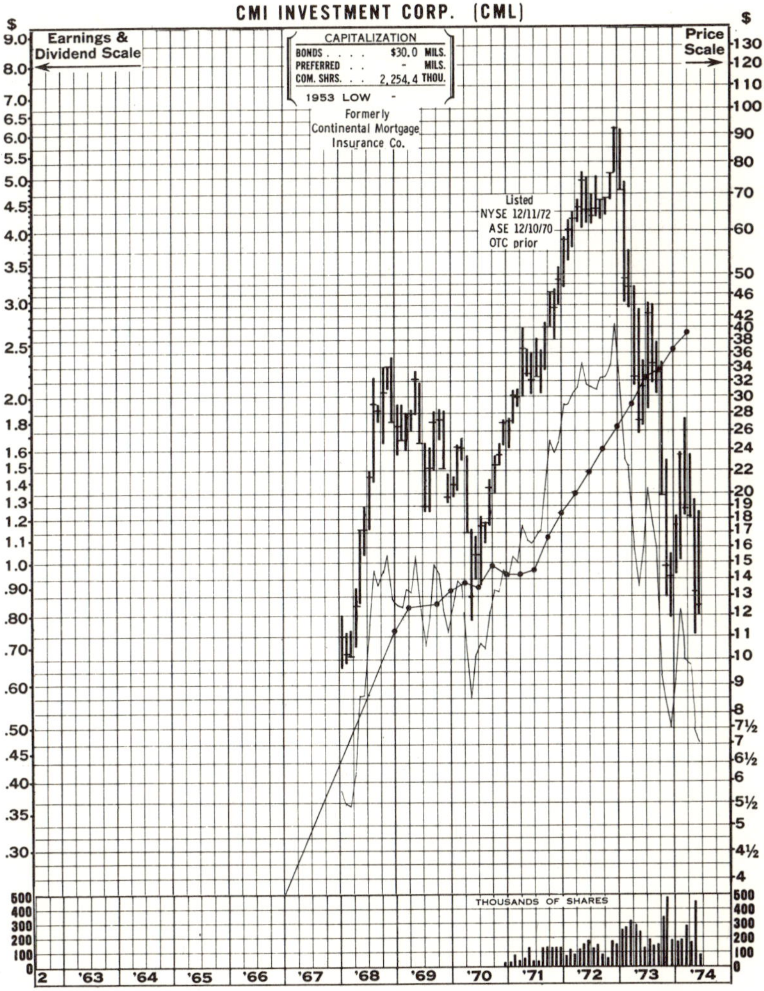

Courtesy Securities Research Company

The Vital Role to Be Played by Technical Analysis

This is not a book on "Technical Analysis of Stocks," so we are moving quite swiftly through some of the most basic concepts in order that we may get to our "Practical Trading Techniques". This writer did publish an extended work on this subject of "Technical Analysis" in 1960, but it is now out of print, and we have refined many of our approaches since that date to what we feel is a much more efficacious level. In a complete study, such important components of Technical Analysis as "Group Movement", "Relative Strength", "Point & Figure" analysis, and "Momentum", to name only some of the most important areas, receive adequate scope. But since we are confining ourselves here to "Trend Line Analysis" only — and we shall soon see that this is adequate for the trading techniques we are going to describe — let us at least take a few more paragraphs to illustrate for the reader the true beauty of the interplay of Trend Lines as they picture not only the movement of a stock over a period of years, but in much shorter periods of time as well, and in many different ways. It is important to realize this *because weekly and monthly charts are going to be the most important weapons in our armory as we shall soon see.*

Here is Cluett, Peabody common, for example, in a truly ordinary chart, there being hundreds comparable to it. But look closely at each "leg" of each move and note how significant Trend Lines come into play, and give important guidance. Starting at the extreme left in what remained of 1962, an upside Trend Channel carried the stock from about 12½ to 28. The lower Trend Line broken, there ensued a deep drop to about 14¾ and the start of another upside Trend Channel which carried forward to a high of 39.

Following the breaking of the lower Trend Line of that Trend Channel the stock returned to its 14¾ starting place and we next draw the reader's attention to the single Trend Line which

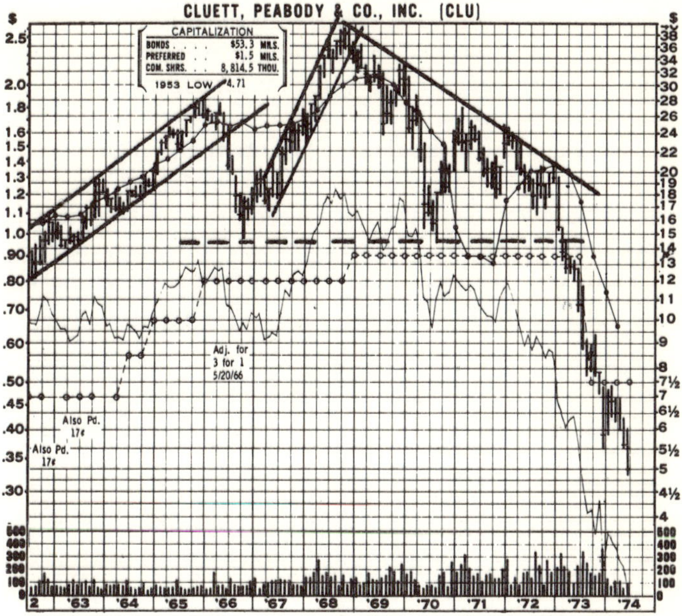

Courtesy Securities Research Company

ticked off 5 tops in a 5-year period, those tops starting with 39 in 1968, moved to 34 in 1969, 27 in 1971, a whole series of tops in the first half of 1972 bunched around the 22-24 level and, finally, a top at 21 at year-end 1972 from which a toboggan slide to a 1974 low of *4* commenced.

Note now the dashed line representing a sideways Trend Line was formed by the 14¾ lows in both 1966 and 1970. In 1973 Cluett, Peabody common dropped precipitously through that Trend Line, which was indication enough of the severity of the decline which then actually followed.

Trend Lines, Trend Lines, Trend Lines — we trust readers are beginning to more fully absorb their usefulness. In all of our descriptions of these Trend Lines in the previous pages, we have stayed away from the obvious parallel discussions about the *Fundamentals* in each case of Balance Sheet and Income Account. In actuality, the factors of intrinsic value and present earnings and future earnings potential must *always* be analyzed side-by-side with such a technical tool as the Trend Line. And there are some dozens of important additional technical tools which come into play. But we repeat once more that if we followed the admittedly desired end of completeness, this book would run to 1,000 pages! And our immediate goal is to get to our "Practical Trading Techniques". So, negating the excessive claim that Trend Lines can do the job by them-

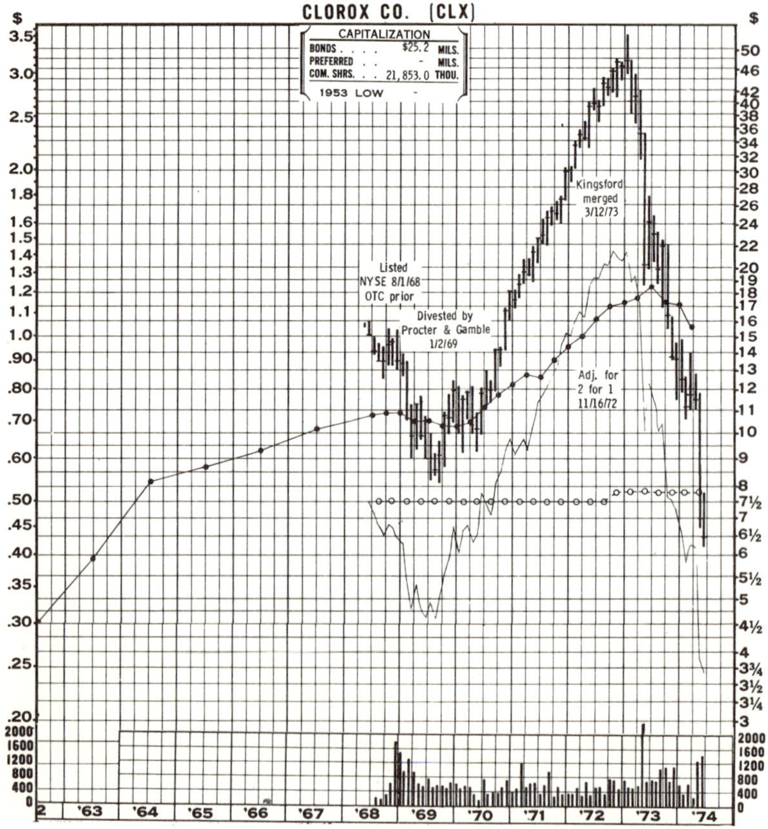

Courtesy Securities Research Company

selves, we still want the reader to appreciate the great help they *do* give.

Our last chart of a stock for this section is that of Clorox Co. common, and it illustrates once again the *explosive* nature of many common stock moves from a profound market bottom. When Clorox common took off in 1970 from an adjusted level of 9⅜ to reach an early-1973 high above 50, it carried the advance through with hardly a backward glance, and this type of move will assume a place of first importance in our discussions of "Practical Trading Techniques" to follow. When the quite narrow, sharply tilted-to-the-upside Trend Channel was broken in the first weeks of 1973, a plunge back to the 4 level took place, again with only minor interruptions. The two Trend Channels, side-by-side, are a fitting end to this part of our discussion, placing Trend Lines and Trend Channels securely into the framework of great usefulness they surely deserve.

A Pause To Look At Some Remarkable Long-Term Trend Channels

Very shortly now we are going to turn to the quite *short-term* Trend Lines which will provide much of the basis for our "Practical Trading Techniques", but we don't wish to do this without taking a few paragraphs to reprint some very *long*-term Trend Channels which should do two things: (1) impress upon the reader the true beauty, and real mystery, of Trend Lines (*how* can they be so accurate over so long a period of time!), and (2) the serious economic and stock market difficulties underlined by the clear message of those long-term Trend Channels and which we feel sure will stay with us for quite some time to come.

First, there is a chart from an investment service of which this writer is Editor, The R.H.M. Warrant & Stock Survey + Stocks Under 10. The chart is from the issue dated February 16, 1973, where we discussed "Interior Trend Lines," and let us present the appropriate, although abbreviated, explanation for readers. "Straight" Trend Lines run *outside* the chart, touching highs and lows but never crossing any part of the chart itself. *"Interior"* Trend Lines also touch highs and lows, but run *through* portions of the chart being analyzed, and provide guidance of at least equal importance as "Straight" Trend Lines — a judgment which we can corroborate with our own thirty years of studying market movement during which we are sure we must have studied some tens of thousands of market charts of all descriptions.

In the chart shown we see an Interior Trend Line starting with two lows in 1962, picking up the important 1966 low with exactness, and being almost exactly touched by the 1968 low. But in 1969 something happened. Up to that point, the Trend Line had been of the "Straight" variety, remaining outside the chart, but when the 1969 market *crashed through* that line, it signaled something important was happening, and our next chart will tell us more about that "something important" category.

Continuing with that Trend Line, now turned "Interior", look at the 1971 top. You will find it virtually touching the Trend Line, and when we continue up that Trend Line we find the *very important January 1973 top* penetrating that Interior Trend Line only slightly. A truly remarkable performance for a Trend Line, but we have had to use that word "remarkable" on innumerable occasions in studying all manners of charts, of individual stocks, stock Groups, and market Averages. Trend Lines and Trend Channels are inherently remarkable in the way they work, even though *why* they work over *long* periods of time remains in the realm of mystery. (How can 2 points in 1962 hit the 1973 top 11 years later?)

The dashed line on the same chart illustrates this efficacy on a shorter-term scale. Starting with two tops in 1968, 1969, the line touches the 1971 top, passes *through* the 1972 recovery, which gave good indication of the 1972-1973 market rise to follow when the market went through that line on the

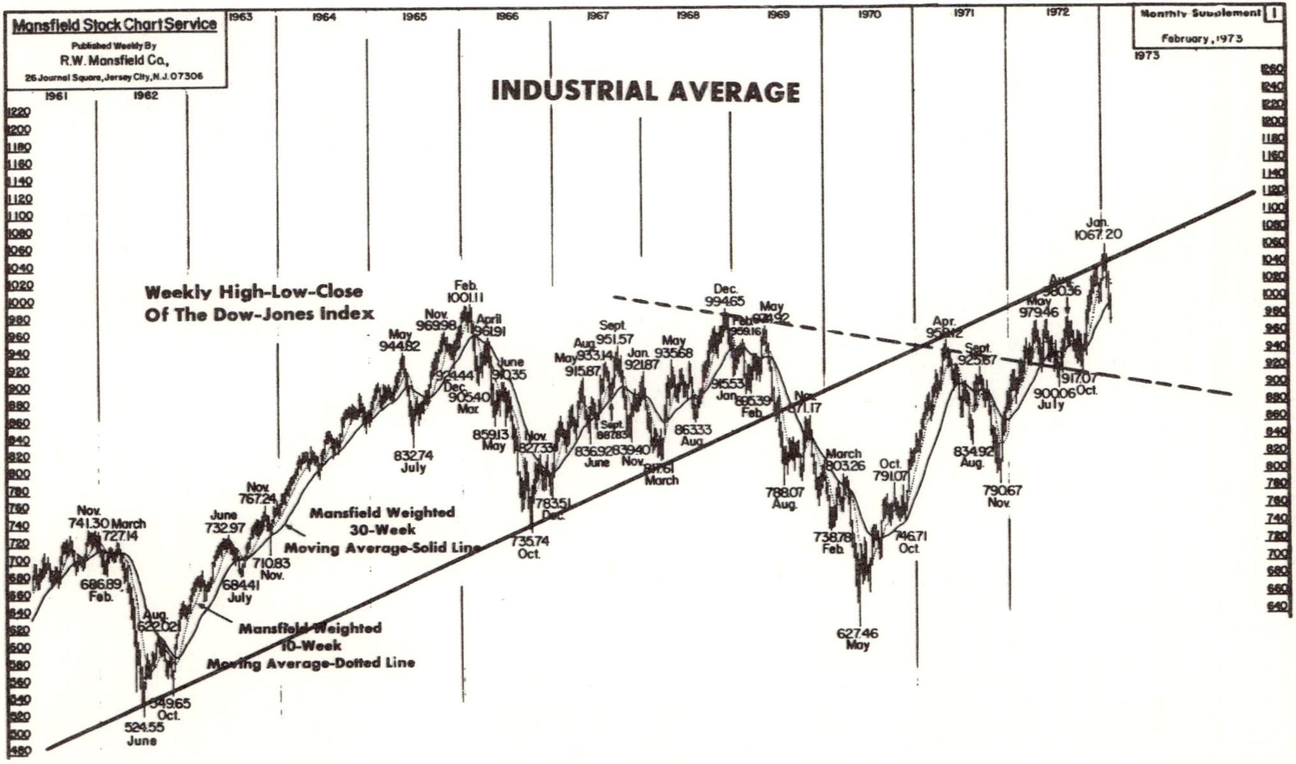
Mansfield Stock Chart Service
Published Weekly By
R.W. Mansfield Co.,
26 Journal Square, Jersey City, N.J. 07306
Monthly Supplement 1
February, 1973
INDUSTRIAL AVERAGE
Weekly High-Low-Close
Of The Dow-Jones Index
Mansfield Weighted
30-Week
Moving Average-Solid Line
Mansfield Weighted
10-Week
Moving Average-Dotted Line
1961
1962
1963
1964
1965
1966
1967
1968
1969
1970
1971
1972
1973
Nov. 741.30
March 727.14
686.89 Feb.
Aug. 622.02
524.55 June
549.65 Oct.
June 732.97
684.41 July
Nov. 767.24
710.83 Nov.
May 944.82
832.74 July
Nov. 969.98
Feb. 1001.11
April 961.91
924.44
Dec. 905.40
Mar.
June 910.35
859.13 May
Nov. 827.33
783.51 Dec.
735.74 Oct.
May 915.87
Aug. 933.14
Sept. 951.57
836.92 June
Sept. 867.83
839.40 Nov.
Jan. 921.87
May 935.68
863.33 Aug.
March
Dec. 994.65
May
Feb. 969.16
915.53 Jan.
895.39 Feb.
Nov.
788.07 Aug.
March 803.26
738.78 Feb.
627.46 May
Oct. 791.07
746.71 Oct.
Apr.
Sept. 925.67
834.92 Aug.
790.67 Nov.
May 979.46
900.06 July
917.07 Oct.
Jan. 1067.20

upside, and then was touched by a number of lows in 1972. That Trend Line has since been broken on the *down*side, which gave another indication, this time of the market devastation that was to follow in 1973-1974.

A REALLY Long-Term and MOST Remarkable Chart

Our good and long-time friend, Samuel J. Auerbach, who was head of technical research at Oppenheimer & Company prior to his recent and very untimely death, used to keep a long-term chart (which started when he was a member of this writer's staff at R. H. M. in the 1950's). It was of the Standard & Poor's 425 Industrials, and it was in Point & Figure, a very valid technical tool and quite as authoritative as the "bar" chart which we described in a previous paragraph. There is neither space nor time for a detailed description of "Point & Figure", so we will merely state that it dispenses with the regularity of *time,* and moves to the right only when a change of a certain magnitude has occurred. Thus, since our chart is a "One Point Reversal", as long as the stock (or "Average") keeps moving in the same direction, an "x" is placed in the appropriate box, above or below, depending on whether the direction is up or down *until* the chart changes direction by more than 1 point, whereupon the posting moves over to the next column on the right. We apologize for this brief description, and ask the reader to accept our statement that the ultimate picture given by the Point & Figure chart bears a strong family resemblance to the more familiar bar chart, and very often can be used to corroborate what the bar chart is telling us, in addition to other strategic uses in its own right.

Now on to the *remarkable* Trend Lines in this Point & Figure Chart of the Standard & Poor's 425 Industrials going back to 1929! (We were forced to present it sideways because of length.) When two highs at 1929 and 1956 are connected, the subsequent highs in 1959 and 1962 are well within reach and the important 1966 top is touched with exactness 37 years after

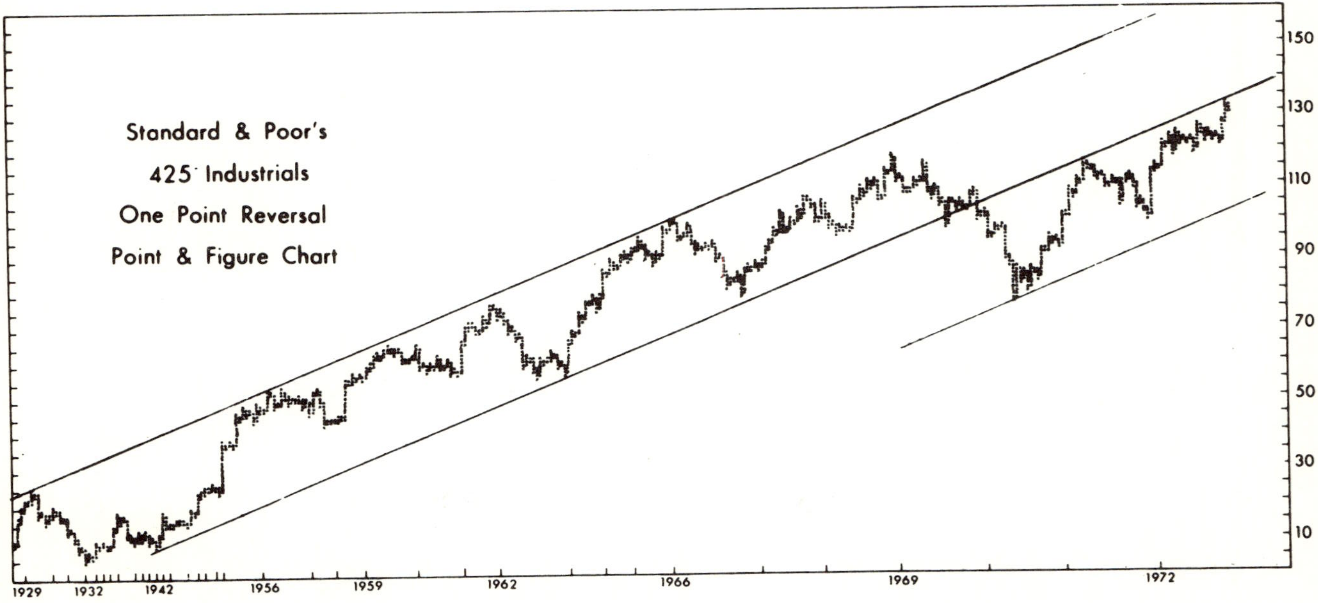
Standard & Poor's
425 Industrials
One Point Reversal
Point & Figure Chart
150
130
110
90
70
50
30
10
1929
1932
1942
1956
1959
1962
1966
1969
1972

the starting point in 1929! Drawing a line through the 1942 bottom parallel to that upper Trend Line, what is the next point to be touched with exactness? The 1962 bottom, and then the 1966 bottom with only a tiny bit of white space showing.

Now we are not only pointing out here how remarkably Trend Lines worked once more in delineating important market turning points, and over such a long stretch of time. We bring to the reader's attention with utmost seriousness this one overriding observation: From 1929 through 1969, a period of 40 years, the stock market stayed totally within the Trend Channel. This is clearly visible. The breaking of that very long-term lower Trend Line on the downside spelled trouble in very big letters. We have gotten quite a bit of that trouble already. We may get a good deal more.

One final point before we turn to our very short-term Trend Lines and their so useful contribution to successful and profitable trading in *today's* market. The lower Trend Line which was broken became the *upper* Trend Line of subsequent market action — a typical occurrence. The 1971 top touched the Trend Line with exactness and the 1973 top as well, corroborating the same market high with the chart discussed just previous to this one. One last look at this 45-year chart. The Standard & Poor's 425 Industrials recently touched a low of *79*, decisively breaking the new lower Trend Line we drew through the 1970 low, parallel to the other two Trend Lines, and constituting a flashing Warning Signal which readers would do well to keep in mind for some time to come, regardless of what encouraging market rallies may take place from time to time. We are *far* from out of the woods with our over-all economy, and the stock market must be considered to be in the same precarious boat for some time to come.

A Transition From Very Long-Term Trend Lines To Very SHORT-Term Trend Lines

We trust that each reader now agrees with us as to the value of carefully watching long-term Trend Lines. We could at this point introduce any number of charts from past markets, *thousands* of such charts, if this were necessary, to demonstrate over and over again the remarkable insights into market movement detailed by these Trend Lines. But we feel, as we now turn to our "Practical Trading Techniques" utilizing relatively *short*-term Trend Lines, that the logic and usefulness of these later Trend Lines will be quite unmistakable.

You have just looked at a 45-year Trend Line (the one which went from 1929 to 1974). What would you think of a 45-*hour* Trend Line? This is not an attempt at humor. When we were an active professional trader for a well-known securities firm in the early-1950's, we kept, as an indispensable tool, a roll of cross-section graph paper which we had to extend across the floor of an office to provide enough room, the chart running anywhere from 6 to 12 feet, and we had to draw Trend Lines with a 3-foot carpenter's rule. We were charting the *hourly* figures for the Dow-Jones Averages to help us arbitrage Convertibles against common stock (a technique which belongs in another book).

We *had* to intelligently estimate the trend of the market literally hour-by-hour and these short-term *hourly* Trend Lines were most helpful — indeed invaluable. The beauty and mystery of Trend Lines, whether they extend for 45 years or 45 hours, is that *they work*. We can build logical explanations around this judgment which could have a good deal of persuasiveness, but not certainty. Do the biological rhythms so pervasive for all living things, and the unquestioned rhythms in all the world about us, the movement of the Planets and other heavenly bodies, the tides, waves of sound and light and so much else, have a family relationship to the rhythms of Trend

Lines and Trend Channels? Perhaps, but we still come back to our own conclusions, based on daily study for more than 30 years in the most practical sense in almost every phase of the securities industry, that Trend Lines and Trend Channels and the associated techniques in the entire field of "Technical Analysis" *work.* It must quickly be said that no tool of Technical Analysis stands by itself, and no technical method can give an assured answer every time, because Technical Analysis is an *art,* not a science, with the skill and experience of the analyst playing a large part. But wedded to a thorough study of applicable Fundamentals in each case, great additional power is added by those tools of Technical Analysis to the thrust for stock market profits.

Short-Term Trend Lines With "Breakout" Low-Price Stocks

We are now directly at an approach to what we believe will be spectacular profit opportunities in low-price stocks and low-price Warrants in coming markets, and to work toward our advice toward success in those opportunities permit us to look back at another period, 1966-1967, when a devastated market righted itself and commenced a definitive recovery. The manner in which low-price stocks behaved in *that* year of market recovery was about the same in which low-price stocks have behaved in *any* year of market recovery, the degree varying only to reflect the extent of the previous market washout. What we shall learn about 1966, then, will be completely applicable to what we can expect to happen when the 1973-1974 market smash-up begins to heal its wounds and prepares for a new upsurge. The fact that we expect a considerable period of sideways movement with *this* bear market because of the extent of the collapse makes what we will describe of even greater importance, because we look for the high-profit trading opportunities to be numerous and frequent in such a sideways-moving market as well as along the lines we shall now describe.

Low-Price Stock "Breakouts" in the 1966-1967 Recovery

Kleer-Vu Industries

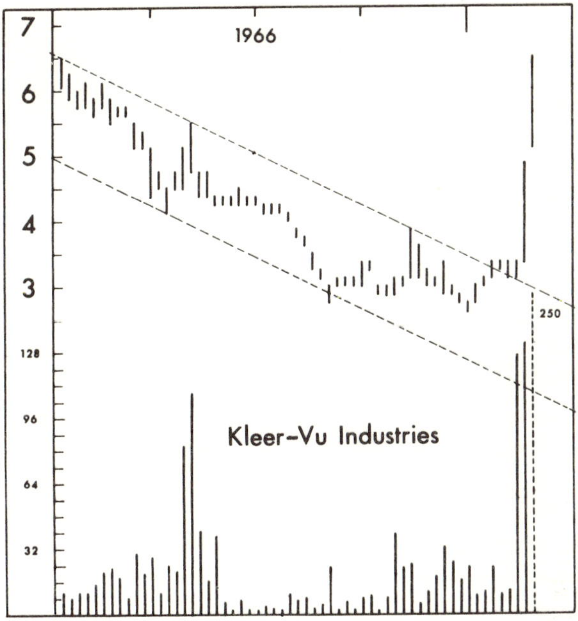

In early-1967 a modestly-sized company on the American Stock Exchange, Kleer-Vu Industries, moved outside of the Trend Channel which had been defining its price movement for all of 1966, first "peeking" through the upper Trend Line of that Trend Channel, and then "breaking out" with a strong surge. This was accompanied by a heavy increase in volume of trading. This first chart shows the weekly highs and lows, the "tick" marks representing three-month intervals, the volume given in hundreds of shares, and a dashed volume line indicating volume in excess of the scale, with the actual volume given in the figure alongside.

1967 was slated to show a high in earnings for Kleer-Vu Industries of $0.80 per share, but the speculative excitement

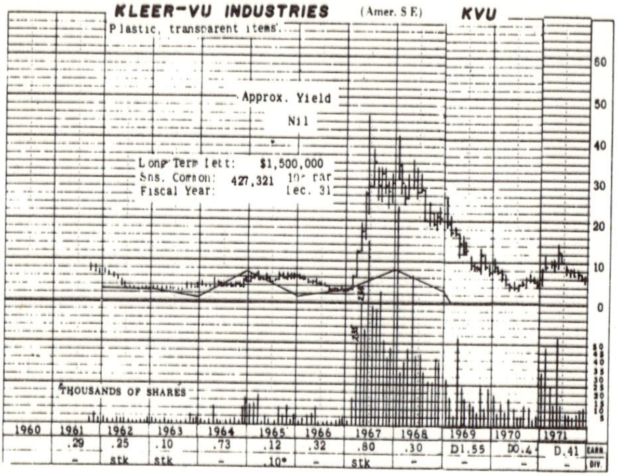

which developed in 1967 (often typical of a recovering market after a profound decline) carried the stock far beyond reality. When we look at the *long-term* price chart (courtesy of Graphic Stocks) we see a fast run-up from the breakout level of about 3½ to *46* in 1967, with hardly any significant backtracking prior to that high — a fact which will play a large part in the trading techniques we shall be describing and recommending for use in subsequent markets when sideways convalescence and a new later upsurge come into play. 1968 saw diminished earnings and 1969 a large deficit, with the entire price advance disappearing by 1970, but the move here was a *trading* move to be utilized with the techniques of Technical Analysis, and since the rise quickly outstripped any rational relationship to intrinsic value and earnings, present and potential, the pre-eminence of technical factors is unquestioned, and leads directly to the Trading Techniques capable of taking best advantage of exactly such a move as took place with Kleer-Vu Industries.

AMREP Corp.

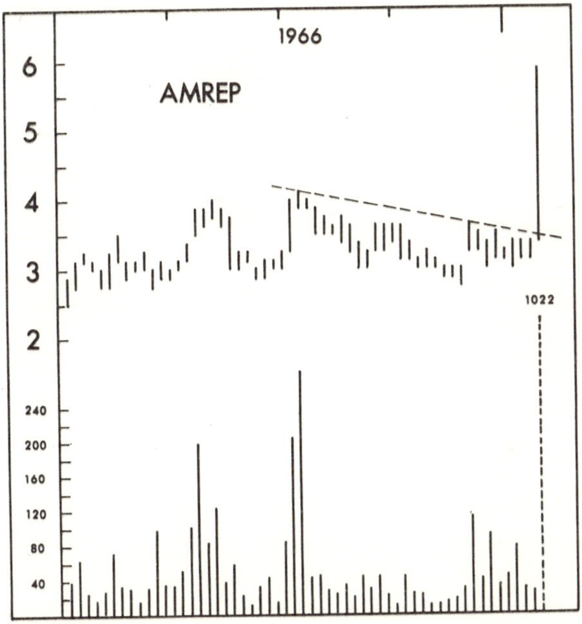

With AMREP, a real estate developer with oil and gas interests, the six-month Trend Line shown in a dashed line on the chart was shattered by a "breakout" early in 1967 on very high volume. If we now look at the long-term price chart we see a fast run to the 10 level, sideways movement for some months, another run to *30,* more sideways movement, with two more repetitions of this process reaching a high of about *60.* The stock has since transferred to the New York Stock Exchange and there have been many wide price swings, but we are pointing only to the "breakout" period.

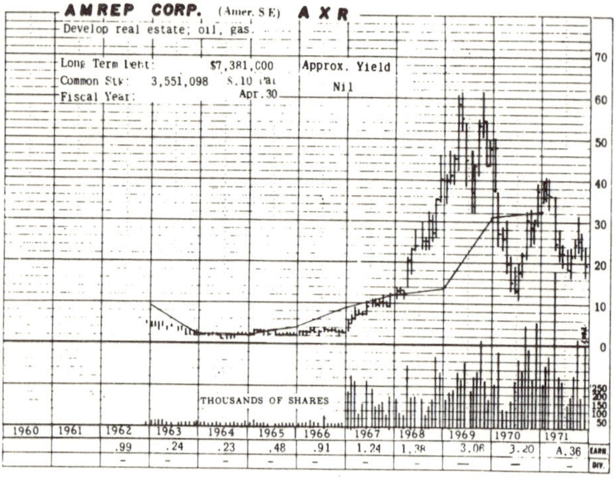

Guerdon Industries

Here the stock had its breakout much later in 1967 than the other two examples — and we shall soon be describing this very helpful characteristic of *rotation of opportunities* in a recovery market. An upper Trend Line running for almost two years through all of 1966 and almost all of 1967 saw the Trend Line broken on the upside to the accompaniment of distinctly higher volume of trading, as shown clearly on the chart, and then the stock was "up and away", as can be seen on the long-term chart, with no significant reaction until the 40 level was reached, representing about a five-fold multiplication in price

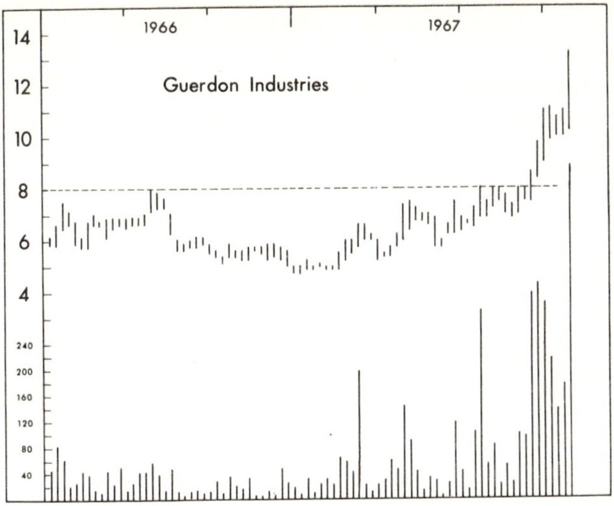

in a matter of months. Readers can note that in 1970 came a duplicate performance, from a somewhat higher level, for both AMREP and Guerdon, the common stocks again breaking out of downtrend channels to rise from about 10 to 40 in the case of AMREP and 8 to 38 in the case of Guerdon Industries. If we reproduced the short-term charts of the "breakout" periods in 1970, they would look exactly like those of 1966 in their general performance.

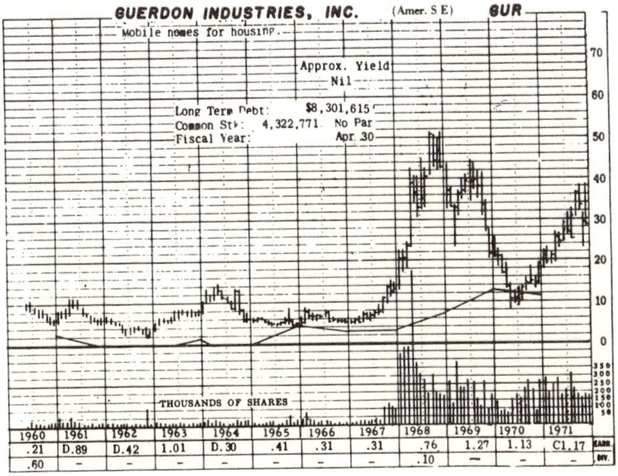

Coca-Cola Bottling

Continuing, we learned about "Trend Lines" from the giant in the soft drink industry, Coca-Cola; now let's look at one of its satellites, the Coca-Cola Bottling Co. (N. Y.), itself a large entity in its field.

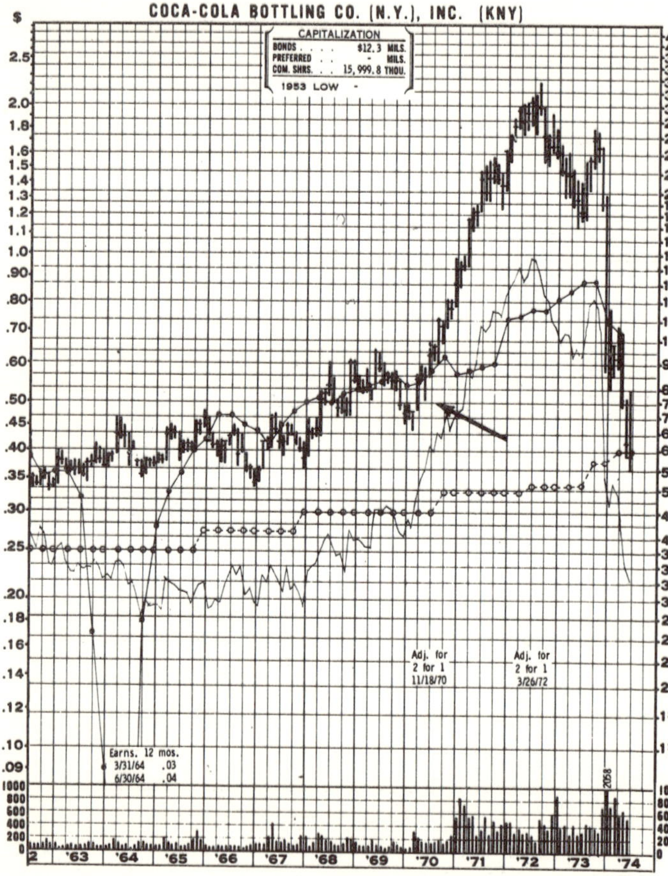

Courtesy Securities Research Company

If we look at the chart, we note an unmistakable Trend Channel to the downside in 1969, with the upper Trend Line broken on the upside in March 1970 (arrow). There then followed an uninterrupted climb to about 23, when there was a sideways pause, followed by another climb to a top near 33. When the entire uptrend channel which saw a five-fold multiplication in the stock from 6¾ to 33 was broken in late-1972, there followed the destruction of the stock's price structure as shown. The significance of such wide swings for our "Trading Techniques" will shortly be apparent.

Maremont Corp.

Another example which comes quickly to hand is Maremont Corp. whose long-term price chart shows a rise starting in 1970 from the 4¼ level, this advancing Trend Channel then continuing to higher levels without significant reaction until the 20 level, not much less than a five-fold appreciation, continuing

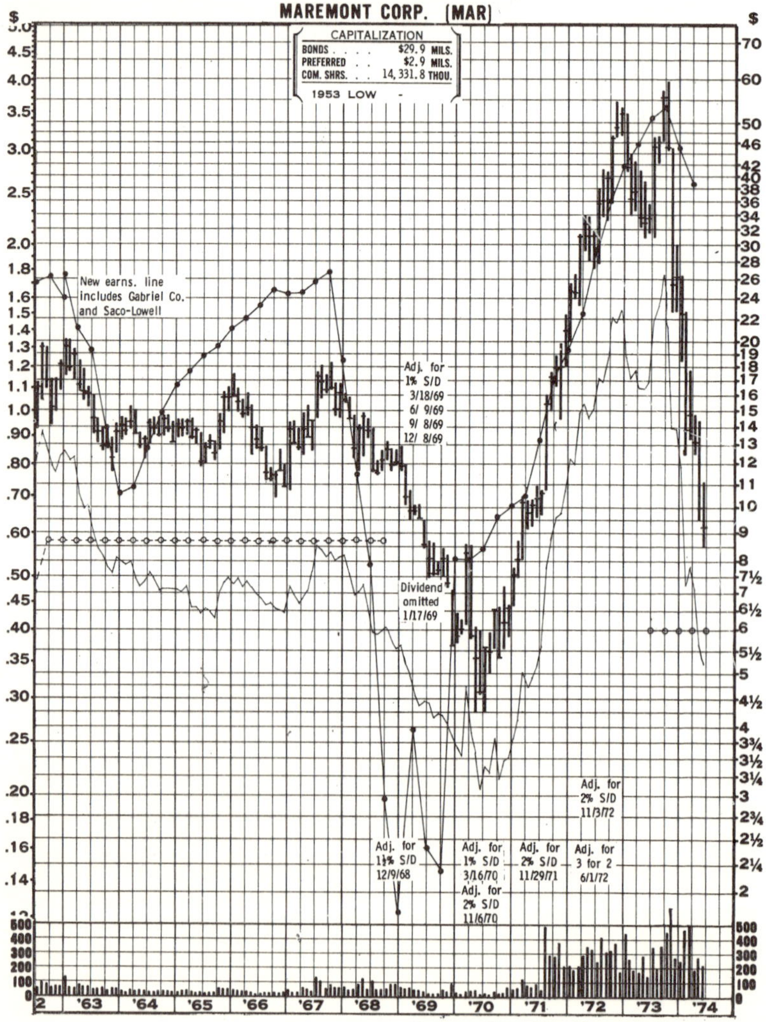

Courtesy Securities Research Company

to a top of 55 after that, or about a 12-fold appreciation. There followed a "double top", a quite bearish technical development, and a virtually uninterrupted slide thereafter to a low of 6½, as we write.

Our Trading Techniques Come Into View

Study any period of market recovery after a severe decline, such as we have pictured for 1966 and 1970, and you find a large number of highly emotional moves in which recoveries measured in three-fold, five-fold and even ten-fold multiplication in price become quite frequent. Momentum tends to carry much too far in recovery in many cases so that even many *under*valued securities quickly become *over*valued securities. Also to be noted is the fact that in the highly-charged emotional atmosphere of market turnarounds, analysis of Fundamentals of Balance Sheet and Income Account hardly ever, by itself, points to the correct vehicles for the largest percentage moves, and certainly is of limited help in the all-important factor of *timing*. We shall shortly return to the large and important role which *is* played by Fundamentals, both in a Trend Channel upsurge once it has commenced, and when we consider long-term commitments for leveraged upside profit, and particularly in low-price Warrants, but here we are talking about *initial Trading techniques,* and the very techniques themselves, as we now look at them quite explicitly, leave Fundamentals for later consideration. Let us see why this is so.

Trend Line Breakout — The Most Relevant "Signal" in Trading

Having watched many market turning points, some of large magnitude, others of smaller magnitude, in the past thirty years of professional market activity, the most descriptive term we can use of what takes place at such turning points is "Follow the leader." A stock which moves out of a downside Trend Channel with decisiveness, making a run to the upside, attracts a following, first small, then larger. The continuing rise of such a stock, far from discouraging new buyers, *attracts* them, higher prices being paid even more enthusiastically than when the prices were lower. Momentum develops as the advance proceeds, volume of trading typically enlarging as the upside leaps increase in scope.

As with understanding the Trend Lines themselves, there is no complete answer as to *why* this should be so. But it is quite enough to have thirty years of close observation tell us that there are invariably large numbers of exactly such occurrences, with low-price stocks breaking out of downside Trend Channels, one after the other, in rotation, and ascending to many times their starting prices after destructive market declines have run their course.

The simplest and best procedure to take advantage of such periods of market behavior is to — *go with the Trend once the breakout has taken place.*

One must, of course, be keeping hundreds of likely candidates in the low-price stock field in careful view. Whenever such a low-price stock is locked into a definitive downside Trend Channel and is approaching the upper Trend Line, there is created the possibility of a breakthrough, and we must watch the *daily* trading result for each such issue. If the breakthrough of the upper Trend Line *does* take place decisively, a purchase is immediately made, such purchase supported by three other steps if success is to be achieved. There are, indeed, four simple steps to the Trading Techniques we recommend for use, as follows:

(1) Buy on the breakout;

(2) Set an initial "Stop Loss" order to sell and get you out if the advance fails to take hold;

(3) If the advance *does* take hold and forges ahead, establish a specific scale by which the "Stop Loss" order

moves up with the price of the stock in "ratchet-like" fashion; and

(4) If the advance continues and moves ahead substantially, use Trend Line Analysis to activate a selling point.

It is our opinion that the above four simple steps will have a large measure of success in drawing profits from a market turnaround, and a later rising market, and the largest measure of financial reward will be enjoyed, as we see it, when applied to low-price stocks, and low-price Warrants, for reasons we outlined on a previous page.

Looking More Deeply Into The Four Steps of Our Recommended Trading Techniques

First Step: Buy On The Breakout

We have never found it wise to attempt to *anticipate* a breakout of a particular stock. All the factors might seem to be in favor of such a rise, and yet the stock might stay in the doldrums for many more months while a low-price stock which might have escaped your attention entirely would suddenly burst through an upper Trend Line and take off like a rocket, such as occurred with the examples we previously cited. Furthermore, it is the very act of the "breakout" which attracts buyers and commences the buildup of speculative momentum. Once low-price stocks have begun, in rotation, to begin the process of breakout and upside run, a larger and larger speculative following begins to develop for *such low-price stocks* as a whole. *Group Movement* then becomes pervasive, "Breakout Low-Price Stocks" attracting a large following just as would any "hot" Group such as Oils, or Computers, or Shipping, or any of the other hundred-plus Groups into which stocks can be identified.

Group Movement is a very important branch of Technical Analysis, and while an adequate description is impossible within the space limitations of this particular study (a separate book, and not a short one, could easily be written just on Group Movement itself), we will mention that once a Group has enjoyed enough of an advance, it begins to attain that aura of "good magic" which sees any analysis of fundamentals pushed into the background in favor of simple emotion which recognizes the Group and all its components as "good" and "powerful" and never mind why. Certainly this leads to overvaluation and that "stretching of reality" which later brings the price edifice crashing down, but this merely means we should go with the rise *while* it is taking place, and watch our Trend Lines carefully to catch the later quite unmistakable signals that the move is approaching its end.

So it is then with "Breakout Low-Price Stocks" that when enough such stocks have succeeded in mounting an upside run with the "feeling good" characteristic of rising quotations, the speculative search commences for *additional candidates* for such profitable moves, and the process takes on the character of "self-fulfilling prophecy." The game of "Follow The Leader" begins in earnest and the Four-Step Trading Technique we are describing moves into view to take best advantage of the large number of profit opportunities which then appear in rotation, and very often for a long period of time.

Second Step: "Stop Loss" Order To Sell If The Advance Fails To Take Hold

Looking at the chart for Nytronics, we see some clearly positive technical indicators pointing to a "breakout". Note that the stock broke out from the Trend Line decisively (arrow) and probably would have run to about 5 before a "Buy" order could be executed. The purchase point could have been lower because this is a weekly chart and we would have been following such movement on a *daily* basis, but for the time being this is only a detail and we ask the reader to focus instead on the efficacy of a "Stop Loss" order, with the definition of this term certainly due at this point.

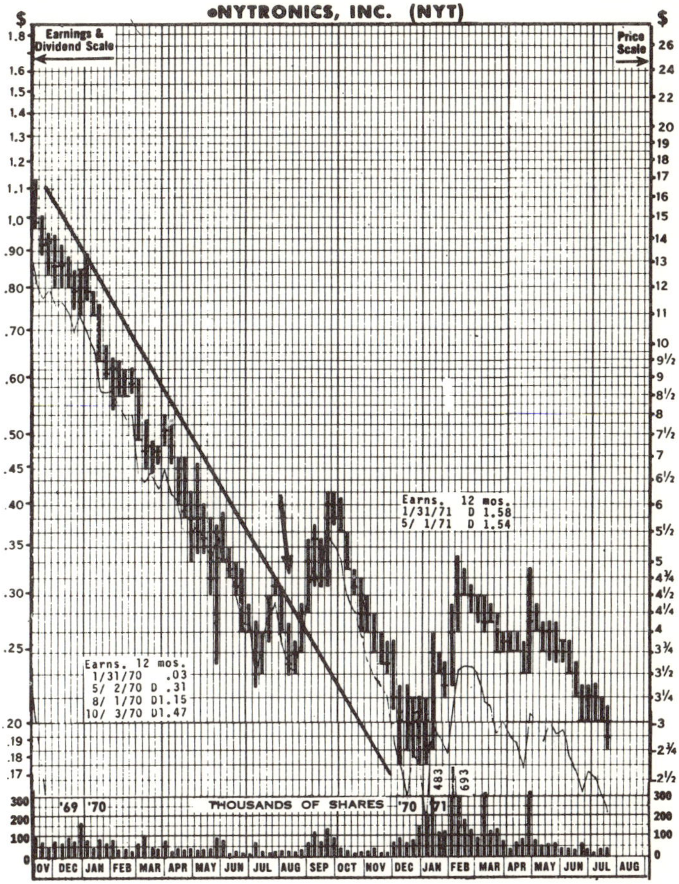

Courtesy Securities Research Company

A "Stop Loss" order is given to one's broker, good-till-canceled, putting into operation a "sell at the market" order if the stock sells at a certain price. The order, then, is initially given when the stock is still selling *above* that particular price. Thus, when purchasing, say, 100 shares of Nytronics at 5, one would immediately put into effect a "Stop Loss" order at a predetermined price, which would become a "market" order and effectuate a sale, if and when the stock fell to that price. If it never fell to that level, but continued merrily on (we shall shortly be looking at the happily plentiful such occasions in the proper market climate) the "Stop Loss" order would never be executed.

The Nytronics chart shows us exactly what we are protecting ourselves against. Following the "breakout", the stock reached only to 6¼, after which it turned around and commenced a slide to 2¾, following which it recovered but never got beyond the 5⅛ level for the period of the chart. Staying with the stock would have tied up capital to no avail and perhaps produced a greater loss if need for the money had necessitated a sale. The most harmful result of "holding on", however, would be to make the funds unavailable for *another* low-price "breakout" stock which might have much better fortune. Thus, the unquestioned (in this writer's experience) validity of simply accepting a loss if the "breakout" does not take hold.

Where To Place The "Stop Loss" Order

In studying a large number of "breakout" moves over many years, this writer has arrived at a pragmatic conclusion that a 20% figure works out well, both for a "Stop Loss" order to get out if the "breakout" does not follow through, and also for the next step of advancing the "Stop Loss" order, "ratchet-style", as we shall soon describe. In the case of our purchase of Nytronics at 5, a 20% decline would take it to 4, down 1 point, and the moment the stock ticked at 4, the "Stop Loss" order would become a market order to sell at the best possible price after that initial 4 sale. If trading was active in the stock, a sale at 4 would probably take place. If trading was less active, such a sale might take place at, say, 4⅛, or 3⅞. But trading usually is quite active around a "breakout" period, and sale at the desired level should present little difficulty.

Let us make an important observation at this point. In following many "breakout" stocks during a few decades of intensive observation, during the periods of market turnaround and the early phases of a new bull market, we have found that there are *very few* instances where a "breakout" is followed by an immediate return to the downside, and new lows, such as shown on the Nytronics chart. If we did indeed purchase at 5 and sell at 4 on the "Stop Loss" order, the 20% loss plus commissions would still be a desirable policy because of the general validity of "Cut your losses and let your profits run" philosophy, which is the foundation of the logic of the Trading Techniques we are recommending. But *much more likely* would be enough of a run to produce a small profit, or at least break even, along the lines of the move in Greyhound Computer common, which we now describe, and which takes us to our vital *Third Step* in our Trading Techniques.

Third Step: A 20% "Ratchet" For The Initial Part Of A Rise

Greyhound Computer Corp.

Assume a stock has "broken out" in decisive fashion, has not reversed itself immediately again to the downside but—much more likely—has made further upside progress. If the rise still falters at some point and turns into decline, this writer recommends the following policy: Accept the hypothesis that a 20% decline would have violated the short-term Trend Lines, active even in *daily* markets as we discussed previously with our own professional trading experience, and signaled a change in trend. A "Stop Loss" order should be used to (a) protect whatever profits have developed, (b) get you out of a situation where the trend had very possibly changed for the worse, and (c) make the funds available for other "breakout" situations which might be developing, which could be heading for substantial profits.

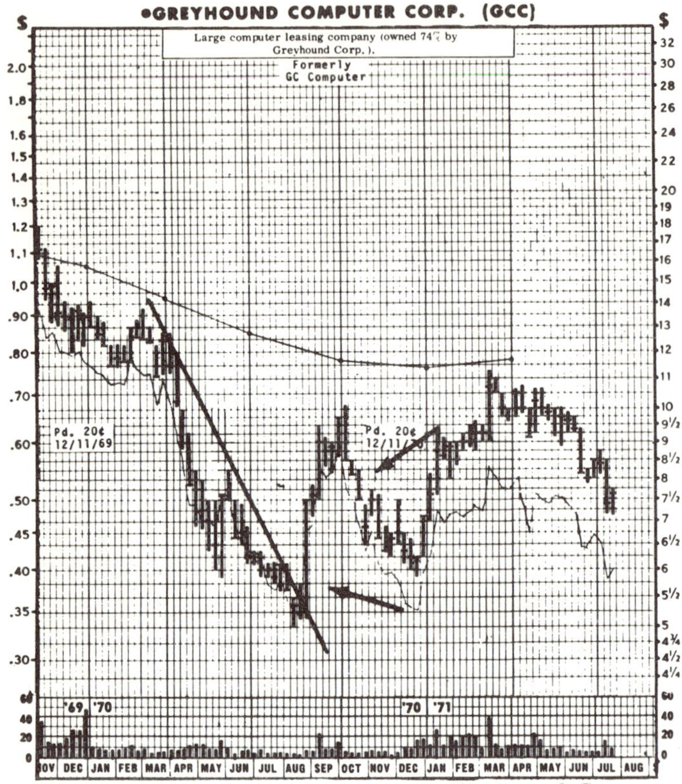

Courtesy Securities Research Company

Look at Greyhound Computer to see the logic of this approach. A "breakout" near the 5½ level (arrow) could have seen a purchase triggered at, say, 6. An uninterrupted rise to 7½ is visible in that first week's record, and let us now consider what "Stop Loss" orders would have been instituted for the move thus far. When the purchase at 6 was made, since 20% of 6 is 1.2 points, a "Stop Loss" order to sell at the nearest fraction to 4.8, or 4¾, in this case would have been instituted. Since the stock did not retreat to this level, but quickly moved on to 7, a new "Stop Loss" order would have replaced the older one in this manner: 20% of 7 is 1.4 points, or 1⅜ points. A 1⅜-point drop from 7 to 5⅝ would activate our next "Stop Loss" order. If the stock managed to make it to *8,* a new "Stop Loss" order would have come into play, calculated at a projected decline of 20% of 8. This would be 1.6, or 1⅝ points, making the new "Stop Loss" order 8 minus 1⅝, or 6⅜.

It being practical to work only with integers (changing a "Stop Loss" order every ¼ point would hardly be desirable or necessary!) the 20% "ratchet" would be moving up with each point advance. Looking once more at Greyhound Computer, we see that no 20% decline occurred from integers 8 or 9, but did occur from 10. This is an important point, so look at the chart with care. After reaching 8, the greatest decline from that point was only to 7½, while it would have taken a drop to 6⅜ to trigger the "Stop Loss" order. After reaching *9* with a new "Stop Loss" order of 7¼ (1¾ points being the closest fraction to 20% of 9) the greatest decline from that level was only to 8⅛, failing once again to trigger the "Stop Loss" order. On to 10 and to a new "Stop Loss" order of 8. Here, finally, the trend did turn, and 8 was reached at the point shown by the arrow. The "Stop Loss" order at 8 was triggered, the order became a *market order,* and the stock would have been sold at 8, or a small fraction above or below that figure. Buying at 6 and selling at 8, which is what actually occurred with the above recounting, was not a tremendous profit, but certainly a decent percentage move for about a two-month period, and served our primary purpose of immediately *getting out* of a situation where the Trend had very likely changed.

Fourth Step: Use Trend Line Analysis To Select a Selling Point After A SUCCESSFUL "Breakout" Move.

Thus far we have discussed *protective devices* against losses to quickly, and without much damage, or many more times a modest profit, get out of situations where a "breakout" has fizzled and the trend turned. But in the base-building portion of a turn from a bear market, and more so in the "foothills" of a new bull market, and *emphatically so* when the bull market picks up momentum, we are going to get many occasions when an advance continues for a considerable, and *quite profitable,* period of time without triggering a "Stop Loss" order. This is where the profits begin to come in—very *handsome* profits—constituting the goals of this entire recommended process of "Cut your losses and let your profits run." A few examples are in order.

Levitz Furniture Corp. Common

In mid-1970 Levitz Furniture Corp. common stock broke out of a downtrend channel which took it from 8⅝ to 4½ and then set off on a boom-and-bust path which took it to a high of about 60 and back down to a 1974 low, as we write, of 2½! There are some extremely important lessons here in the overall market action which specifically point up the value of the "technical" approach, but let us first apply ourselves to our immediate discussion of the Fourth Step in our "Trading Techniques."

Analysis of the daily chart would probably pinpoint the first purchase at 5½, but the exact starting point is not vital to this discussion, and we switch now to a *weekly* chart to follow the progress of the stock more closely, taking that starting price of 5½.

With the initial purchase at 5½, the first "Stop Loss" order would have been at 4⅜ (20% of 5½ is 1.1, putting the "Stop Loss" at 4.4, with 4⅜ being the closest fraction). There was no retreat to that level, so 6 was the next integer reached with a "Stop Loss" order at 4¾. Let us now present a table of Stop Loss Orders at successive integers, which table will be useful for readers in later trading programs.

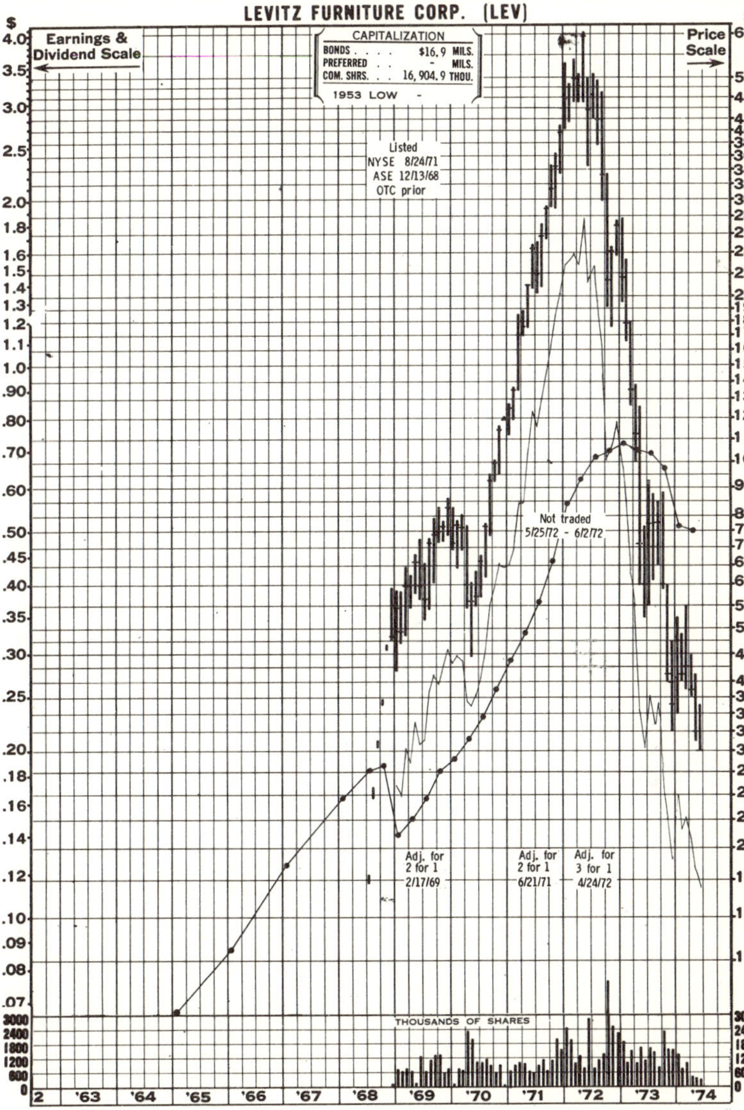

Courtesy Securities Research Company

Integer Level Reached	*20% of Integer*	*Resulting "Stop Loss"*
6	1.2	4¾
7	1.4	5⅝
8	1.6	6⅜
9	1.8	7¼
10	2.0	8
11	2.2	8¾
12	2.4	9⅝
13	2.6	10⅜
14	2.8	11¼
15	3.0	12

Let's follow the integers up the price advance to see if any of the "Stop Loss" orders were activated along the way. It will be noted easily on the chart that the initial run reached 11 without any backtracking worthy of observation, little more than ½-point declines interrupting the surge. Such action after a "breakout" is not uncommon in the early stages of a market revival. At 11, the "Stop Loss" order was at 8¾, but run a ruler across the grid and you will see that the lowest the stock fell to was 9¾, a full point above the "Stop Loss" order. On went the stock to hesitate around the 11½ area, but never remotely touching off a "Stop Loss" order, and then another surge to 19.

This is beyond our Integer Level table and for good reason. Once a "breakout" move has gone a substantial distance, in this case *tripling* the initial price of the stock when purchased, our experience has been that we should move ahead from "Stop Loss" orders and return to Trend Line Analysis to await a selling signal. For after such an advance, the time elapsed and the distance covered, has in most cases (in almost *all* cases, in our experience) produced an intelligible chart amenable to Trend Line Analysis which, falling back on our thirty years of virtually daily study of market movement, provides excellent guidance in the selection of a selling point. Look again now at the

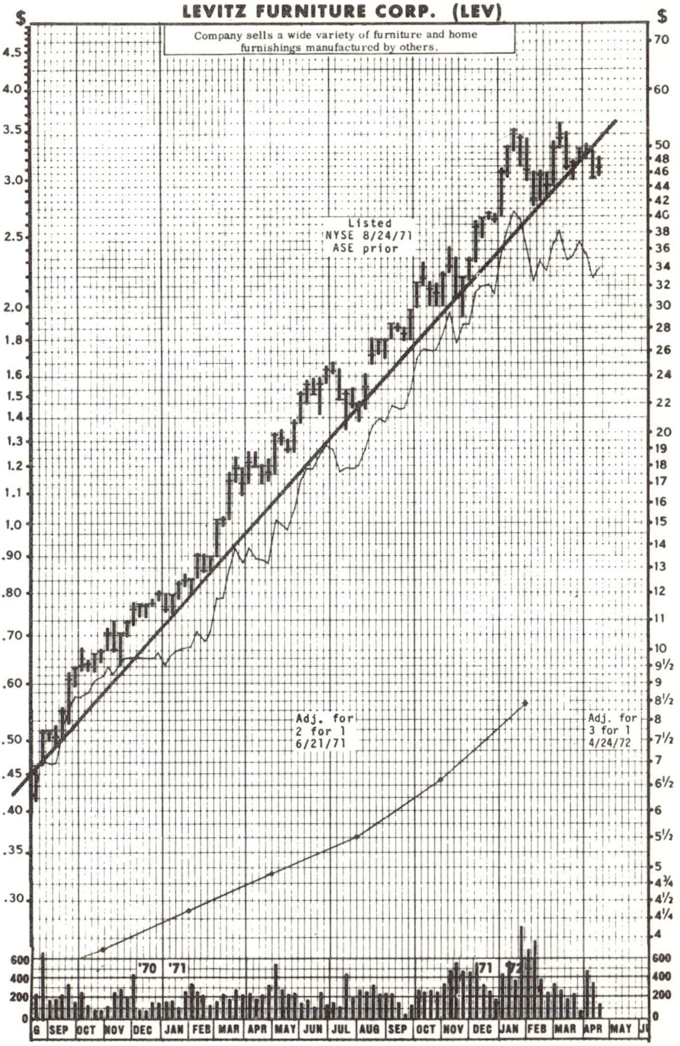

Courtesy Securities Research Company

same Levitz Furniture common stock price chart, with the clear lower Trend Line drawn in. Let us make the point here that, in drawing Trend Lines, one goes through the *closing price* for the day, week or month, usually indicated on the chart by a horizontal bar, rather than taking the extreme high or low for the particular unit. This is to avoid the distortion of a momentary swing during, say, one day's trading, which could show up even on a monthly chart as an irrelevant momentary high or low. On the Levitz weekly chart our lower Trend Line goes through quite a number of closing weekly points, forming a quite perfect Trend Line.

In April 1972 Levitz Furniture common stock dropped through the lower Trend Line at about the 48 level. This is even more dramatically visible when we return once more to the monthly chart which will give us also the dramatic plunge which followed. We have drawn in an unmistakable lower Trend Line which clearly shows the termination of the upside move and the changeover to a sideways movement. The upside Trend Channel has been broken on the downside and the unfailing policy we recommend in all such cases is—Sell.

An additional comment: The truly meteoric rise of Levitz Furniture in 1970-1971 was supposed to be based to a considerable extent on speculative excitement over the "warehouse-showroom" approach to retailing which did indeed see sales moving up in heroic fashion from about $100 million in 1970 to $326 million in 1972. A more realistic explanation of the move in Levitz Furniture, in our view, stemmed from the general market recovery in those years following the severe 1969 decline and the development of the typically strong "Group" move in low-price stocks in rotating fashion. During such periods there are always "reasons" set forth in print which are supposed to explain each individual move with elaborate analysis. But we are much more interested in the fact that the move is taking *place,* a move which should be tracked through technical factors, and *taken advantage of* in the Four-Step Trading Technique that we have described.

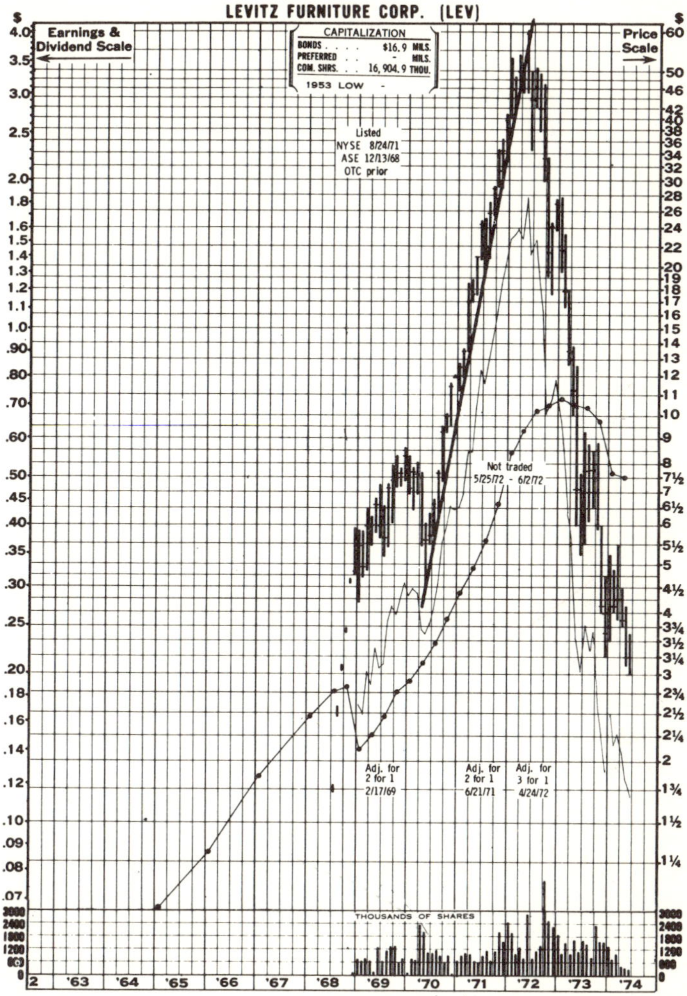

Courtesy Securities Research Company

Earnings for Levitz Furniture did not decline drastically during the 1972-1974 price debacle. An earnings high was recorded in 1972 of $0.72 per share—which meant that at its high the stock was selling at more than 70 times earnings, an obviously dangerous level—and in 1973 there was a moderate decline in earnings to $0.51 per share, with 1974 expected to possibly see a small *increase* in those earnings, and *a new high in sales*. Despite this, there is the catastrophic decline to 2½, and surely it must be recognized that earnings or any other aspect of "Fundamentals" had little to do with the extent of the move, up or down. We should mention here that the Net Equity per common share was about $4 in 1972, further diminishing the value basis of the move.

It adds up to this: Stock market "reality," the reality of intrinsic worth and present and potential earnings, is always being stretched to some extent, often to a *great* extent, by the emotional factors we have described on previous pages. During the more extreme periods of bear markets and bull markets (but many times even during more prosaic periods of general market movement for individual stocks and Groups of stocks) the reality is stretched paper thin and must break at some point. This break is signaled by a change in Trend, the breaking of a lower Trend Line, and when this occurs you do not attempt to find "reasons" one way or the other. You simply "get out," just as you very simply "got in" when an upper Trend Line was broken on the upside during the start of the move. Following this simple principle would have gotten you *into* Levitz Furniture at about 5½ and *out of* Levitz Furniture at about 44, utilizing Steps 1 and 4 of our recommended Trading Techniques. Steps 2 and 3 were necessary to give you the "Stop Loss" protection in the earlier part of the rise, but once the move developed sufficient momentum, simple Trend Line Analysis took over and performed an admirable job—as it has done so many, many times in our experience.

Western Air Lines

Our chart here demonstrates quite well the efficacy of Trend Line Analysis in selecting a "Sell" point. The "breakout" point from the first Trend Line shown, somewhere around 8, is very clear, and there then followed two intervals around the 13-14 level where the "Stop Loss" order failed to be activated by about ¼ point or so, after which there was clear sailing until the 26 level (a better-than-tripling of the stock in about six months). Drawing a dashed upper Trend Line through the relevant tops, we then draw the lower Trend Line parallel to this upper line, from the lows. This line was touched in October 1970 and again in March 1971 with no weekly close getting outside of the Trend Line. This did happen in May 1971 at 30 where the lower Trend Line was clearly violated and a "Sell" signal given, shown by the arrow.

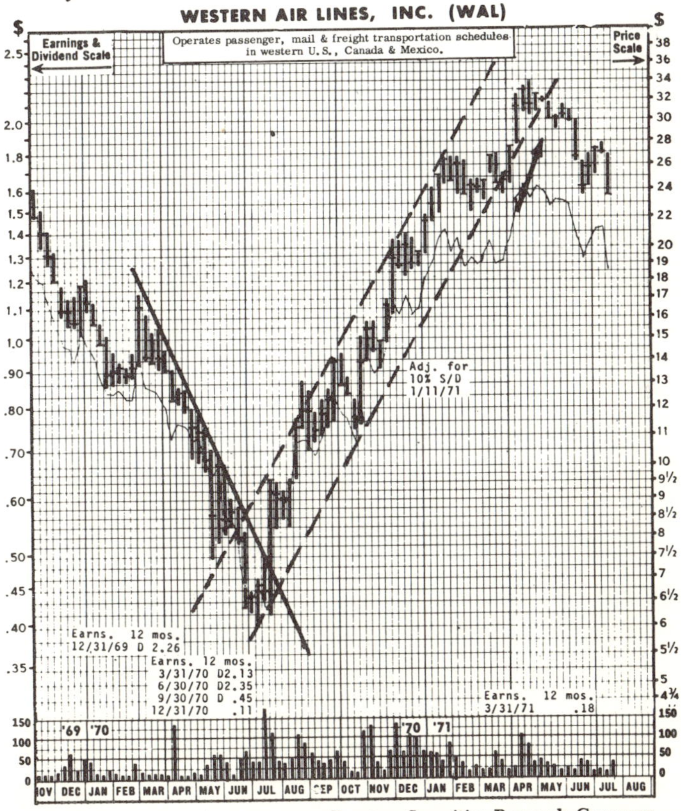

Courtesy Securities Research Company

An Early "Knockout"

Along with the stocks that "run," there are those which are cut off quickly by large fluctuations which activate the "Stop Loss" order.

Looking at the chart for Tyco Laboratories on the American Stock Exchange, the breaking of an upper Trend Line on the upside is clear at about the 8 level. Escaping one "Stop Loss"

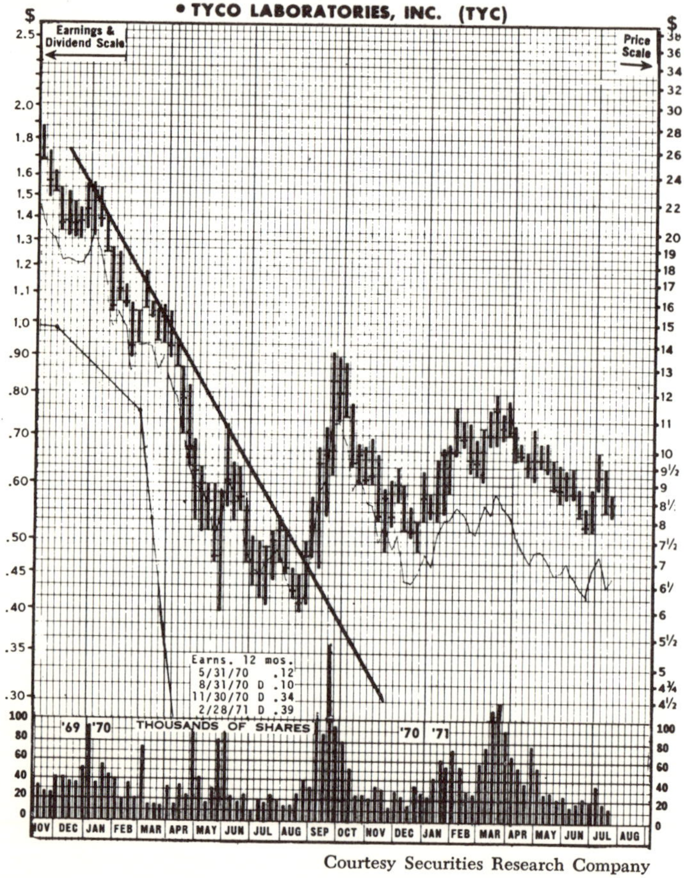

Courtesy Securities Research Company

activation at 10 (the stock sold no lower than 8⅛), the stock moved quickly to 13 where the "Stop Loss" order moved up to 11.4, or 11⅜, which was touched off in the following week. A purchase at 8 and a sale at 11⅜ in four weeks is not unpleasant and it immediately removed funds from an investment which then simply moved sideways for the balance of 1971.

This once again emphasizes the logic of the "rising ratchet" of the "Stop Loss" order which immediately takes you *out* of a situation where the Trend Line has turned.

"Whipsawing" Doesn't Carry Much Pain In the 4-Step Trading Technique

There are occasions—but we must say we simply haven't found it happening very often during our three decades of observation, and *very* seldom in market turning points— when one gets pushed in and out of a stock several times.

Thus, a four-month slide for FAS International was terminated by a breakthrough of the upper Trend Line with a purchase at about 8. When the stock reached 9, the "Stop Loss" order moved up to 7¼ which was touched off two weeks later. Buy at 8, sell at 7¼: result, a small loss. When the stock stopped at 6 (arrow) and commenced to the upside again, the "double bottom" at 6 could have been considered a valid technical reason for another purchase at 8. This time the advance ran to 11 and the "Stop Loss" order moved up to 8¾, which was touched off a few weeks later. Buy at 8, sell at 8¾: a non-productive result.

Certainly the above can happen on some occasions, but it serves to emphasize our major thesis—that the 4-Step Trading Technique with the rising "Stop Loss" order *automatically* cuts losses and lets profits run. This company got into a variety of difficulties with trading suspended in May 1971, as noted on the chart, and with the stock falling to about 5¢ (!). What did the automatic "Stop Loss" order accomplish? It produced two swings in and out around the $8 level with a small net loss, but there was no way in which the humiliating toboggan slide to 5¢ could have been inflicted on a reader using the 4-Step Trading Technique, for the "Stop Loss" order simply takes you out—automatically. We trust the virtue of the "upward-ratcheting" Stop Loss order is becoming very clear.

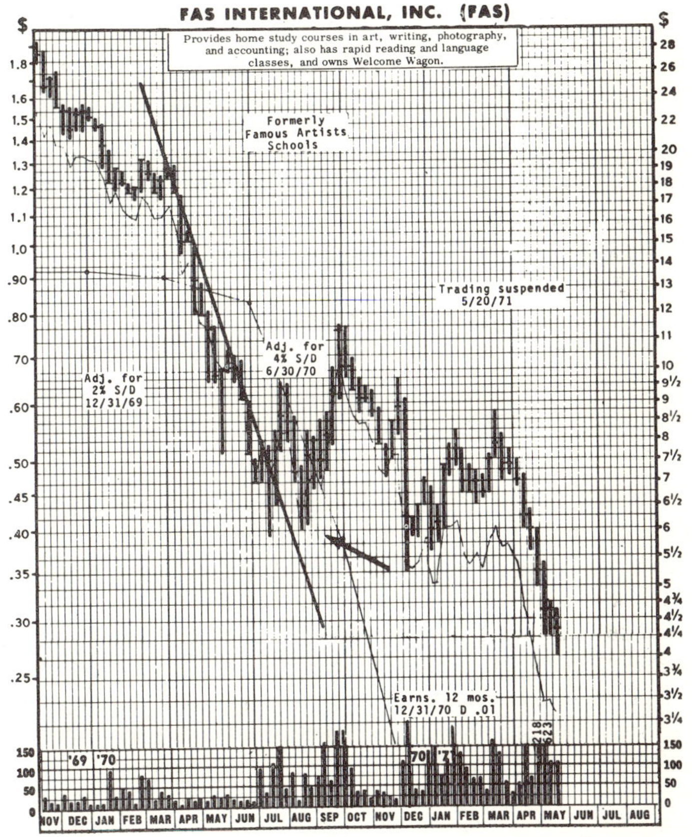

Courtesy Securities Research Company

Don't Ignore the Dynamic $10-$15 Group

Throughout our market experience we have found that well-known companies listed on the New York Stock Exchange, whose stocks have fallen to the $10 to $15 price range from much higher levels, give dynamic performances indeed, and particularly in the earlier stages of both a sideways base-building movement, and the early foothills of a new bull market. These moves are completely amenable to the "Four-Step Trading Technique" we have just described as, indeed, is *every other segment of the stock market,* and it will be valuable for the reader to study the 1970-1971 advance of the three following stocks in this category to observe the very clear "breakouts" for each, the manner in which each moved steadily ahead thereafter, never suffering the 20% decline from an integer which would have aborted the moves in the early stages, and then staying within the appropriate trend lines until a later break through that Trend Line gave a clear "Sell" signal. The three stocks were picked very much at random, there being literally hundreds of charts showing similar configurations.

In these charts—Howard Johnson, Outboard Marine and Vornado—we advise the reader to follow the advance up, point-by-point, in each case to observe the manner in which the early strong rise avoided the 20% "Ratcheting" Stop Loss Order. When the advance had gone a sufficient distance, with a 50% advance being a good guide, Trend Line Analysis took over. We have deliberately selected three contrasting charts to demonstrate that one should not make a *fetish* out of Trend *Channel* perfection. Thus, the Outboard Marine chart is the only one showing such perfection, while the Vornado Trend Channel did not begin taking shape until the first vigorous, almost perpendicular, rise was out of the way, and the Howard Johnson chart sees the December 1970 rise poking through the upper Trend Line with a rise of special force in that month. *In all cases it is the lower Trend Line which gives us our "Sell" advice,* and the Trend Channels have been drawn in by us to emphasize the significant

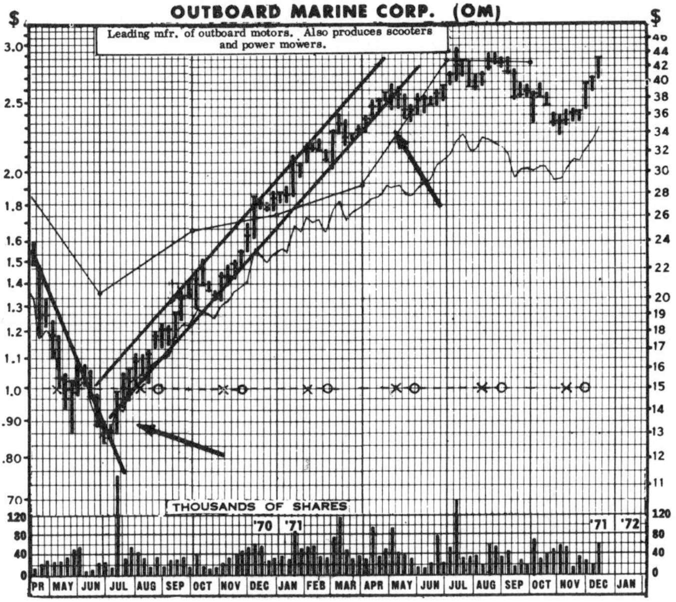

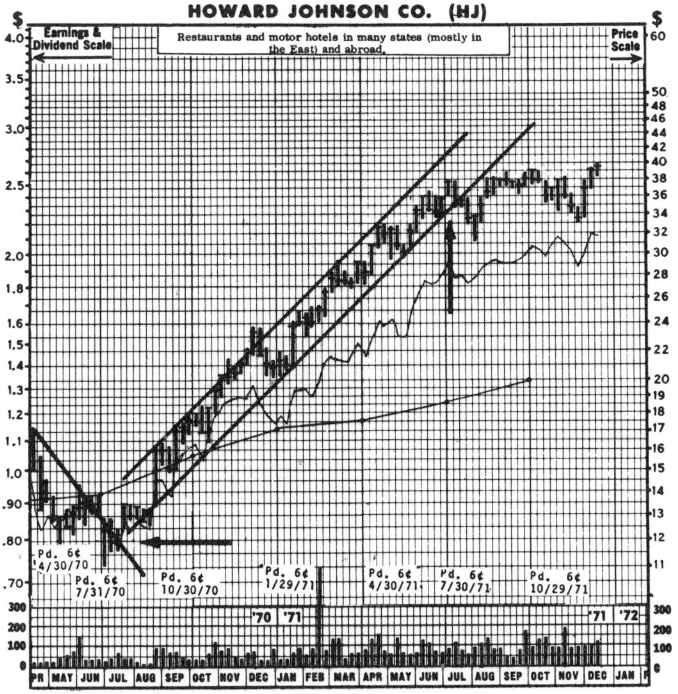

Courtesy Securities Research Company

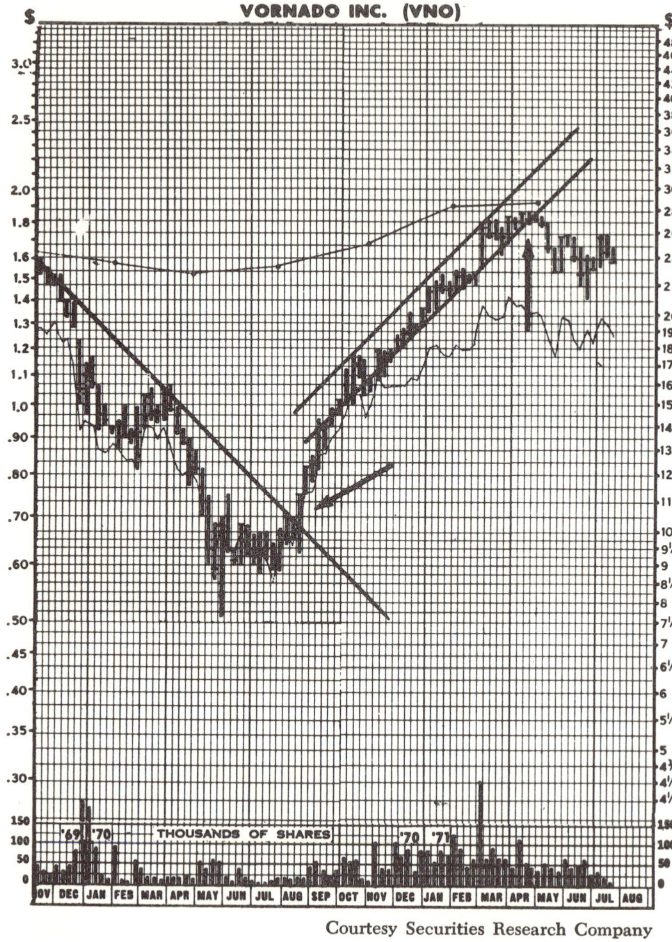

Courtesy Securities Research Company

regularity of the advance once "breakout" has become established. For each chart, we have indicated the "Buy" and "Sell" points with arrows, and readers can note how clearly the respective Trend Lines were broken in each case.

We now present three very well-known stocks indeed which have broken down into the $10 to $15 price area from much higher levels and, as of this writing, let us update the declines to show that Bell & Howell has reached 10⅞ on the downside, R.C.A. 11⅛ and Westinghouse 9⅜. Dozens of similarly well-positioned stocks in the $10-$15 price area are very visible in current markets, providing the raw material for future opportunities.

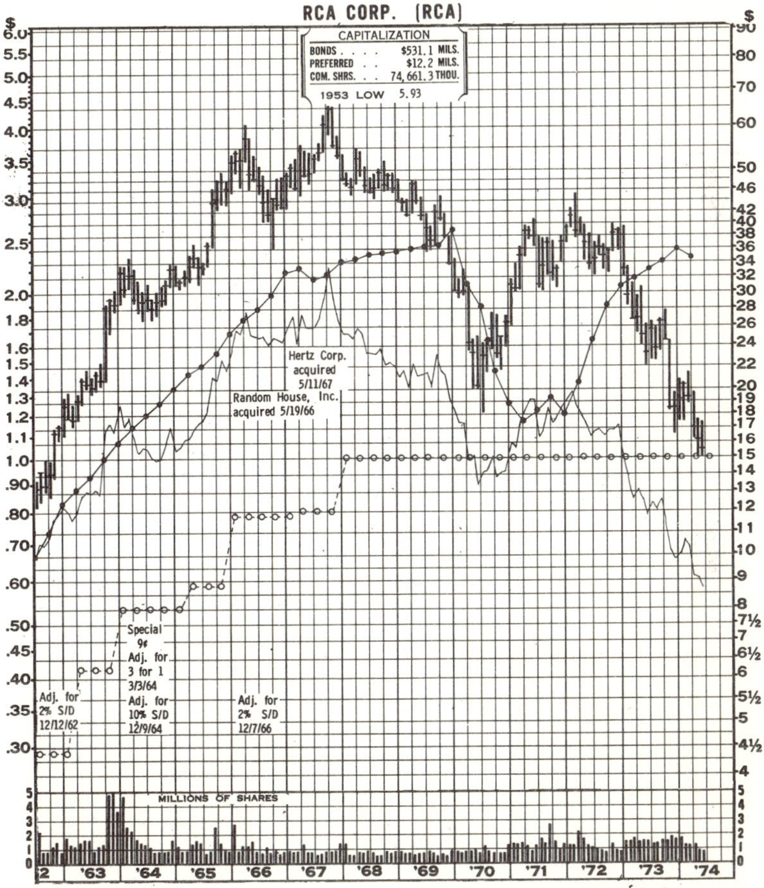

Courtesy Securities Research Company

BELL & HOWELL CO. (BHW)

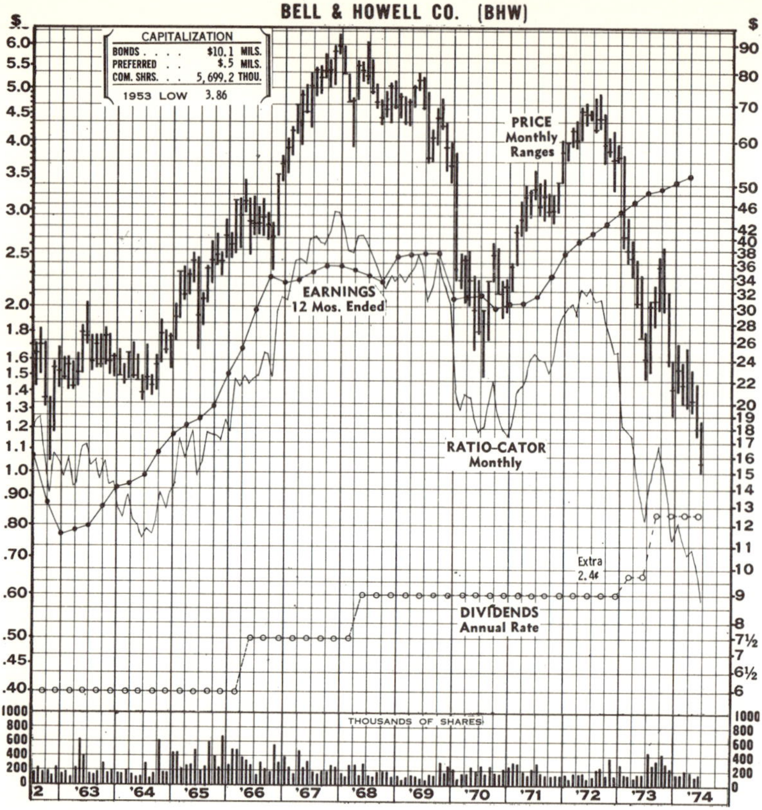

★ WESTINGHOUSE ELECTRIC CORP. (WX)

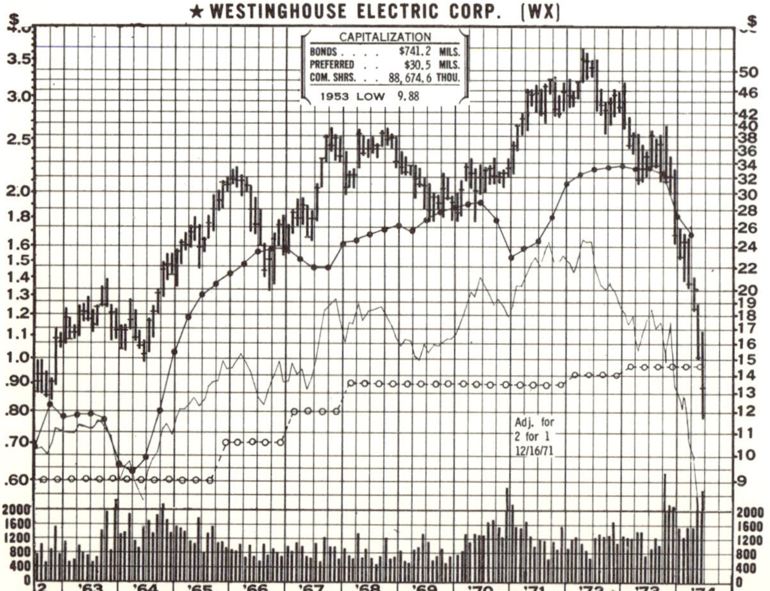

Courtesy Securities Research Company

Turning to the many more stocks—literally thousands of them when the Regional Stock Exchanges are included—which have reached drastically lower levels, we merely turn to the A's in the most recent quarterly edition of Securities Research Charts and quickly select the following examples.

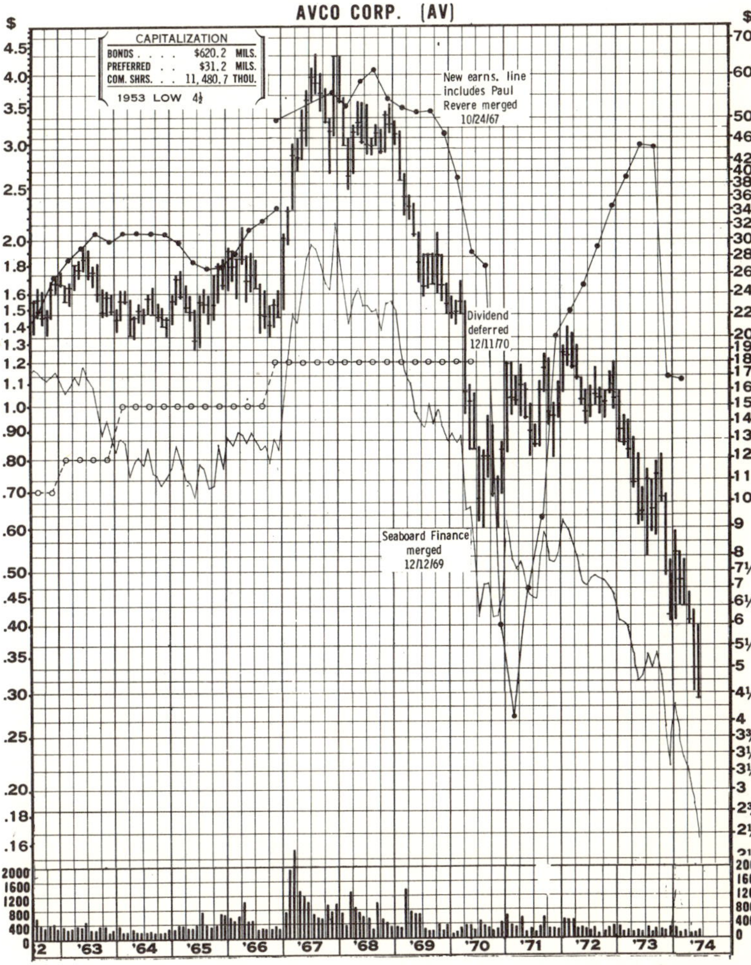

Courtesy Securities Research Company

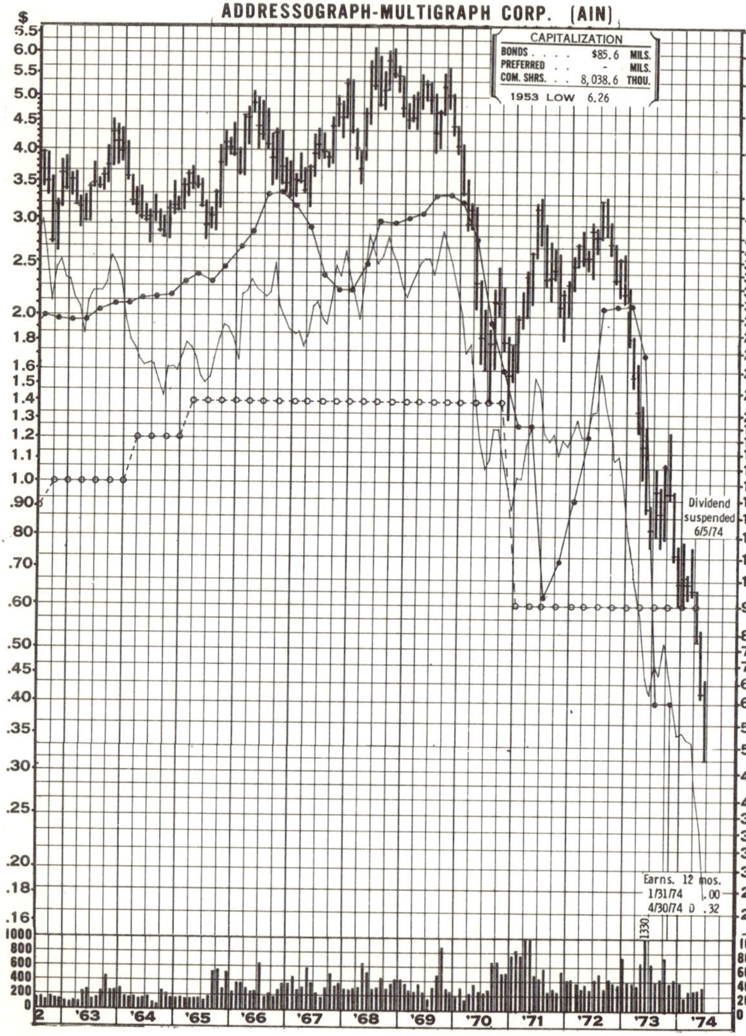

Courtesy Securities Research Company

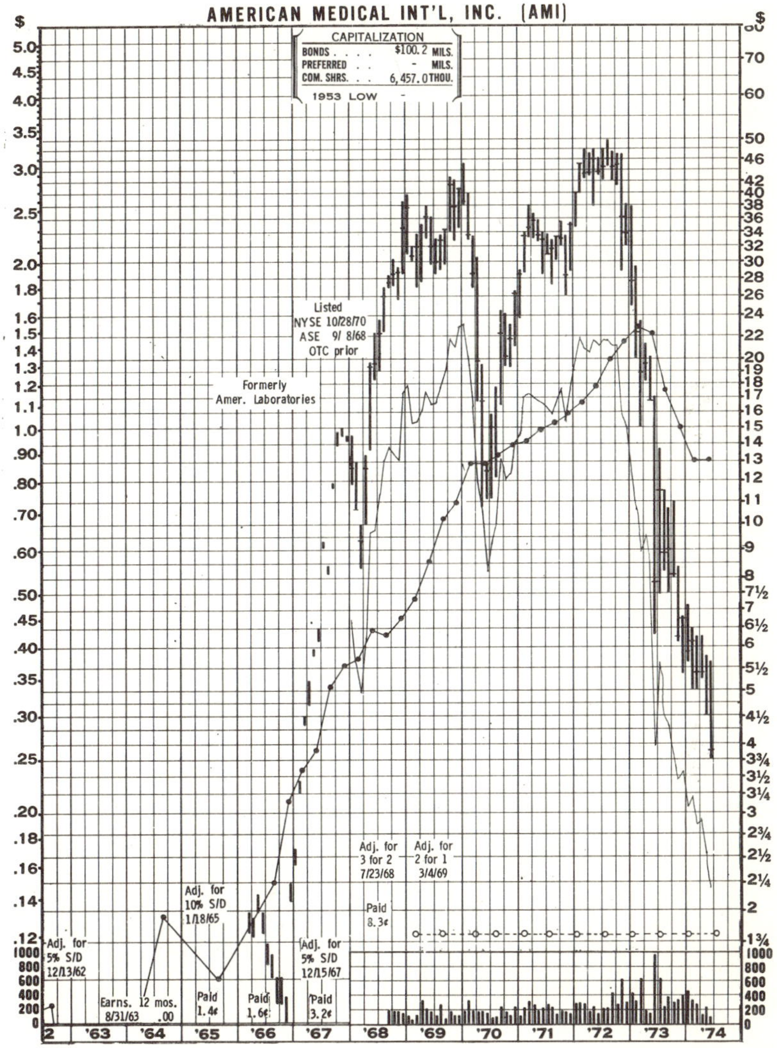

Courtesy Securities Research Company

The fact is that a major bear market hit in 1973-1974 and we have previously referred to a computer study which arrived at the conclusion that the general price damage in the market had been the worst seen for the past 40 years. To this we add the evidence from an article in Barron's Financial Weekly for August 26, 1974, appropriately entitled "Poppa Bear Market," with the informative sub-title: "Since 1968, the Average Stock Has Plunged 70%." In the body of the article, which represented some quite exhaustive statistical studies over a long period of time (77 years of market history!), we find the statistical information that the 1968-1974 bear market is the longest period of decline since 1897, and that ". . . the unweighted American Stock Exchange Index, off more than 85% from its December '68 top, comes close to rivaling the losses recorded during the Great Crash of 1929-1932. . . ." The writer of this article in Barron's has properly ignored the supposed "bull market top" of January 1973 because the Dow-Jones Industrials, loaded with institutional favorites, was giving a highly distorted view of the general market. In recognition of such an indisputable fact, this writer stated in the Survey of January 26, 1973 just after that Dow-Jones Industrials "record high" as follows: "What is the most important factor to be kept continually in mind by subscribers? It is that *most* Warrants and low-price stocks enter a more precarious market period at or very near their 1972-1973 lows! This sets up any number of possibilities of truly outstanding profit opportunities on further market retracement. . . ."

Opportunity Knocks—Very Loudly

Let us take a quick look at two strong upside runs from market lows—Hunt Foods & Industries and Rexall Drug & Chemical, recovering from the 1957 market decline—and White Consolidated Industries and National Airlines from the drastic 1962 decline. There is nothing especially significant about these charts. Hundreds of others from 1957 and 1962 would have looked the same. And look back at the charts from the 1969-1970 recovery and you will note they look the same as well.

Recovery from 1957 Low

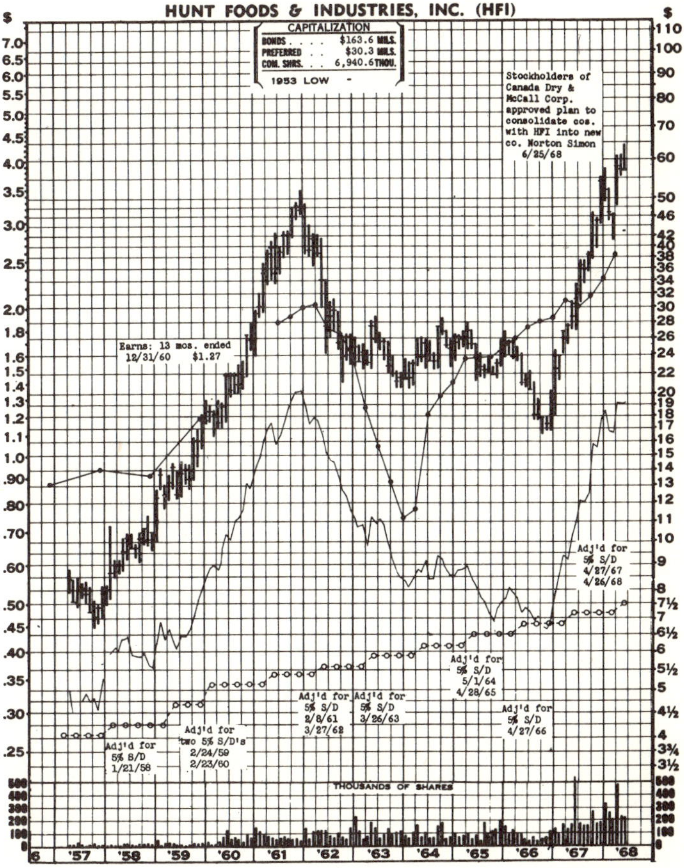

Courtesy Securities Research Company

Recovery from 1957 Low

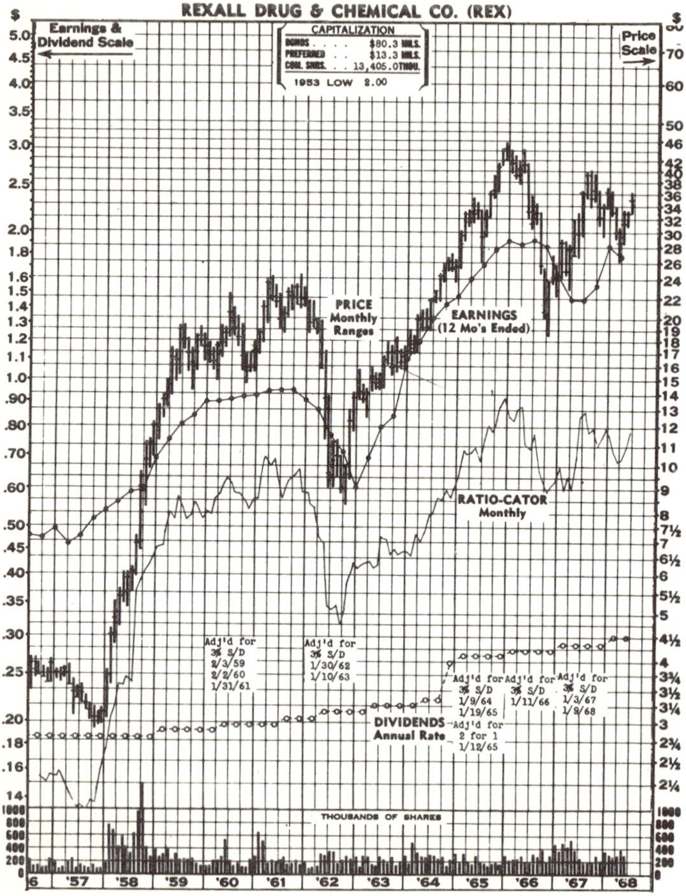

Courtesy Securities Research Company

Recovery from 1962 Low

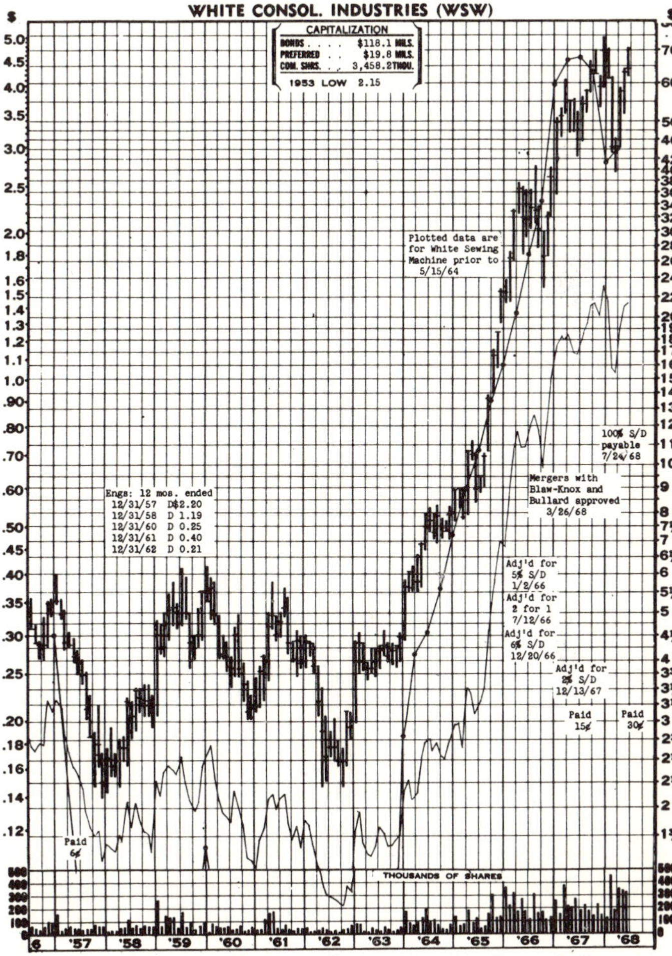

Courtesy Securities Research Company

Recovery from 1962 Low

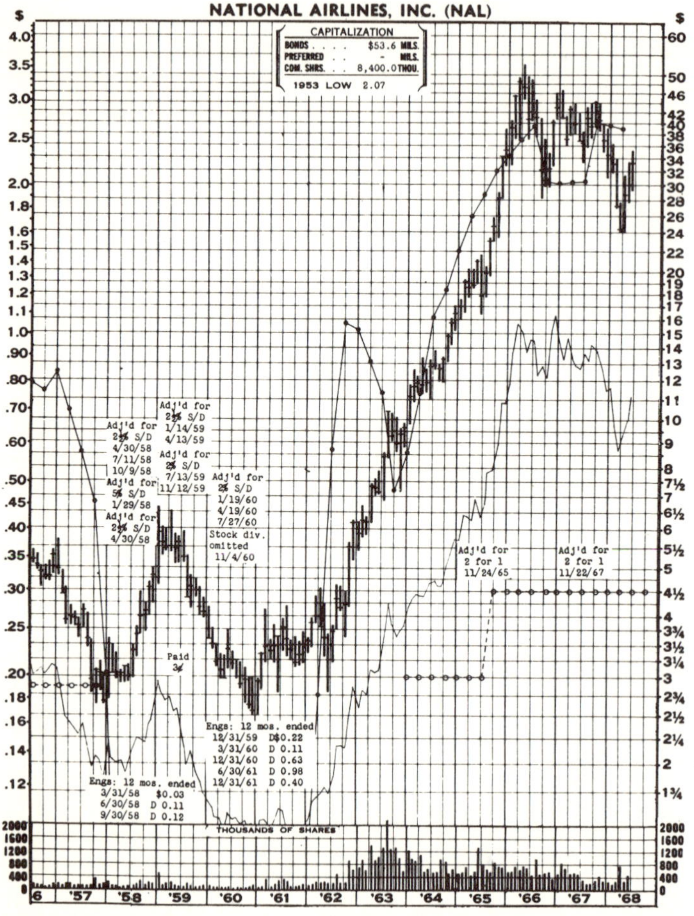

Courtesy Securities Research Company

The point that we are seeking to emphasize is that in the last portion of *all* bear markets we have experienced in almost 30 years of involvement as a stock market professional in many capacities, and in even earlier markets which we have studied closely, emotion very simply takes over and plumbs the depths, sweeping onto the market floor value-filled stocks with promising earnings potential right alongside other stocks which are debt-ridden, bankruptcy-prone and with indifferent prospects at best. Such sweeping declines are quite indiscriminate in their destructive effects and exactly this process occurred in 1973-1974.

All bear markets end—they always have—and when recovery sets in you get the type of market action we have shown for 1957, for 1962, for 1966 and for 1969, all with large emotional overtones and, therefore, *most amenable to Technical Analysis,* with the "Four-Step Trading Technique"as outlined by this writer in the previous sections ideally suited to take advantage of the profit opportunities. There are virtually no differences in the market action of the stocks illustrated from the various years precisely *because* the psychological elements were, and are, so strong in the final periods of decline and in the recoveries that follow.

The extreme destruction which has been visited upon the price structure of the 1973-1974 market sets up the "Greatest Stock Market Opportunities In Forty Years," not only in low-price stocks, *but for about 350 Warrants* which are now capable of producing historic market profits in the next few years.

Three Vital Guideposts, Each With Two Clear Alternatives, Leading To Recovery or Depression

This writer does not believe that the pain, indeed the terror, of Inflation, and the threat it poses to our country, came upon us at all by accident. We trust we have helped to demonstrate that fact in the preceding pages.

Nor will the future be accidental!

The policies we will follow in just the few short years ahead (events will move quickly) will determine whether we pull ourselves out of our difficulties and thereby give real leadership to the entire non-Communist world which has fallen into the same hole to varying degrees, or whether even greater disasters will come upon us.

Those policies will, indeed, determine whether we move to recovery, in our economy and the American spirit, with a new bull market in stocks also eventuating thereby, or whether we sink into the worst economic depression seen in the United States since the 1930's, with an additionally shattered stock market an automatic consequence.

We have put these "Three Guideposts", which follow, in a strong light with the above words, because we believe they deserve all the emphasis we have at our command. Let the reader judge at the conclusion of this discussion whether he feels the emphasis was deserved.

The three Guideposts are:

(1) *Corruption:* Accept its devastating consequences, or fight it.

(2) *Public Employment Policies:* Eliminate unemployment, eliminate budget deficits, and meet vital national needs all at the same time, or inflate endlessly.

(3) *The Automobile Culture:* Bring it back to reasonable proportions, or find all other problems insoluble.

We begin with our First Guidepost.

Corruption: Accept Its Devastating Consequences, or Fight It.

This is the most important of the three Guideposts, explaining its length. Without correcting our course in this area we will inevitably slide, in this writer's strongly-felt opinion, toward economic depression because the disease has invaded all the vital parts of our America and cannot be dallied with. There isn't enough time to do so. Only strong action will suffice, and at the conclusion we outline such possible actions which are easily available to us—only the will being needed, and a true love for what this country has been, and can be again.

As you read what follows in this section, understand that *each* of the areas of corruption covered deserves at least 100 times the space we have given it to project its dimensions with even an *approach* to completeness. We, of course, haven't the space to do this. But we think you will also soon agree with us that even presenting as much as we do outlines enough of the deep crisis we have fallen into to adequately make our point and call loudly for the remedies we shall then discuss.

No Statistical Measure For Corruption!

Many parts of Inflation are well-charted with statistical accuracy. So too are many economic factors which have a widely-acknowledged bearing on the progress of that Inflation.

Interest rates, commercial borrowing, retail sales, housing starts, money supply, consumer price indexes—all come in for thorough, even minute, scrutiny with carefully prepared formulas from government bureaus, financial institutions and educational and research organizations.

But we are aware of no "Index" which tells us how much "Corruption" is abroad in the land—what percentage of our Inflation is composed of plain stealing—the shorter, sharper word for "corruption".

The Connection Is Immediately Apparent

It is simplicity itself to see the connection between corruption and higher prices. Here, for our first example, is the cozy relationship between unions and management at Kennedy International Airport in New York, where they have been running a large-scale but quiet stealing business, according to the following news reports: Journal of Commerce, February 12, 1970: "Rackets at Kennedy Confirmed; Two Agencies Agree That Pilferage, Theft, Etc. Are Ordinary." Paul Curran had been chairman of the New York State Investigation Commission in 1968 which brought out "serious problems of theft, pilferage and hijacking around John F. Kennedy Airport" but, in this article in 1970, Mr. Curran was saying that ". . . it appears that theft and pilferage within the airport itself have not subsided since our report and may have indeed increased. It appears that *the same trade association and union people* we referred to in our report are still in business, and that no housecleaning has been undertaken . . ." (our emphasis—SF)

One year later—business still going on as usual. New York Daily News, July 20, 1971: "The Air Cargo Crime Crisis: The Waterfront Commission of New York Harbor released yesterday an impressive position paper which it has sent to Gen. Benjamin O. Davis, Jr., Ret. . . . Cargo thefts at Kennedy, La Guardia and Newark airports, said the commission, have 'reached crisis proportions,' and are especially bad at Kennedy. A striking sentence from this urgent message to Gen. Davis throws a bright light on the situation: 'The New York State Investigation Commission adduced proof that both the dominant union for air freight trucking employees and the dominant air freight trucking associations are controlled by criminal elements, so that at the airports it is a case of racketeers dealing with racketeers and the airlines are compelled to use truckers who enjoy the favor of such union and such association . . .' "

Let us go from the airport to the shipping piers of New York and an article from the Wall Street Journal, May 14, 1971: "New York—The dock worker blithely steals a carton of transistor radios off a ship. He walks off the pier, puts the carton in his car and drives off. An elderly port watchman sees the theft but takes no action to nab the culprit. . . . The steamship company that brought in the cargo of radios won't sign a criminal complaint to establish that a theft took place. . . . The watchmen are scared stiff. The shipping industry doesn't give a damn. That's how the Waterfront Commission of New York Harbor describes the systematic looting of the huge Port of New York . . . The extent of the looting is unknown—though it's believed to run into the millions of dollars yearly. Every type of merchandise among the $20 billion in general cargo annually passing through the big port is a candidate for theft. A dock worker steals a live lobster, concealing it under his shirt; another walks off the pier with a stereo set tied with rope to his back; another hides 58 brassieres inside his coat. The theft of whiskey and cigarettes is commonplace . . . Others besides longshoremen steal. Crewmen and officers on cargo ships have taken merchandise. A port captain for a steamship company in New York was once caught in a theft of goods. A Mafia-run gang, in cahoots with truck drivers, steals from the pier. Even some pier guards steal goods they are paid to protect. Guards have stolen sewing machines, frozen foods, tape recorders, pharmaceutical supplies, auto tires, liquor and clothing, the commission says . . ."

And now, the point of all this, in the same article: "Waterfront theft has forced up insurance premiums on cargo . . . A source on the Senate's Select Committee on Small Business, which has studied cargo theft, says insurance rates on radios and TV sets have soared as much as 200% in the past five years. The increase, of course, *tends to push up retail prices of the products . . .*" (our emphasis—SF)

Has there been any improvement? Quite the reverse. Here is the U. S. News & World Report for October 2, 1972, dealing with the nationwide situation: "Hijackers, burglars, thieves and other criminals are costing U. S. business close to *16 billion dollars a year*—and an official study indicates that the situation is steadily getting worse. Some authorities believe the direct loss to commercial enterprises may actually be *three times higher* than the 16 billion dollar estimate of the Federal Bureau of Domestic Commerce . . ." (our emphasis—SF)

In addition to the stealing by hijacking, burglaries and other criminal acts, whose costs were estimated in the article just quoted at possibly as high as $48 billion annually, consider this article from The Journal of Commerce for July 6, 1972: " 'White collar' workers who 'rip off' an estimated *$10 billion a year* from American business won't be stopped until management decides to do its own policing, according to Edgar Lion, Jr., San Francisco resident vice president of Firemen's Fund America. Mr. Lion spoke at a U. S. Department of Commerce seminar held recently in Burlingame, Calif. He said 'white collar' crimes—pilfered paper clips to million-dollar embezzlements to burglarized Xerox machines—have become common. *'Thirty per cent of all business failures each year result from employee dishonesty.'* " (our emphasis—SF)

The vast impact of crime leads with obvious directness to an increase in inflationary pressures because the cost of everything stolen must necessarily be added to everything bought by those of us who do *not* steal. But we are only at the beginning of outlining the possible dimensions of such contributions to the cost of living, to Inflation. Corruption in government is the fountainhead of civilian crime and to see the direct connection we need only once again bring it all down to a small scale.

Thus, if in the house across the street both mother and father steal, would we be surprised to find that as soon as their children can get around they would steal too? Of course we would not be surprised; we would *expect* that "the apple does not fall far from the tree." Put another way, the conscience of our young citizens are formed not only by what their parents say and do but, and particularly in this age of ever more rapid communication, by what they become aware of *government* doing.

What are such young citizens to think then when they read such articles (or hear the same reports on television) as this one from the New York Times, June 26, 1973: "Thirteen of 16 former members of the Newburgh (N. Y.) police force, convicted on conspiracy, attempted-burglary and other charges, were sentenced today to terms ranging from four years in jail to five years' probation . . ." The 16 included the *Chief of Police* of Newburgh, New York, who was sentenced to an eleven-year jail sentence.

From Newburgh, New York to the state capitol, Albany, New York, and another article in the New York Times for September 20, 1973: "A former policeman told the State Commission of Investigation today that he had committed 16 burglaries with 11 fellow policemen, including a lieutenant and two sergeants still on the force . . ." Across the country to Seattle and back to 1970, the New York Times, July 20, 1970: "A classic police shakedown and bribery scandal has been exposed here in the Federal court conviction on perjury charges of an assistant chief of police . . ."

Ahead to 1973 and Chicago, Illinois, the New York Times, December 6, 1973: "Chicago Faces Push for Police Reform; . . . The clamor for change from civic leaders and community organizations has been intensifying since the long summer trial and conviction of Capt. Clarence Braasch and 18 lower-ranking policemen for extorting money from nightclubs, bars and taverns . . . the office of United States Attorney James R. Thompson . . . has indicted 60 policemen for extortion and bribery. To date 40 of the policemen have been convicted."

Finally, an editorial from the New York Times for March 12, 1974: "Another Rotten Barrel; After a year and a half of studying wholesale corruption in the Philadelphia police force, the Pennsylvania Crime Commission has reached conclusions even more dismaying than those the Knapp Commission drew from its 1972 investigations into police graft in New York City. The Philadelphia finding that systematic payoffs, extortion and other criminal practices existed at every level of the city's principal agency of law-enforcement was made worse by the commission's report that the 'law and order' administration of Mayor Frank L. Rizzo had obstructed the inquiry . . . The shake-up now under way in Chicago's police force, with half of its top officers forced out of their jobs, and the scandals besetting the police in dozens of smaller cities make it plain that corruption has become a way of life for many of those charged with community protection against crime."

Let us now continue up this ladder of evil to cite examples of the collusion of corrupt elected officials with businessmen who are indispensable partners, and we see the "bill" for such corruption mounting, to be added to the already huge "bill" we have described from "ordinary" crime.

On "local" levels: Newsday, Long Island, New York, 7-12-74: "A Suffolk County grand jury yesterday indicted former county personnel commissioner Richard Wyssling, Babylon Town's deputy highway superintendent and a Nassau carter who law enforcement authorities say has ties to organized crime . . ." New York Times, 7-12-74: "A former Suffolk County official was indicted today on a charge of perjuring himself before a grand jury that was investigating his land transactions with associates allegedly having ties to organized crime . . ." New York Daily News, 1-20-74: "Brooklyn Rep.

Frank J. Brasco (a four-term Democratic Congressman—SF) was found guilty last night of peddling influence to help reputed mobster John (Gentleman John) Masiello get Post Office mail-hauling contracts . . ."

New York Times, 8-4-74: "In Jersey, Only The Names of the Indicted Change . . . J. Edward Crabiel, the New Jersey Secretary of State, has been indicted on bid-rigging charges . . . Mr. Crabiel is the third New Jersey Secretary of State in the last three administrations to be indicted on corruption charges . . ." New York Times, 5-3-74: "Key Cook County Democrat Is Indicted in Land Deal." Journal of Commerce, 3-14-73: "A precedent-setting verdict in federal court here may serve as a warning to insurance brokers in politics that they are in peril if they use their public offices to place insurance coverages. The verdict involves Cook County Clerk (Chicago) Edward J. Barrett, a veteran Illinois state and Cook County official, who was convicted of multiple counts of accepting bribes, income tax evasion and mail fraud in connection with his acceptance of $180,000 in bribes from a Pennsylvania voting machine company to buy the company's voting machines for Cook County."

As is quite well known to those involved—but hardly at all to those who ultimately pay the bills (*all* consumers)—corruption can enmesh an entire industry and become woven into its every strand. Thus, a survey by the New York Times, 6-26-72: "New York City's vast, multi-billion-dollar construction industry pays at least $25-million a year in bribes to city building inspectors, highway officials, policemen, state safety inspectors, agents of the Federal Housing Administration, clerks in various city agencies, union representatives and certain powerful blue-collar workers. Hardly a skyscraper is built, scarcely a change is made in the world's most celebrated skyline, hardly a brownstone is renovated or a restaurant expanded without the illegal payoffs, ranging from $5 to $10,000 each. . . ."

Moving up to an entire federal national program: Newsweek,

5-20-74: "The scandal has gone nearly unnoticed because of Watergate, but is considerable in its own right. It has tarnished the image of a government agency—the Federal Housing Administration—that has helped finance millions of U.S. home buyers in the last four decades by insuring their mortgages. Since the troubles started to surface, the former top FHA official in Philadelphia has been jailed and 26 persons have been sentenced to prison in Detroit. In Chicago, two former officials of Kaufman & Broad, a large U.S. home builder, have pleaded 'no contest' to charges of bribing FHA inspectors with cash and cases of liquor. The FHA finally had to close a scandal-rocked office in Hempstead, N. Y.—and the man sent to clean up the mess later admitted to being on the take himself. . . . Federal investigations throughout the country have turned up hundreds of similar but unconnected cases of conniving among FHA employees, builders, real-estate speculators and mortgage bankers to defraud the housing agency. So far 239 defendants have been convicted and 227 others are under indictment. . . ."

Some idea of what this type of corruption is costing the taxpayer? Newsday, Long Island, New York 3-23-74: "The Department of Housing and Urban Development is spending *$2 billion a year* to bail out housing subsidy programs from a massive wave of defaults on federally insured mortgages. . . . Extensive fraud, mismanagement and bribery in many of these cases have been uncovered in the last two years. . . ."

We turn now to well-known events of the past two or three years to see how the shadows of corruption have progressed from the most local of local levels to the Oval Office in the White House.

Vesco

An attaché case carrying $200,000 in $100 bills is sent to the Committee to Re-elect the President by Robert L. Vesco, who is under intensive investigation by the Securities & Exchange Commission at the time, accused of misusing $224 million from mutual funds managed by I. O. S. Ltd. The Wall Street Journal of 5-6-74 has filled in the details, reporting that: "Erlichman Talked of 'Quid Pro Quo' Over Vesco Gift, Transcript Shows." The article went on to say: "The White House transcript of President Nixon's conversations with adviser John D. Erlichman on April 14, 1973 adds a surprising footnote to the acquittal a week ago of John N. Mitchell and Maurice H. Stans. The 10-week trial of the two former Cabinet officers, on obstruction-of-justice and perjury charges, might have gone differently if the prosecutors had known how Mr. Erlichman described the Robert L. Vesco affair that day. But the White House withheld the tape recording from them. Mr. Erlichman told the President that Mr. Vesco had asked former Commerce Secretary Stans, who headed the President's 1972 campaign fund raising, for a 'quid pro quo' in return for a $200,000 campaign donation in April 1972. The 'quid' Mr. Vesco got was a date with former Attorney General Mitchell, who headed the Nixon campaign. . . ."

How do some of the highest luminaries in the Administration, a former Attorney General of the United States and a Secretary of Commerce accept $200,000 in a cash contribution for the President's campaign from someone known to be in serious difficulties with another arm of the government, the Securities & Exchange Commission?

Milk

Newsday, Long Island, New York (Sorry—we forgot to date this article when we put it in our files, but since pictures of then President Nixon's attorney, Mr. St. Clair, are on the reverse side of the article, it must have been early-1974—SF):

"Washington (AP)—President Nixon's former personal attorney, Herbert L. Kalmbach, has testified that a top dairy cooperative official was asked at a midnight meeting for confirmation of a $2,000,000 campaign pledge the night before Nixon announced increased milk price supports, according to informed sources. Investigators for the House Judiciary Committee are seeking more information about the meeting. Kalmbach said in the secret testimony that the session took place on March 24, 1971, in his suite at the Madison Hotel in Washington, the sources said. The alleged meeting, which took place after a Republican fund-raising dinner attended by dozens of dairy cooperative officials, included Kalmbach, the late Murray M. Chotiner and Harold S. Nelson, according to the Kalmbach testimony. Chotiner had quit three weeks earlier as Nixon's special counsel to enter private law practice and was receiving a retainer of $75,000 a year from the nation's largest dairy cooperative, Associated Milk Producers Inc. Nelson was the chief executive officer of the cooperative. According to the sources, Kalmbach testified that Chotiner told Nelson that John D. Erlichman, who was Nixon's chief domestic adviser, wanted Nelson to reaffirm the milk producers' promise of $2,000,000 in light of a milk-price increase that the President had just authorized. Kalmbach said Nelson agreed, the sources said. The next day the administration publicly announced the price increase of 27 cents per hundredweight, which added hundreds of millions of dollars to the income of dairy farmers. . . ."

Getting some estimate of what the dairy farmers got for their $2 million contribution to President Nixon's election campaign, Mr. William A. Powell, president of the Mid-American Dairymen, Inc., reported to a member of that organization that the deal ". . . added $500 to $700 million to the dairy farmers' milk checks. . . . Whether we like it or not, this is the way the system works. . . ." (This last quote from the New Republic for 3-17-73).

How does one allow an Administration-initiated $500 to $700 million increase in costs to the consumer to follow on the heels of a $2 million political contribution from the benefiting group to that same Administration?

I. T. T.

In 1971 the International Telephone & Telegraph Corp. agreed to pay $400,000 toward the financing of the 1972 Republican

National Convention scheduled, at that time, for San Diego, California. This was exactly the time that a huge antitrust action against I. T. & T. over its acquisition of the Hartford Insurance Company was coming to a head. These events did not come out fully until early-1973, reported in a page 1 story in the Wall Street Journal of 3-19-73 as follows: "An internal working paper of the Securities and Exchange Commission indicates that several key Nixon Administration officials were instrumental in helping International Telephone & Telegraph Corp. reach its controversial 1971 antitrust settlement with the Justice Department.

"The officials include Vice President Spiro Agnew, former Treasury Secretary John Connally, former Commerce Secretary Maurice Stans and former Commerce Secretary Peter Peterson, who was on the White House staff when the settlement was in the works.

"The settlement allowed ITT to retain the huge Hartford Insurance Co. in exchange for other divestitures.

"In addition, the SEC working paper indicates that former Attorney General John Mitchell discussed the ITT-Hartford Fire relationship with President Nixon, which tends to contradict congressional testimony by Mr. Mitchell that he had never talked about the ITT case with the President, only about general antitrust policy.

"These and other insights into the administration-ITT relations were revealed in a confidential SEC staff summary of ITT documents—mainly letters and internal memos—that the SEC had subpoenaed during its two-year investigation of the company. The documents themselves—34 boxes full—are currently in the possession of the Justice Department.

"One thing the summary of the ITT documents makes clear: ITT mounted a major effort, with the help of administration officials, to pressure Richard McLaren, then assistant attorney general in charge of the antitrust division, into backing down. Mr. McLaren had brought three antitrust suits against ITT and had solidly refused to settle out of court unless ITT agreed to divest Hartford Fire. . . ."

The I. T. & T. merger with Hartford Insurance was the largest merger in corporate history, involving hundreds of millions of dollars of potential profit or loss, depending upon which way the Justice Department's antitrust suit went. How could President Nixon's associates agree to let ITT pay $400,000 in costs of its upcoming National Convention at the same time the above-recounted events were in full swing?

Vesco, "Milk" and ITT were obviously just symptoms of a disheartening lowering of standards of political morality which thrust itself fully into public attention with the political earthquake called "Watergate." But it had been there and growing all the time.

When Harry Vaughan, an official of Harry Truman's Administration, was found to have accepted presents of a deepfreeze and a fur coat for his wife from a businessman who was seeking some political favors, newspaper headlines screamed across the country and Mr. Vaughan resigned. Sherman Adams, high in Dwight Eisenhower's Administration, took a now-famous "vicuna coat" as a gift. Again, nationwide publicity and anger and Mr. Adams resigned. But from that point on the transgressions seem to have steadily mounted and public anger to decline. Did this run parallel with the growth of Inflation? In this writer's opinion, the connection is certain. Please recall this quotation, first given on a preceding page:

From Andrew Dickson White's "Fiat Money Inflation in France," first published in 1876: "Out of the speculating and gambling of the inflation period grew luxury, and, out of this, corruption. . . . It was first felt in business operations, but soon began to be seen in the legislative body. Bribery of legislators followed as a matter of course. . . . Even worse than this was the breaking down of the morals of the country at large. . . ."

In the course of our work as Editor of two investment advisory services, and in recognition of the fact that to understand the stock market you have to keep up with everything happening in current history, sociology, and politics *as well as* economics, this writer's major activity is reading—newspapers, periodicals, special reports, books, a growing mountain of all of these—and as we read we add to files and take notes. As we look through our *bulging* files labeled "Corruption" (we became convinced of the major impact of this phenomenon many years ago), anywhere our hand goes finds an all-too-typical news item.

New York Times, 8-12-71: "Itkin Testifies Two Light Concerns Got Millions by Fixing City Bids; Accusations that the Broadway Maintenance Corporation and the Welsbach Corporation rigged bids to obtain millions of dollars in street-lighting contracts with the city were made yesterday in testimony at a perjury trial in Federal Court here. The testimony came from Herbert Itkin, a Government informer, who quoted a Broadway Maintenance official, Milton Lipkins, as having said that 'they had been fixing their bids' for many years to divide city contracts for maintaining street lights. . . ."

Wall Street Journal, 1-20-72: "Former Sen. Daniel R. Brewster of Maryland and a mail-order house lobbyist were convicted on charges of exchanging $14,500 to influence the Democratic Senator's vote on postage-rate legislation. . . ."

Newsday, Long Island, New York, 10-11-71, in an award-winning investigative series on former Senator George A. Smathers (Democrat, Florida): "Early in 1968, Sen. George A. Smathers (D.—Fla.) led a group of Florida Congressmen in a behind-the-scenes effort to save a multi-million-dollar defense contract held by Aerodex Inc., a Miami firm whose 'poor quality' work, the Air Force said, was 'endangering Air Force pilots and aircraft.' One year later, shortly after he had retired from the Senate and returned to the full-time practice of law, Smathers was named a member of the Aerodex board of directors and was allowed to purchase $435,000 worth of stock for only $20,000. . . ."

New York Daily News, 3-30-73: "Banks Invested 100 G in Pet Candidates Last Year; New York candidates cashed in on at least $100,000 in campaign contributions last year from banking industry conduits and bankers, a survey by The News disclosed. Some of the campaign cash has been collected by banks from their employees and used to buy tickets to political dinners —sometimes secretly and in possible conflict with the election law, yet another indication of the banking industry's Hidden Interest in the Albany (N.Y.) Legislature. In addition to the cash, which went to Republicans over Democrats by nearly three to one, banks loaned hundreds of thousands of dollars to candidates and debt-ridden party committees. . . ."

What Part Does Corruption Play In The "Cost of Living" Index?

When airport freight-handling personnel steal $1 billion in cameras, liquor, cigarettes, and all other manner of goods, who pays for it? The insurance companies initially—but then the insurance rates go up to the companies sustaining the losses and they add the increased costs to the over-all costs of what they sell. The cost of what is stolen is paid for by all of us in higher prices. Similarly for the shoplifter who walks into a department store without a coat and walks out *with* one, without benefit of payment to the store.

We have seen that the "numbers" for out-and-out stealing are very large. We quoted the U. S. News & World Report as saying in its issue of October 2, 1972 that "Hijackers, burglars, thieves and other criminals are costing U. S. business close to *16 billion dollars a year*—and an official study indicates that the situation is steadily getting worse. Some authorities believe the direct loss to commercial enterprises may actually be *three times* higher than the 16 billion dollar estimate of the Federal Bureau of Domestic Commerce . . ." (our emphasis—SF) If the possible loss in 1972 went *as high as $48 billion,* the rising trend in all crime since 1972 almost ensures that this figure is bigger today.

We also previously pointed out that the estimates just quoted had to do with direct criminal action. Additional estimates of "white collar crime" were estimated at *$10 billion a year* in a Journal of Commerce article from its issue of 7-6-72, previously quoted.

Already we are near the $50 to $60 billion area on an annual basis. *And every dollar of it pushes up the cost of all the goods and services we buy, dollar-for-dollar stolen.*

Turning to the cost of government, realize that the Federal government itself takes almost one-fourth of our Gross National Product. Add the costs of running State and municipal governments and you are up to a considerably higher percentage. When "millions of dollars in street-lighting contracts" are subjected to "fixed" bids by paying off public officials in New York City, as reported in an article quoted a few paragraphs back, the cost of government goes up.

Also mentioned previously, the $180,000 in bribes taken by a Cook County (Illinois) official to favor purchase of voting machines from one particular company meant that those machines would cost much more than if purchased without collusion.

And the mail-hauling contracts for reputed mobsters which a four-term Democratic Congressman reportedly helped them obtain also had to cost the citizens more than if free bids by honest companies had prevailed.

Suppose we had to multiply these few examples by tens of thousands of similar occurrences as indeed we know we must? What kind of total figure for this type of "stealing in government" would emerge? U. S. News & World Report had an article in its 6-4-73 issue as follows: "Corruption in Politics, How Widespread? It's not only Watergate. All across the country, official skullduggery keeps surfacing—at national, state and local levels. . . ." Pictured on the first page of the long article were a U.S. Senator, a Federal Judge and the former Mayor of a large city.

All three had gone to prison. And in the article was case after case similar to the few we have described, many involving very large sums.

More evidence which cannot be argued with:

Vermont Royster in the Wall Street Journal, 10-17-73, discussing the resignation of Spiro Agnew as Vice President and public morality in general: "Mr. Agnew did not invent the payoff system from state contractors when he became governor of Maryland. As Mr. Agnew pleaded the other evening and as the Justice Department agrees, Mr. Agnew found it 'customary' for engineers to make substantial cash payments in return for state engineering contracts. And nobody familiar with state government politics is going to deny the prevalence of the custom. . . ."

We are trying to get across to readers some estimate of what the total costs of such public corruption might be and another contribution to this attempt surfaces in an article in the U. S. News & World Report dated 10-29-73, as follows:

"Bribes that make headlines are only the tip of the iceberg. Billions go undetected each year, say crime authorities—with consumers footing the bill. Charges and countercharges that swirled around the case of Spiro Agnew are raising questions anew whether kickbacks and payoffs have become a way of life in the U. S.

"Many experts in Washington and elsewhere say 'Yes'—and, what's more, they claim the practice is getting worse year by year. . . .

"Leaving aside the merits of the Agnew case, it is the opinion of Norman Jaspan, head of a New York-based firm specializing in detection and prevention of white-collar crime, that: 'Never before have kickbacks, bribes and conflicts of interest been such a dominant factor in U. S. society.'

". . . Kickbacks paid by business alone are conservatively estimated by authorities to exceed 5 billion dollars a year—practically all of it passed along to consumers in the form of higher prices for goods and services.

"Herbert Robinson, an attorney handling many cases of white-collar crime, estimates the annual cost at 1 per cent of the gross national product—10 billion dollars—but adds: 'Many of the executives I work with say the real total could be *more like 20 or 30 billion dollars*.' . . ." (our emphasis—SF)

We have reported estimates thus far as high as $48 billion per year in stealing by crooks, gangsters and racketeers and $20 or $30 billion for "white-collar" crime, most of the latter involving public corruption on State and local levels. Who pays these billions of dollars? *All of us,* through higher prices. The connection between Corruption and Inflation cannot be questioned.

We Move Higher, To The Federal Level

It must be recognized immediately that the entire political structure in Washington, both Executive and Legislative, *develops from and remains an intimate part of* the local political structure on the State and county levels. This applies to members of the House of Representatives, the Senate, and the President and most of his aides. We cannot adduce a morass of corruption on the local level—and its existence is indisputable—and find purity, wholesomeness and a selfless desire to serve only the public good in the national politicians in Washington. We must rather expect to find self-seeking at best, and various shadings of corruption at worst—albeit with bigger numbers—and in the following paragraphs we try to give some idea of its size and extent, and the *immense* part it plays in fueling our Inflation.

We have to understand that much of the self-seeking and corruption is often much more difficult to recognize as such with clarity. If someone bursts into a bank wearing a mask and carrying a gun and calls out loudly, "This is a stick-up!", we know exactly what we are dealing with. In politics as it is carried out on a national level in Washington, what happens to the taxpayer's money can vary from outright giveaways (a legalized stick-up!) to policies which are truly debatable.

Consider, for example, a protective tariff to make certain goods coming into the country are higher-priced than the same American product, the stated objective being to protect the jobs of American workers. It must quickly be stated that to accomplish this end *all* consumers pay to attain this objective through higher prices for the goods in question. But if these American workers have been suffering depressed wages and are brought up to the approximate living standards of other workers by making it more difficult for "cheap labor" foreign products to flood the country, one could certainly debate the merits of this approach, and on this level no one will speak of corruption.

What if, however, labor union and management have gone into collusion to apply political pressure in Washington to attain their protected position, and that after this objective is attained, the union easily obtains wage increases, with only token argument from management, far above the national average when its next contract comes due, and management, for its part, raises the prices of its product sharply, causing its profits to swell?

What if, further, it is demonstrated that both union and management have raised large amounts of money which found its way into the pockets of Administration people pushing that protective tariff, and/or Senators and Representatives voting for it?

Not only are we right back at completely recognizable corruption, but whereas a shoplifter might make off with $100 in goods and a bank robber $10,000, corruption in Washington *starts* at the million-dollar level, and gets up into the billions of dollars very quickly.

Let's consider a few areas, one-by-one, and the scope of the attack on the U. S. dollar by mountainous Federal spending will become all too clear.

Tung-Nut Oil

In the Wall Street Journal of 2-16-73 there was a heading: "Price-Prop Program for Tung-Nut Oil Comes Under Attack; Government Buys Entire Output at Twice World Price. . . ." The article then went on to say: ". . . U. S. taxpayers are ankle-deep in tung-nut oil. It is used as a drying agent in paint and industrial coatings. It was popular, even considered critical for defense, until synthetic substitutes came along and, strategically speaking, tung-nut oil went down the drain some time ago.

"Yet, under a mandatory price-support law, U. S. taxpayers are still buying the entire American tung-nut oil production—at more than twice the price being quoted on the world market. . . .

"Rep. Paul Findley (R.—Ill.), a member of the House Agriculture Committee, calls the price-support program unneeded and costly, with losses running between $1 million and $3 million a year since 1967. He wants Congress to phase it out over four years.

"Similar legislation died after a hearing last year, with a spokesman for the American Tung Oil Association testifying: 'The tung industry is small but in proportion to its size it keeps workers off the relief rolls and furnishes a market for supplies and equipment.' "

Think *that one* over for a while!

Peanuts

Another headline in the Wall Street Journal, 11-26-73: "Peanut-Subsidy Slash Set by Administration Stirs Counterattack by Southern Democrats; Washington—Influential Southern Democrats are launching a major attack against the Agriculture Department—over peanuts . . . The fuss is over the administration's decision to cut back the subsidy the government pays peanut farmers. The cost last year was around $70 million. The administration's actions are aimed at trimming that back about $6 million.

"Foes of the cost-cutting effort include Speaker of the House Carl Albert (D. Okla.); Chairman Herman Talmadge (D. Ga.) of the Senate Agriculture Committee; Chairman W. R. Poage (D. Texas) of the House Agriculture Committee; Gov. Jimmy Carter of Georgia and nearly all other Congressmen and Senators from peanut-growing states . . .

"The original peanut law was aimed at keeping supply in line with demand. But because of technology, farmers have increased their yield far above consumption. What they couldn't sell on the open market, the Agriculture Department buys through the Commodity Credit Corp. The unit then sells most of the surplus overseas, but at the prevailing world price, which is always lower than the price it paid to farmers . . ."

The American consumer pays *twice* in this particular operation. First, he pays *as* a consumer by prices for peanuts and peanut products in the store at a higher level than would be the case if the law of supply and demand were allowed to work. And, secondly, when he takes off his "consumer" hat and puts on his "taxpayer" hat he pays millions of dollars to peanut growers for peanuts they cannot sell in the open market, the loss to taxpayers coming to about $70 million annually in recent years.

Sugar

An editorial in the New York Times, 6-17-74: "The scream of the outraged consumer has finally penetrated the storm cellar in which Congress has been hiding from the hurricane called inflation. With a considerable assist from makers of candy, soft drinks and other confections, consumer groups succeeded this week in persuading the House to junk the intricate structure of subsidies, quotas and excise taxes that has kept the price of sugar artificially high for forty years."

For the Inflation-harried reader wishing to permit himself a wan smile, consider this additional quotation from a news article on the same subject in the New York Times of 6-7-74: "Washington, June 6—Supporters of sugar-control legislation seemed stunned today following their surprise defeat in the House of Representatives but determined to find ways to fight back, and their opponents were under no illusion that they had scored a knockout. . . . 'When the pork barrel breaks, you don't abandon the pork, you scoop it up and put it in a new container,' said the head of a New York brokerage firm, an opponent of the bill who asked not to be identified. . . ."

The Over-All Farm Subsidy Program

In previous pages we discussed how a $2,000,000 contribution to President Nixon's re-election committee garnered the dairy farmers of the nation a reported $500,000,000 to $700,000,000 in higher milk prices and, after hearing about Tung-Nut Oil, Peanuts and Sugar, the reader might be wondering exactly how much this form of Washington, D.C. payouts cost the taxpayer when *all* farm commodities are considered. Let's turn to a feature article on the Wall Street Journal's editorial page for 7-21-72, by John A. Prestbo, one of the Journal's agricultural experts. Said Mr. Prestbo: "A funny thing happened to President Nixon's farm program on its way to getting the government out of agriculture: The government will spend a record $5.5 billion this year on farm subsidies and related expenses, up a whopping 49% from last year. A near-record $5.4 billion is budgeted for next year."

On to 1973 and something new appeared in the farm bill—escalator clauses, tying certain support price levels to the cost of living index. Business Week expressed its editorial anger in its issue of 8-4-73: "Meanwhile, Congress has been putting together a 1973 farm policy bill that is loaded with unnecessary and highly inflationary price support features. At first the Administration put on a brave front and threatened veto. In a moment of common sense, the conference committee returned the bills to House and Senate for further consideration. But instead of pressing the advantage, Agriculture Secretary Butz now says the Administration will accept a compromise that is, in effect, a capitulation.

"The revised bill passed by the Senate would give dairy farmers a guarantee that prices will be supported at the present inflated level for another two years, even if costs come down. And it would add an escalator clause to the formula for calculating support prices for grain and cotton in the last two years of the bill's four-year life. This means that the price floors would rise with any increase in the cost of living—thereby generating a further rise in consumer prices the next time around the spiral.

"Farmers are entitled to share in the nation's prosperity. But this is not sharing. It is extortion."

As we previously stated, the direct cost to the taxpayer for farm subsidies is only one-half the story, the other half, coming into the open when we get to the checkout counter in the supermarket. A Wall Street Journal article for 5-9-73 sheds some light on the numbers involved in the higher prices emanating from farm subsidies. ". . . Former U. S. budget director Charles Schultze estimated some time ago that consumers would pay $4.5 billion less for food annually if all government farm programs were abolished. . . ."

Four to $5 billion for direct farm subsidies in taxpayer money; another $4 to $5 billion in consumer money when the higher prices come through at the supermarket; the total cost of farm subsidies alone would seem to be about $9 billion to $10 billion annually. Big numbers indeed! The connection with corruption? We will weave this in during our later summary.

The Maritime Industry

Total maritime industry subsidies are not large in comparison with, say, agricultural subsidies, but they throw a particularly bright light on how subsidies work in Washington, how money flows one way, and favorable laws the other way, with the taxpayer, as usual, footing the bills, and Inflation via government budgetary deficits taking another upside whirl. Because of its instructional effects, we will permit ourselves some lengthy quotations here.

Newsday, Long Island, New York, had a particularly fine series of articles on this subject in July 1970, written by its Washington chief, Joseph Albright, starting off its article for 7-21-70 as follows: "Washington—The maritime lobby has erected what amounts to a perpetual motion machine to keep the taxpayer's dollar flowing into merchant marine subsidies. . . . Every year Congress pumps about $300,000,000 into direct subsidies for American shipyards and shipping companies. Through the grace of Congress, the industry also gets another $400,000,000 a year in indirect subsidies. The theory behind subsidizing the merchant marine is that the federal government should serve as a crutch to keep the maritime industry on its feet in the face of low-wage foreign competition. As it turns out, the subsidy program has been so generous lately that it has pushed up the wages and benefits of American seamen twice as fast as those of workers in American manufacturing industries. . . ."

We pick up this important thread with the Newsday article for 7-22-70: "Operating Differential Subsidies: Largely because of overmanning and high American wages, labor costs about four times as much on an American flag ship as on an identical foreign ship. To make sure that American ships engaged in foreign commerce can compete on an even basis with foreign ships, the Maritime Administration gives American shipowners cash subsidies to make up the difference between foreign and U. S. wage costs. . . . Operating subsidies are set up in such a way that seagoing wages are bound to skyrocket—and they do. At the bargaining table, the subsidized shipping companies have not had the usual incentives to take a hard negotiating line because they and the unions knew that the wage cost would be quietly absorbed by the U. S. taxpayers. And this has been no secret to the Maritime Administration.

"It is little wonder that during the last five years the costs of seafaring labor have risen more than twice as fast as the labor costs in typical manufacturing industries. By the Maritime Administration's own calculations, the rate of increase between 1964 and 1969 was nine per cent a year for the seamen and four per cent a year for all manufacturing industries. On a standard American cargo ship the total labor cost is now about $18,000 a year for each job.

"Lately the cost escalation has speeded up. The maritime industry has now finished calculating the effects of last summer's maritime labor settlement. Although it has never been publicly bruited about, the increase in labor costs amounted to 18 per cent this year, 11 per cent next year, and 12 per cent the third year. Compounded over three years, it comes to 46.7 per cent—clearly one of the more inflationary wage packages of the year. . . ."

Back to the 7-21-70 article: "The circle of subsidies is completed when election year rolls around. Then Washington representatives of the maritime union dole out close to $1,000,000 among the 200 or so of their favorite congressional candidates. Anyone in the House who has faithfully voted for maritime subsidies can almost certainly get $500 from the Seafarers donation committee just by asking. Any friendly senator or any of the 37 members of the House Merchant Marine and Fisheries Committee can usually get $1,000 or more from the Seafarers. In 1968, Sen. Daniel Brewster (D.—Md.) got $20,000 but lost his election. . . ." (The same Senator Brewster who was convicted in 1972 for taking $14,500 from a mail-order lobbyist for favors done on postage-rate legislation—SF).

"Rep. Edward A. Garmatz (D.—Md.), the chairman of the House Merchant Marine and Fisheries Committee, is proof of how dependent upon a special interest lobby a congressman can become without violating congressional ethics.

"Records filed by Garmatz in Annapolis, Md., indicate that he received $134,000 from campaign contributions in his last two election years including primaries. Of that, Newsday has traced $75,191 to executives and union groups in the maritime industry who had business before his committee. . . ."

The golden flow of taxpayer subsidies to the maritime industry continued through 1971, 1972 and 1973, but let's jump to 1974 to conclude this section with some current happenings.

For years the Maritime industry-union combine had been trying to get a law passed to order that a certain percentage of oil reaching our shores be carried by American-built, American-manned tankers. Rather remarkably, Inflation-wracked 1974 was when success seemed closest. A bill was introduced with a good public-relations title—"The Energy Transportation Security Act of 1974"—and started making its way through the appropriate committees of Congress with breathtaking speed. The bill would mandate that 20% of the oil and oil products imports to the United States be carried on U. S. flag ships, this percentage to rise to 30 per cent by mid-1977. While the proponents of the bill emphasized the additional jobs it would create in the shipyards and on the high seas (all high-cost and subsidized), what was *not* stressed was that using U. S. carriage would be more expensive and would immediately translate itself into higher costs to the consumer for all oil and oil products.

The House of Representatives passed the bill in lightning fashion, followed a few months later by the Senate. Two Wall Street Journal editorials summarize the meaning of the bill quite well, one before the Senate vote and one after:

Wall Street Journal editorial, 8-18-74, entitled "Superboondoggle."

"When the Energy Transportation Security Act of 1974 arrives on the Senate floor today, Senators who have committed themselves to vote for this superboondoggle would be wise to phone in sick. There's no way they can justify supporting this bill, except if they wish to argue that the rate of inflation in the United States is now too low.

"In the name of 'national security,' the proponents of the bill would require that 30% of all petroleum imported in the U. S. be carried in American tankers. By 1977, some 40 supertankers would have to be constructed in American yards at a cost of $4 billion. The U. S. would then presumably be secure against a joint economic attack by the Panamanians, Greeks, Liberians and Swedes. . . .

"The legislation is so bad President Ford should not even threaten to veto it. He might more effectively bring the Senate to its senses by threatening to sign it."

Wall Street Journal editorial, 9-9-74, entitled "Shame on the Senate!"

"On the very day President Ford was meeting with some of the nation's leading economists in search of a strategy to fight inflation, the U. S. Senate shamelessly approved the Energy Transportation Security Act of 1974 by a vote of 42 to 28. This super-boondoggle, which would require that at least 30% of oil imports be carried in American-flag ships by 1977 is nothing more than a colossal, inflationary gift to the maritime unions and shipbuilders. . . ."

Let's add a few lines from the Newsday series dealing with Senator Russell B. Long (D.—La.)then, as now, chairman of the Senate Commerce subcommittee on merchant marine, after pointing out that Senator Long was one of the chief proponents of the "Energy Transportation Security Act of 1974." The Newsday article for 7-21-70 reported that the Senator ". . . had been loyally supported in past political wars by certain executives of Lykes Brothers Steamship Co., a New Orleans firm which has in its time received $276,000,000 in operating differential subsidies. . . ."

We found enlightening as to the typically free-spending mood in Washington the following two sentences quoted from Senator Long in that Newsday article in responding to Commerce Secretary Stans during a hearing on a Maritime subsidy bill: "As far as I am concerned, may I say, with the kind of business we are voting on in the Finance Committee, I know it would not make a difference to put another $1 billion in there. That is a very small item."

The entire Federal budget for 1932 was $4 billion. By 1970, $1 billion had become "a very small item" to Senator Long.

Housing

In a previous context we described "One-Way Keynesianism" as "feeling so good"—blown-up prosperity for the Electorate, votes for the politicians—that the only thought was to keep it going without regard to the reckoning which must one day come. In the same way, new techniques developed in the past few decades to stimulate housing, introduced on a small scale at first, suddenly were found to "feel so good" by so many influential groups, that the programs commenced to grow and grow, again without regard to an "ultimate reckoning."

Let's take a quick look at the "reckoning" first. The chief ingredient by far in federal housing programs is the government-guaranteed mortgage. Mortgage bankers, Saving & Loan institutions and other commercial banking enterprises are encouraged to make long-term mortgages on houses or apartment houses easier to obtain and finance through the federal government accepting the final liability. There are many varieties of such programs, some including additional forms of aid such as construction subsidies, interest payment subsidies, and let's not forget tax subsidies to wealthy investors. But any sober analysis of the programs as a whole must concentrate upon the extent of government liability, which really means the liabilities of future taxpayers.

Business Week for 5-27-72 computed the relevant figures up to that time and came up with the following: "Awareness is dawning in Congress that when the government commits itself to interest payments on 30-year or 40-year mortgages, the federal budget is obligated for years ahead. Even if no additional housing subsidy commitments are made, existing obligations *would total $200 billion during the next 40 years.*" (our emphasis—SF)

The same article went on to describe what was taking place with Section 235 (single and double family houses) and Section 236 (apartments), each Section relating to the "Housing Act of 1968." With the stated objective of making it possible for people without the necessary means to own houses, Section 235 put a requirement on a low-income family of only a *$200* down payment, with a 40-year mortgage obtainable on which the government would pay interest charges down to one per cent. Section 236 was aimed at helping the renter, with rents as low as $75 per month because the government subsidy program on mortgage interest charges to the owner of the building made it possible for that owner to drastically lower rentals.

Is there any wonder that, along with other types of help for housing mortgage needs, a housing boom developed in the early 1970's, the over-all statistics soaring to two million units annually? And shall we wonder at the soaring wage demands of the building trades unions meeting little resistance when government subsidies would fill the gap in so many cases for the builder? (This was exactly similar to the taxpayer-subsidized shipbuilding industry's token resistance to maritime union wage demands.)

More low-income and middle-income people had houses or apartments, builders were happy, mortgage bankers were ecstatic, the economy was being greatly "stimulated." Who could argue with such success?

Only those who bothered to analyze what was really taking place.

Firstly, such analysis soon revealed—to take one area—that subsidized apartment housing under Section 236 was running about 20% higher in cost than unsubsidized comparable structures. (A desultory attitude toward cost *always* accompanies subsidy.) Secondly, the wildly generous terms of subsidy invited fraud, and these began to show up with increasing frequency. Here were some of the cases described by Assistant Attorney General Henry E. Petersen, many cases involving bribery of F.H.A. appraisers, as quoted in that 5-27-72 Business Week article:

"A young couple in Detroit bought a house under Section 235 for $17,500, a 'bargain' because the FHA had appraised it at $18,500. Three weeks after they and their small children had moved in, a city inspector found so many code violations that he condemned the property and ordered them to move.

"A speculator one morning paid $3,300 for a house that carried an FHA appraisal of $11,600. In the afternoon, he sold the house to a mother on welfare for the appraised value. He made the $200 down payment for her and gave her $20 in merchandise from a nearby store to sweeten the deal.

"A third speculator eliminated buyers altogether. He bought several houses, carrying FHA appraisals of about $10,000, for around $4,000. He then prepared false papers and submitted applications for FHA guarantees for fictitious persons. At the closings, he would hire people to pose as buyers, and pick up his $5,000 or so profit per house. No payments would ever be made on the houses, which, like most houses in such examples as this would be repossessed by the FHA. . . ."

Continuing:

"Families that are cheated into buying defective houses or ones they cannot afford generally stop making their payments and walk away from them; after all, they have little equity to hold them back. HUD (Housing & Urban Development—SF), therefore, has been forced to repossess thousands of dwellings. In some cases, vandals do an average of $2,000 damage per house. In many inner-city neighborhoods whole blocks are standing abandoned. In Detroit one two-block stretch contained 84 houses a few years ago, of which 52 changed hands under federal subsidies. At present, 24 of these houses have been repossessed, another dozen are in foreclosure, and six have been burned down. A Chicago suburban subdivision called Forest Heights consisted of 270 houses built under Section 235. Today, 52 of them are abandoned and boarded up."

As mentioned on a previous page: Some idea of what this type of corruption is costing the taxpayer? Newsday, Long Island, New York, 3-23-74: "The Department of Housing and Urban Development is spending $2 billion a year to bail out housing subsidy programs from a massive wave of defaults on federally insured mortgages. . . . Extensive fraud, mismanagement and bribery in many of these cases have been uncovered in the last two years. . . ."

The Remarkable Benefits of the Housing Programs To Those Who Are Not In Need

On October 2, 1972, the conservative banker's periodical "The Money Manager" (formerly "The Bond Buyer") ran an informative article headed "Public Housing Programs Near Bankruptcy; Another Administration Scandal Threatens." In the body of the article was a revealing complaint from Chairman Wright Patman of the House Banking and Currency Committee which was responsible for housing bills. " 'Many of these (housing) programs start out with high-sounding purposes,' Chairman Patman complains, 'then someone comes along and insists that we add in the profit margin for each real estate interest. There's a little bit for the land speculator, the builder, the lender, the closing attorney, the title company, the insurance company and on down the line,' the Texas Democrat charges. 'By the time the project reaches the end of the line, it is so top-heavy, you can't be sure just who did get the subsidy.' "

Further on in this same article:

"There are other sordid aspects to the housing mess that reflect anything but credit on Congress for its discharge of its responsibilities. Investigators have developed, for example, such facts as these:

"Strangely close ties link commercial interests that want to see the housing programs continue unchanged, with members of Congress most responsible for drafting housing legislation. . . .

"Key members of both the House and Senate Banking Committees rely heavily on private housing interests for campaign contributions, and these are rewarded by the sort of legislation private operators want most to see.

"For example, a few weeks ago a Housing Department official commenting on the public housing section of the Senate-passed bill said, 'That section of the law is just like Carl Junior wrote it.' No one batted an eyelash.

"The official was referring to Carl A. S. Coan, Jr., a lobbyist for the National Association of Homebuilders and the son of Carl A. S. Coan, Sr., the staff director on the Senate Banking Committee. (!!!—SF)

"Committee Chairman John Sparkman, aged 72, who is up for re-election this year in what may prove to be a tight race in Alabama, often falls asleep during public hearings. But this causes him no worry, since he delegates most of bill-writing authority to Mr. Coan, Sr.

"Whenever Sen. Sparkman runs for re-election his campaign coffers are fattened with sizable contributions from such organizations as the NAHB (National Association of Home Builders—SF), savings and loan associations, and other banking and building interests.

"But Senator Sparkman is not alone. Other powerful Senators on the same committee, such as John G. Tower (R.—Texas), and Thomas J. McIntyre (D.—N.H.), have been the recipients of what politicians like to call 'sweeteners.' "

The article then went on to describe a similar situation in the House of Representatives which it called ". . . somewhat different, but equally noxious. . . ."

Our files are full of articles such as the following: The New York Times, 5-12-72: "U. S. Helped Finance Relief Housing Here for Speculators, Senate Panel Discovers. . . ." Wall Street Journal, 3-19-74: "Ailing Agency; The Once-Proud FHA Is Beset by Scandals. . . ." New York Times, 12-4-71: "U. S. May Lose $200-Million in Detroit Mortgage Scandal," etc.

But we will conclude this section with two quotations, one serious, and the other good for another of those "wan smiles."

A Wall Street Journal editorial, 10-2-73: "Congressional liberals have been having great sport with Mr. Nixon's housing message. House Majority Leader Tip O'Neill had a good line: 'The President is telling us that eight months of housing limbo will be followed by a year of suspended animation.' But the best was Rep. Henry Reuss' observation that the administration had labored mightily and brought forth not a mouse, but the promise of a mouse by 1975.'

"Suspended animation more or less describes the Nixon decision to have the government stop building or subsidizing public-housing units, at least after a few remaining commitments are met. The government will no longer subsidize mortgage interest for low-income families; HUD is already stuck with 200,000 units in default. And it will halt the Section 236 rental program, the noble Great Society experiment that prodded the construction of lower middle-income apartments by offering a bonanza to mortgage bankers, land developers and wealthy investors in search of a tax shelter. . . ."

Now for the "wan smile."

New York Times, 7-23-74: "LeRoy Barnes, accused of murder and listed by the police as a top narcotic dealer, emerged in a court hearing yesterday as principal owner of a Michigan housing project under construction with a $4.6 million Federal loan guarantee. . . ."

Defense

If we take a figure of $80 billion for the defense portion of the federal budget for the current fiscal year, we will be somewhat under what we think it will ultimately cost, but that figure is close enough to project the scope of the possible problems with waste and corruption when we realize that $80 billion comes down to *$219,000,000 per day.*

Further demonstrating with ease the potential scope of problems, consider just one typical article from our files as follows: Business Week, 5-26-73: "Panic in the face of a Navy exodus: A couple of Saturdays ago, a handful of businessmen from Aquidneck Island in Rhode Island's Narragansett Bay led about 5,000 irate fellow citizens to Washington to stage a protest on the Capitol lawn. Their goal: to get the Navy to roll back its Apr. 16th decision to pull the fleet out of Newport and sharply cut back the Naval base there, as well as other military facilities at nearby mainland Quonsset, all by June 30 of next year.

"It was a futile move—but it is easy to understand the desperation behind it. Cutbacks around the Newport area are the heaviest reductions being carried out as part of a wide-reaching Defense economy move . . . nowhere will Defense's economy move bite more painfully into a community than in the Newport area. As the Navy departs over the next year, it takes with it 41% of the jobs, 50% of the payrolls, 33% of the population, and 40% of the school children of Newport, Middletown and Portsmouth, the three towns that comprise Aquidneck Island. The area will lose some 22,000 jobs, 17,000 of them military and 5,000 civilian, with a $205 million payroll. . . ."

This is one of the more extreme examples of defense impact on communities for good or ill—more jobs or less jobs—and one can imagine without any difficulty whatever the meaning of such a routine newspaper release as follows from the Wall Street Journal for 7-9-74: "United Aircraft Gets Job Costing $102.4 Million; Pentagon Also Gives Work to Pan Am, Lockheed, Rockwell, Other Concerns." The news item then commenced: "Washington—United Aircraft Pratt & Whitney Aircraft division got a $102.4 million addition to an Air Force contract for jet engines. The engines will be used in flight-test programs for the F15 fighter, built by McDonnell Douglas Corp., and the YF16 lightweight fighter prototype, developed by General Dynamics Corp.

"Pan American World Airways received a $39.2 million addition to an Air Force contract for operation of the Eastern test range in the fiscal year that started July 1.

"Lockheed Aircraft Corp. obtained a $13.5 million addition to an Air Force contract for maintenance of F104G aircraft used in the West German pilot-training program. The award is for fiscal year that started July 1.

"Rockwell International Corp.'s Missile System division was issued an $11.3 million addition to a Navy contract for the Condor air-to-surface missile. . . ."

The release went on to name multi-million-dollar contracts for 9 additional companies, and such releases appear throughout the year.

Every one of those contract awards means jobs for the personnel of a specific company, and money for a specific community. Can we imagine that the Representative or Senator representing that particular community is unaware of, or disinterested in, whether the contract is awarded or not? A rhetorical question to end all rhetorical questions!

What then are we to expect when the defense budget comes up for a Congressional vote? Are we to expect the average Representative or Senator to seriously question the recommendations of the Pentagon as to (a) the size of the military budget, and (b) its composition? Two things assure us that there will *not* be serious opposition to either (a) or (b). First, weapons technology in a nuclear world beset with international tensions has become so incredibly complex that Congress as a whole does not have the capability of ongoing research on a scale making it anywhere near possible to second-guess the Pentagon, let alone an individual Congressman being able to do so. Secondly, political realities work strongly towards the same end. The companies and their workers back home want those contracts.

So it is that only a very few defense issues at the very top of national awareness, such as the "ABM" debate of a few years ago, ever involve controversy, along with pro-forma debates to cut some small percentage out of the over-all defense budget, perhaps $2 or $4 billion—a yearly debate which can easily be handled, we can logically assume, by the Defense budget merely containing some few billions of padding which can later be given up to be labeled "economy."

Thus it is that $291,000,000 per day is spent via the defense budget, and when we come up against the task of imagining some estimate of what portion of the $291,000,000 per day is lost to the country's military defense shield through corruption, we find it necessary to consider additional areas of concern, which we feel we can do quickly by referring to a representative study made by Senator William Proxmire in 1970. Issued in book form under the title: "Report From Wasteland," the work is actually the conclusions drawn from hearings on the military budget conducted by the Subcommittee on Economy in Government of the Joint Committee, of which subcommittee Senator Proxmire was Chairman.

The Foreword to the book, written by former Senator Paul H. Douglas (Illinois), is immediately illuminating.

"Everyone interested in public affairs should read this book. It shows with solid evidence how we are wasting at least $10 billion a year on our weapons systems. Until Senator Proxmire began his investigations less than two years ago, this field was treated as 'off limits' as far as congressional scrutiny was concerned. Because the subject was highly technical as well as crucial to physical and national security, Congress deprived itself of any adequate means of finding out what was going on. . . .

". . . Beginning with the C-5A cargo plane, Proxmire discovered that the actual costs of the plane were not the $3.37 billion authorized but would be at least $1.9 billion more, or $5.33 billion. Further inquiry revealed that this overrun of actual costs was the rule rather than the exception. Despite the strenuous efforts of the military to cover it up, some of the truth came tumbling out. . . .

". . . In the course of his investigations, Proxmire found out the submarine rescue vehicle had experienced an even greater expansion of cost than the C-5A. Originally authorized at an outlay of $36 million for twelve vehicles, the price skyrocketed to $460 million for only six of them, an increase of from $3 million to $77 million per unit, or twenty-five times. In addition, the total cost of the strategic missile (Minuteman I and II, with Minuteman III to come) will expand from $3 billion to $7 billion.

"An assistant to McNamara has said that the ultimate cost of a weapons system is, in 90 per cent of the cases, double the original estimate, and another expert says that the typical cost overrun is from 300 per cent to 700 per cent.

"Proxmire punctures the usual excuses for such excesses. He proves that inflation was a relatively minor cause and that, if improvement in design were a factor, they were relatively ineffective. Of thirteen aircraft and missile systems with electronic equipment begun since 1955, only four, costing $5 billion, were as much as 75 per cent effective. Five more, costing $13 billion, broke down at a performance level 75 per cent or less of that fixed in the contract. Two more systems, costing $10 billion, were dropped after a time because of 'low reliability.' Finally, the contracts for two systems were canceled. Their cost was $2 billion. . . ."

A few quotations from Senator Proxmire's book itself:

"What is most appalling is the uncritical way in which cost overruns and supply surpluses are accepted by the Pentagon. They treat a $2 billion overrun as if it were small change.

". . . One of the most dangerous and shocking aspects of the military-industrial complex is the ease with which military officers retire and move into big jobs in the defense industries. It matches the way in which high-ranking civilians in defense or defense-related industries move into the Pentagon—and out again into industry. There is, in fact, an active, ever-working, fast-moving, revolving door between the Pentagon and its big suppliers. . . .

". . . As of February 1969, some 2,124 former high-ranking officers were employed by the 100 biggest military contractors. . . ."

We pause here for an example of this important area, in a news item taken from the New York Times for 12-16-72: "Air Force General Maxwell Joins Boeing. Major Gen. Jewell C. Maxwell, who retired from the Air Force on Nov. 1 after more than 30 years of service, joined the Boeing Company as a vice president on Nov. 30. . . . During his Air Force career, the 55-year-old officer was assigned to the Federal Aviation Administration as director of supersonic transport programs from 1965 to 1969. . . . Boeing was the prime contractor for the SST, which was killed by Congress last year. Boeing was awarded the contract in December 1966. . . ."

Without ascribing any wrongdoing to General Maxwell, or to any of the other 2,124 former high-ranking officers who went to work for "the 100 biggest military contractors" after retiring from service, we take note of the fact that General Maxwell headed the supersonic transport program at the time Boeing got the contract for the SST, and that General Maxwell later went to work for Boeing. We see below that this was a quite common occurrence.

Continuing from Senator Proxmire's book:

"North American Rockwell is a huge aerospace company. It handles almost $700 million a year in defense contracts and many hundreds of millions of dollars more in space projects. On its payroll is retired Air Force Lieutenant General W. A. Davis, who is a group vice president in charge of aircraft. Altogether, North American Rockwell employs 60 former high-ranking Air Force officers, of whom there were seven generals and 53 colonels. . . .

". . . There is something else wrong about present practices. This is the subtle and unconscious temptation to the officer still on active duty. He knows that over 2,000 of his fellow officers work for the big companies. . . . The point is this: How hard a bargain does an Air Force lieutenant colonel drive with Lockheed or Boeing or General Dynamics when he is representing the Air Force at one of their plants? He knows that shortly he will be forced to retire and that hundreds of his fellow officers work for these and other companies. Is he really going to bite the hand that may feed him? How hard is he going to buck the welfare system operating in the United States for the military-industrial establishment? . . .

"The meaning of all this is simple. The significance is there for everyone to see. When the bulk of the nation's budget goes for military purposes, when 100 companies get 68 per cent of the defense contract dollars, when cost overruns are routine, and prime military weapons system contracts normally exceed their estimates by 100 to 200 per cent, when these contracts are let by negotiation and not by competitive bidding, and when the top contractors have over 2,100 high-ranking retired military officers on their payrolls, the public interest is threatened. . . ."

The Larger Meanings of Corruption

Those who steal come in many guises. The criminal who robs with a gun is threatening life as well as property. The shoplifter who walks out of a store with goods without paying for those goods, the longshoreman who takes a carton of transistor radios from a pier, the white-collar worker who puts office equipment into his briefcase, all steal without the threat of force, but steal they do. The middle-management executive who juggles bills of lading on the company's books to embezzle moves up a considerable notch in the scope of his stealing.

In the public sector, at the local level, the policeman who "shakes down" a local bar, the housing inspector who overlooks a violation for a fee, the alderman who votes for a zoning change and gets paid off by a grateful builder, the construction company that gets a large State contract and pays off the public official who helped them get that contract in cash, or with "campaign contributions," all represent varieties of stealing almost bewildering in their diverse forms.

In the public sector, at the national level, the highly-placed member of an Administration, or a Senator, or a member of the House of Representatives who helps a multinational giant corporation with a merger, or pushes through a special subsidy for an industry, or a segment of that industry, or who benefits them in some way—and who gets "paid off" in the form of direct cash payments or "campaign contributions" or lucrative retainers for his law firm back home, etc., etc. moves us into a realm of corruption which has reached, for each act, the millions of dollars, sometimes the *billions* of dollars, level, as we have seen.

All the above types of corruption have one thing in common—*they add directly to the cost of goods and services we buy.* The storekeeper who sees 20% of his goods taken by shoplifters, or the company whose goods are stolen, can only stay in business by raising all their prices to bring profit margins back to a workable level. The builder who pays off the dozens of state and local inspectors in order to put up his building, must reflect all those bribes in the rents he will charge, or the price of the home or other structure to be sold. The State politician who swings a voting machine or street lighting purchase to a particular company upon payment of a bribe, ensures that the State will be paying higher prices for the equipment.

We all *pay* for what government buys and that goes into the cost of living for all of us just as directly as the price of a suit of clothes or an automobile.

We have presented some appropriate headlines and news articles on previous pages and let's run down a few of them to set the stage for the thoughts which follow:

"Growing Toll of Crimes Against Business; Losses from crime and the expense of fighting it keep climbing—a huge burden paid by honest tradesmen and customers on every purchase."

"Corruption in Politics, How Widespread? It's not only Watergate. All across the country, official skullduggery keeps surfacing —at national, State and local levels. . . ."

"Kickbacks as a Way of Life: . . . Bribes that make headlines are only the tip of the iceberg. Billions go undetected each year, say crime authorities—with consumers footing the bill."

"Employe Dishonesty Soaring; Employe dishonesty in business has reached an all-time high and far exceeds, both in dollars and number of participants, crime in the streets. . . ."

"In Agnew's Maryland, Payoffs to Politicians Are a Way of Life; Some Funds Legitimately Go To Campaigns, but Others Are Taken for Personal Use."

(Above items taken, respectively, from U. S. News & World Report, 10-2-72, 6-4-73 and 10-29-73; Journal of Commerce, 3-20-73; and Wall Street Journal, 10-12-73.)

What does it all cost? What part of the rising "Cost Of Living," of the Inflation ravaging our country and its way of life, its values—flows directly from the corruption which we have tried to describe as to its type and extent in the preceding pages?

Obviously, this is a very difficult figure to arrive at with any hope of accuracy. We have quoted estimates by recognized experts in their various fields and we have seen that these estimates are somewhere near the $70 to $80 billion level before we get to corruption on the Federal level, which corruption has many shadings and is difficult to define in many cases.

Turning to this area:

Was it corruption for the Nixon Administration to have raised price support levels for the dairy farmers to the extent, as we have previously cited, of raising their income by an estimated $500 to $700 million? As we read the events, and just about everyone is by now familiar with them, consumers *did* pay $500 to $700 million more for milk and milk products—and President Nixon's re-election committee *did* get $2 million. What there is no doubt about is that the Cost of Living went up by $500 to $700 million.

As we write these words, both Senate and House have passed the bill requiring that 20% of oil products imported into the United States be carried in tankers built in the United States and manned by American crews. According to the Wall Street Journal of 9-6-74: " 'In my opinion the President is going to sign it,' Mr. Cotton declared at one point (Senator Norris Cotton, R., N.H.—SF). 'If the President signs it, I'll never listen to another word from the President about all this stuff about fighting inflation.' "

One can argue that requiring more tankers to be built in American shipyards, and manning them with American seamen, will provide many jobs for Americans, and this is unquestionably true. But the American consumer will be dealt two body blows by this legislation. Carrying 20% to 30% of oil products into the United States in this new manner will cost tens of billions of dollars in higher prices—one estimate we have seen puts it near $60 billion in the next ten years. The cost of living goes up by that amount. And then we must take off our consumer hat and put on our taxpayer hat and pay subsidies to keep up the inflated seamen's wages to run the tankers, and subsidies to build those tankers at far higher costs than obtain overseas. Just as with the entire Agricultural subsidy program, all subsidies have a one-two punch: one when you pay the subsidy through Federal taxes, and again when the product reaches you as a consumer—at higher prices.

This tanker preference bill has a huge price tag on it for the consumer, but when Congress passes it, and the President signs it, everything is completely legal.

What shall we say, however, when another article—a very familiar one!—comes along in the New York Times for 9-16-74 entitled: "Maritime Unions Aid Congressmen; Donate $333,300 to Senate and House Members Who Backed Oil Import Bill"?

Whatever you call it, we do know that because of it the Cost of Living will go up by tens of billions of dollars.

We are still trying to approach an estimate of what this type of "Corruption" adds to the Cost of Living, to Inflation, when stemming from the Federal level, from Washington, D.C.

Here is an article from the banking organ, The Money Manager, for 1-17-72 entitled: "Subsidies Written into Federal Law Through The Years Total Something Like $63 Billion Or One-Third of Total Revenue" and went on, quoting Senator William Proxmire as Chairman of the Congress' Joint Economic Committee, ". . . 'This mammoth subsidy system represents a mindless means of spending taxpayers' money,' he charges. 'There is virtually no analysis of economic benefit and little analysis of the cost of these programs. In fact, there is not even the most elementary examination of whether these subsidy programs actually achieve the goals they were designed to achieve. . . .' "

Some of the subsidies do things like shoring up the housing sector by allowing local taxes and mortgage interest to be deducted from federal taxes, but much more of it represents tax money-support to special interests, opening the door to the various shadings of corruption we have described. And let us add that the contemplated federal budget for the current fiscal year is expected to run to *$305* billion and if the same one-third proportion holds, the over-all subsidy programs, direct and indirect, would run to *One Hundred Billion Dollars.*

Can we place a figure on the misapplication of funds, covering both inefficiency and corruption, that has to be present to some extent in the $80 billion segment of the federal budget which goes to Defense? The total has to be painfully high if only for the fact that the defense industry does not operate in a vacuum, but in the same environment of easy corruption affecting every aspect of American life today. A substantial level of corruption is a foregone conclusion, and almost certainly at an even more expensive level than elsewhere because "it's not real money—it comes from the government."

Another BIG Item—"Agency Financing"

Few Americans know that the budget balance between income and expenditures does *not* include something called "Federal credit programs." Let a Wall Street Journal editorial dated 8-28-74 tell us how these come about: "Once upon a time the federal deficit was a reasonably good measure of federal borrowings and thus demands on the credit supply and expansionary pressures on the Fed. So the conventional wisdom was that deficits cause inflation and budget balance cures it. This created a bit of discipline for Congress, which with its typical ingenuity evaded the discipline by inventing off-budget financing. The idea was that so long as the numbers didn't show up in the federal deficit, Congress could dream up a lot of new agencies that made demands on the credit pool.

"Thus we have Fannie Mae, Ginny Mae, the Federal Home Loan Banks, the Export-Import Bank, the Postal Service, an

Environmental Financing Authority, a new Federal Financing Bank and so on, all making credit demands *but not showing up in the budget*. The Morgan Guaranty Survey dubs this process 'debudgeting the budget.' " (Our emphasis—SF)

For some idea of how huge these programs have become, we turn to Ed Tyng, a leading financial writer for the excellent Journal of Commerce, its issue of 10-17-72:

"The startling growth in federal credit programs—as anybody knows who follows the borrowing and lending policies of Fannie Mae or the Federal Home Loan banks (Fannie Mae is a familiar Wall Street name for a government agency insuring home mortgages, with Ginny Mae being another variety of the same thing—SF)—is something that is deceptively kept out of the federal budget. The American Enterprise Institute this month has come out with a study entitled '$300 Billion in Loans: An Introduction to Federal Credit Programs', written by Dan Larkins, its staff economist. . . . Included in the survey is a table which notes that since 1969 direct government loans have jumped from $48.2 billion to $57.8 billion in fiscal year 1972 while insured loans have risen from $116.4 billion to $163.5 billion. Government agency-sponsored loans have gone up from $18.9 billion to $46.4 billion. All are to go up sharply further in fiscal year 1973. . . . (They are still going up in 1974—SF)

"Government guaranties under insured loans are almost infinite: The guaranties reduce the risks of private lenders who are insured; there is the liquidity guaranty against loss if the lender sells the loan and there is also the guaranty against default. . . .

"As now operated, billions of government or government agency expenditures are wholly outside the federal budget, making the budget misleading and the national debt limit meaningless."

Let's take a quick look at one of the smaller agency loan programs at the bottom of the heap, which is amusing in a painful sort of way. The Money Manager, 9-18-72: "If something isn't done soon, the Administration may find itself encumbered with the nasty ingredients of what soon may become a national scandal involving the handling of the college loan program, designed initially to help poor or near-poor youngsters get educations they otherwise could never afford. The U. S. Office of Education has reluctantly disclosed that about 4% of the student borrowers, scheduled to repay their Federally-insured student loans, have defaulted, sticking the government with more than $50 million in unpaid loans.

"Bank losses on student loans climbed so high and so rapidly earlier this year that the Office of Education was forced to ask Congress for an extra $12,765,000 to reimburse the banks for defaults piled up in the first three months of the year. . . .

". . . there's a substantial minority of defaulting young students who callously disregard their obligations and, to all intents and purposes, thumb their noses at their lenders. For one Washington banker, the first hint that there was something wrong with the Federally-insured loan program came from an 18-year old college freshman. 'When I handed this fellow a check for $1,500, wished him good luck in school and reminded him to keep in touch so he could arrange to repay his loan,' this banker recalls today, 'he looked at me and said, 'Forget it Mac, I don't ever expect to repay you.' "

We go now from the lowest level of federal agency lending to the highest—and by far the most expensive and far-reaching—housing. Again the very informative Money Manager for 2-13-73: "The Nixon budget proposal in announcing cuts in community development and housing outlays has delivered a back of the hand slap to the housing finance sector as well as to the overseeing agencies. Noting that the 'Federal Government has committed itself to . . . assistance payments . . . in the range of $57 billion to $82 billion in direct subsidy payments, as well as additional sums for . . . tax subsidies,' the budget statement lists certain inequities it claims were a result of the programs.

" 'Provided inordinate financial gains for intermediaries in the housing and financial sectors. . . .' "

Translating the above into simple language, a good part of the housing subsidy program was a giveaway, as we described on previous pages, and a near-riskless bonanza for the mortgage bankers, builders and tax-shelter-seeking investors. All of this underwritten to the tune of tens of billions of dollars *without ever appearing in the federal budget.*

The Real Point

We can ascribe, recognizing that these are only educated estimates, something approaching $80 billion annually to crime and corruption before we get to the Federal level, all of which goes without hesitation into the Cost of Living Index. In discussing corruption on the Federal level, we have pointed out there is considerable haziness in the links between bonanzas to various interests which cost consumers billions, the votes of Senators or Representatives or the influence exerted by highly-placed members of the Administration to vote in those bonanzas (whereupon they become "legal"). But when those same special interests openly supply funds to those in power in government who have helped them, we citizens are completely entitled, in this writer's view, to bracket much of what is taking place as corrupt. There is the *spirit* of the law as well as its *letter!*

Our files keep growing even as this book nears completion. Here is an article from the New York Times for 9-20-74: "House Unit, in Shift, Bars Reform Move On Real Estate Tax; Washington, Sept. 19—The House Ways and Means Committee reversed today an earlier decision and decided to permit investors in real estate ventures to keep the special tax advantage they have now. . . . The elimination of the real-estate provision that the committee adopted on Tuesday *would mean an annual tax-savings to real estate investors of about $300-million a year, according to Congressional staff estimates.*" (Our emphasis—SF) By enlightening circumstances, in the same issue of the New York Times, 9-20-74, there was a page 1 article by the excellent Times researcher and reporter, Eileen Shanahan, headlined "Tax Writing Congressmen Aided by Special Interests; Washington, Sept. 19—Special interests that are trying to preserve or enlarge the favored treatment they now receive under the tax laws are contributing heavily to the campaign funds of members of the House Ways and Means Committee, which originates all tax legislation. . . ." There then followed a very long article indeed, giving many facts and details.

But permit us to repeat something we stated on a much earlier page: "It must be recognized immediately that the entire political structure in Washington, both Executive and Legislative, *develops from and remains an intimate part* of the local political structure on the State and county levels. This applies to members of the House of Representatives, the Senate, and the President and most of his aides. We cannot adduce a morass of corruption on the local level—and its existence is indisputable —and find purity, wholesomeness and a selfless desire to serve only the public good in the national politicians in Washington. . . ."

After studying the evidence in our own files on a more complete basis, and fully recognizing that our estimate must be imprecise, but still serving to make our point, we have come to a working conclusion that various shadings of corruption which produce immediately higher costs for the American consumer and go directly into the Cost of Living must be on the order of $50 billion annually at a minimum, on the Federal level, could easily approach the $100 billion level, and might be higher than that, astounding as such totals are.

Adding the top estimate of $80 billion annually in costs from crime and corruption on the local level, which we previously described, to the minimum $50 billion in costs we have adduced for the Federal sector, and coming up with the total of at least

$130 billion being dumped on the backs of consumers annually through such corruption, we are able to draw the following conclusion without any possibility of being contradicted:

Corruption IS the Inflation

Is it not ludicrous to read that President Ford and his advisers are seeking to cool the Inflation by attempting to trim the Federal budget by $5 billion? Or by postponing a scheduled Federal workers pay increase for three months?

The conclusion forces itself in front of us and will not go away. Corruption IS The Inflation, and we will not deal with Inflation until we deal with Corruption.

The Strong Link Between Civil Crime and Political Corruption and How It Further Propels the Inflation

Cynicism about public officials, from the most local of levels right up to the White House, has deepened and widened in the past decade. The younger generations learn by example—how can there be any doubt about such elementary human psychology? And when newspapers, periodicals and television carry an endless stream of stories about public officials being indicted, tried and punished for corruption, when the policeman on the corner and the judge on the bench are caught up in the same net, why should anyone wonder that respect for the law breaks down, as it has, and the numbers of lawbreakers soar?

Look at a headline in the New York Times for 12-28-72 about the New York Police Department: "Report Says Police Corruption in 1971 Involved Well Over Half on the Force" and jump from that to a New York Daily News article for 4-7-74 headed: "An Ex-Top Cop Blames Politicos Over Corruption." This latter article went on to report that "Murphy (former New York City Police Commissioner—SF) said that a cop finds it easy to rationalize his decision to take payoffs when he sees improper political influence playing an important role in other parts of the government. . . ." Just so.

Here is Attorney General William B. Saxbe speaking almost in despair about cascading crime, addressing a conference of big-city police chiefs in Chicago on August 27, 1974, reported in the New York Times for 8-28-74: "Mr. Saxbe said that statistics to be released soon would show that crime in the United States increased by 6 per cent in 1973 instead of the 5 per cent rise estimated earlier. He also noted that in the final quarter of 1973 (note the following startling statistics—SF) crime had risen *16 per cent* above the rate of that quarter in 1972 and in the first quarter of 1974 by *15 per cent* above the first quarter of 1973 . . ." (Our emphasis—SF)

Attorney General Saxbe went on to say: "No one can accurately predict the crime rate for the remainder of 1974. But we can now perceive with shocking clarity that we have suffered a severe setback in the concerted effort to alter one of the nation's most agonizing facts of life. It is a failure of substantial dimensions—harsh, bitter and dismaying, and it may prove to be the prelude of worse things to come. . . . If we go on as we are, there is every possibility that crime will inundate us. . . ."

Was Mr. Saxbe speaking only of the problems of big cities? By no means. The New York Times, 9-6-74: "Washington, Sept. 5 (AP)—Serious crimes rose 6 per cent in the United States last year, *with the biggest increases in suburbs and rural areas,* the Federal Bureau of Investigation reported today. . . ." (Our emphasis—SF)

The meaning of the above cuts deeper when we turn from cold, generalized statistics to a very small segment of the crimes themselves. Here are a series of news reports, all from the New York Times, in the space of 6 days:

8-18-74: "Queens Girl Found Murdered in Yard of Bayside School."

8-19-74: "Garage Employe Slain by Youths."

8-20-74: "A Woman Doctor, 72, Found Slain in Jersey City."

8-21-74: "Mother and Girl Are Slain Uptown."

8-21-74: "Body of a Woman Found in 'Village'—Victim Believed Murdered Elsewhere."

8-23-74: "Four Knife-Wielding Thugs Slay a Brooklyn Father of Six for $7."

In almost all big cities, people are afraid to walk the streets at night in most areas. And people no longer feel safe even in their homes, not only in the cities, but increasingly in all suburban areas.

Again—The Direct Connection of Crime and Corruption With Inflation

In its issue of 9-20-72, the Journal of Commerce had an article entitled: "Industry's 'Steal Doors' Wide Open" and went on to report: "American industry can no longer depend on police and punishment to protect it from crime and internal losses which now approach $10 billion per year. So said Saul D. Astor, president of Management Safeguards, Inc., New York, who spoke at the annual meeting of the American Society for Industrial Security held at the Waldorf-Astoria. The three-day seminar, expected to attract some 2,000 authorities in the field, is addressing itself to security problems in every major area of business. Mr. Astor charged that *theft is no longer a 'deviant outlaw activity.'* Instead, he said, it is almost the norm. 'With one-third of the nation engaged in some form of dishonesty each year, *honesty is not necessarily equated with goodness any longer,'* said Mr. Astor. . . . He also pointed out that the consumer invariably pays for these losses, and that the losses themselves contribute to the price spiral." (Our emphasis—SF)

A feature article on shoplifting from a local town newspaper, GN Newsmagazine, Great Neck, New York for August 1974: "Mr. Levy of Virginia Variety echoed many an aggravated voice when he summed up his feelings on the matter. 'There is a complete moral breakdown in our country; shoplifting in Great Neck has to be symptomatic of this. There's no more golden rule. It's 'what is in it for me,' or 'what can I get away with,' that rules now. You know, for the first time in fifteen years I seriously considered not renewing my lease last month. It's getting that bad.' "

Does civilian crime have any connection with the following string of newspaper headlines?

"Ex-Patrolman Testifies He Committed 16 Break-ins With Other Albany Police."

"Federal Prosecutor Declares That 'Everything Has a Price' in Corrupt Hudson County."

"Jersey Secretary of State Indicted for Bid-Rigging."

"Whelan Is Guilty With 7 Officials in Trial in New Jersey; Mayor and Colleagues Face 20 Years and $10,000 Fine. . . ."

"Brasco (member of House of Representatives at the time——SF) Convicted as Contract Fixer."

"Ex-Suffolk Official Indicted as Perjurer."

Of course, it has every kind of direct connection. And this is the proper time to return to Attorney General Saxbe's 8-28-74 statement that ". . . If we go on as we are, there is every possibility that crime will inundate us. . . ." Mr. Saxbe then went on to say something which hit us with great force when we read it in the midst of doing our final research for this chapter. Mr. Saxbe said: "As a people, we seem to sit like zombies while our problems spread. . . ."

The point is that nothing basic can be done on the "civilian" level.

If corruption *in government* on all levels continues, it can be said with utmost logic that civil crime will continue, and will grow.

We stated our conclusion before that:

Corruption IS the Inflation

Now we see indisputably that political Corruption breeds and accentuates civilian crime, which adds directly to the rising cost of living not only by stealing, but also by contributing to a breakdown of morale and spirit, which surely undermines productivity throughout the economy. On *every count,* the responsibility zeroes in on political corruption, and cannot be placed anywhere else.

The First "Vital Guidepost" and Our "Two Alternatives"

We trust that readers now fully appreciate why we have given so much space to this first Guidepost: "Corruption: Accept its devastating consequences, or fight it." We don't think anyone can seriously doubt that if political corruption is allowed to continue to move along its present course—indeed, if it is not quickly and effectively cut down to a fraction of its present scope—the truly devastating economic crisis we face cannot be solved and a major depression approaching the dimensions of what we experienced in the 1930's will be not too far ahead. Even going *part* of the way toward such an economic catastrophe would completely vitiate our leadership ability in a very dangerous world, and would create social upheavals in our own country with unpredictable results. The fact that it would further wreck the stock market pales a bit by comparison with such consequences but is of importance to the readers of this book. We treat that part of the subject in the last chapter.

Will Political Corruption Be Vigorously Attacked? What Are the Means at Hand?

In September 1974 the new President, Gerald R. Ford, issued a general "pardon" for the former President, Richard M. Nixon, and floated a trial balloon that pardons were "under study" for the other 49 individuals connected with our Watergate trauma. The ensuing public storm of disapproval was of such hurricane intensity that it left Mr. Ford's "credibility" badly impaired and all talk about additional pardons was dropped. As stated before, much of our work in editing two investment services is simply to *read* very widely and this takes many hours a day and covers a long list of newspapers, periodicals and other published materials, giving us a very useful insight into what is taking place, what people's reactions are to current developments. On the basis of such study, let us state a conviction on our part that many influential people, and a growing number of "Average" Americans are ready to work for strong action to deal with Corruption.

The Weapon of "Full Disclosure"

As we write these words, there appears in the New York Times 9-19-74 an article which begins: "Washington, Sept. 18—The Federal Energy Administration is expected to adopt within the next day or two a lobbying regulation under which the names of all those seeking to influence policy in meetings with top officials would be logged and made public. . . . The suggestion that the energy agency adopt a lobbying rule was proposed last April by Common Cause, a publicly-financed group that lobbies for changes in Government policies and procedures it believes are in the public interest.

"The plan suggested by John W. Gardner, chairman of Common Cause, was considerably broader than that included in the pending proposal. One key recommendation that was not adopted would require all persons seeking to influence F. E. A. policy to file a registration statement detailing who they represented and how much they were paid."

Thus, the Federal Energy Administration has gone part of the way—but this writer thinks much more along these lines must inevitably come. The day of the showering (both open, and hidden) of our Congressmen with "contributions" by special interest groups is rather swiftly moving into its evening because of heightened awareness of the major role it plays in fostering political Corruption, made so painfully clear in Watergate.

An item along the same lines from a Wall Street Journal editorial, 7-11-73: "American Airlines is getting high marks for candor for admitting that corporate funds were used in a $75,000 kitty that went to the Committee to Re-Elect the President. We think the marks would be more deserved were it not for suggestions by 'insiders' that the airline was about to be found out anyway . . . the recent revelations do encourage us to think that maybe the tough disclosure requirements in the Federal Election Campaign Act of 1971 have proved to be more effective than anyone imagined they would be. . . ."

Florida, in 1972, passed a "government-in-sunshine" law which opened just about all meetings of public officials dealing with government business to the public.

Illinois has passed a law which requires that public officials disclose financial interests and business connections, which upset many local politicians whose legal counsel fought the law all the way to the Supreme Court. They lost. A similar type of law didn't fare so well in California where the State Supreme Court voided it, but a new approach is being pursued vigorously.

It has remained for the State of Washington, however, to produce the most important omen for future action in the realm of "full disclosure" in political life, as a means of throttling back corruption. Scandals in local government had angered many people, and proposed reforms in the legislature were moving at a snail's pace. Irate citizens groups joined forces behind a Referendum, put the bill known as "Initiative 276" on the ballot, and the bill won with an overwhelming 72% of voters giving it their backing. The law provides for a public disclosure commission which can subpoena witnesses, take testimony and make their findings public. An elected candidate who is proved not to have complied with the full disclosure provisions of the law can find his election set aside, and a new election called. Fines of up to $10,000 are also provided.

As reported in the Wall Street Journal for 7-6-73:

"The law (Initiative 276), as upheld by the trial court, requires enormously detailed reports on campaign spending of every state and local candidate and on financial and business ties of every elected official in the state except precinct committeemen. Campaign reports, for example, must list every donation over $5 by name, address and date. Financial reports of elected officials must show every creditor to whom more than $500 is owed and the source and nature of each portion of income above $500 yearly.

"Lobbyists here for the first time are required to name the legislators and other officials whom they entertain. Each expense above a low minimum of $15 must be itemized, and for the first time spending on a year-round basis must be reported by lobbyists. . . .

"The law also grants the public access to nearly the entire paperwork output of any state or local government unit and requires every agency to adopt clear rules for opening its files and operations to public scrutiny. . . ."

The LARGE Potential of "Full Disclosure"

Following the stock market crash of 1929 and the market devastation that followed, there was much "soul-searching" from which there finally emerged new laws regulating the stock exchanges and the securities industry as a whole. While 100% of former abuses were by no means all eliminated, improvements of large scope indeed came into being, and they mostly rested on the foundation of—Full Disclosure. Brokers and investment advisers had to disclose to their clients any interests they might have in securities whose purchase or sale they were advising.

Corporations selling new issues of stocks or bonds to investors, or making tender offers for securities, or offering securities in pursuit of mergers or reorganizations—had to issue a *Prospectus* in each case in which they had to fully disclose all the affairs of the company in minute detail, including the identity of owners of the company's securities in significant amounts, information about officers and directors, and much more.

Indeed, there was a blanket proviso inherent in all these new laws and regulations that failure to disclose any relevant material fact could represent a failure to fully disclose, which could be held to be fraud and subject to severe penalties.

Other areas of the corporate and securities fields received the same treatment. For example, officers, directors and controlling stockholders of companies had to regularly report any of their own buying or selling of the company's securities, giving full details, and these same principles were applied to other facets of the securities business which could cover many pages of description.

"The "Full Disclosure" principle probably eliminated 50% of former practices which were recognizable as ranging from questionable ethics to downright fraud because the person considering a certain act which might fall into these areas had to consider two eventualities, both having potential for unpleasant results: (1) If I do not fully disclose, I might be discovered and suffer penalties, and (2) If I do disclose, this act will receive immediate attention and the act doesn't put me in a good light and will subject me to criticism or worse. The result was, from this writer's observations of "Street" behavior in many parts of the securities business during the past thirty years, that some questionable practices were virtually eliminated and others severely reduced in their rate of incidence.

The Same Gratifying Procedures May Be on Its Way To Sharply Reduce Political Corruption

Full disclosure requirements in the political sphere would most likely involve an annual report on income, and a "Balance Sheet" report of personal assets and liabilities for all elected officials and all members of the Administration. All fees and other benefits with a cash value above a designated sum would have to be reported. There could be a direct question if the person presenting the report, or any member of his family, or any close associate, had received any consideration for influencing legislation or any other governmental policy in anyone's favor.

Since the *presentation of false or misleading information,* or the *omission of any pertinent information* would be equally punishable offenses, the elected or Administration official leaning to an illegal act of "influence peddling" would have the same quandary as we have just described for those in similar situations in the securities industry. Report the illegal, or quasi-legal act and jump into the pot of boiling water; *Don't* report it, and run the risk of being discovered, with even harsher penalties. Again, we feel there is little doubt that under these circumstances 50% of the illegal acts would be instantly aborted because most individuals would not wish to knowingly walk into such potential difficulties. For those who *would* risk it, the penalties prescribed for false information, or withholding material information, could be brought into play upon discovery of illegal or questionable acts, providing grounds for conviction.

The Role of Harsher Penalties

Newsweek for 2-25-74 had a feature article on "The Good Life in Stir," and the two pictures accompanying the article showed one man reading a book in a comfortable room and another man practicing golf strokes. Both were prisoners! The article commenced as follows: "In the clear, bracing air of the central California coast, the neatly uniformed (denim slacks and shirts) young lawyers, accountants and stockbrokers play a nine-hole golf course, roll boccia balls or plant seedling in their own self-built park. At other times they may jog comfortably around a quarter-mile track or even take their visiting wives and girl friends for a picnic lunch on a pleasant lawn, under gently rippling juniper, oak and eucalyptus trees.

"So pass the more pleasant moments for inmates in the wall-less Federal prison camp near Lompock, Calif., the current residence of Watergate 'dirty trickster' Donald Segretti and 352 other prisoners. At a similar camp called Allenwood in the hills of central Pennsylvania, Egil Krogh, former chief of the White House 'plumbers,' is now serving a six-month sentence. And at Eglin Air Force Base in sunny Florida—a camp prisoners call the "Federal Hilton"—four of the original Watergate burglars . . . were recently released on bond after two months of commodious incarcerations.

". . . The Watergate felons are typical of the inmates at eight minimum-security Federal prison camps, whose clientele consist of heavily 'white-collar criminals' who have been convicted of such crimes as embezzlement and income-tax evasion. At any given time, the roster at these institutions is fairly impressive. 'We once could have formed our own government here,' recalls Eglin superintendent James A. Rhodes. 'We had an ex-governor, two ex-state attorneys general, an ex-senator and Lord knows how many lawyers.' "

Short sentences, and easy-to-take jails are clearly poor deterrents to political crime. So, too, is the fact that many caught at such crimes avoid jail altogether and get off with very little punishment.

George M. Steinbrenner, 3rd, chairman of the American Ship Building Company, pleaded guilty to two Federal charges whose maximum possible punishment was six years in prison and $15,000 in fines. The violation of law was in illegally expending corporate money for campaign contributions. Mr. Steinbrenner did not get six years in jail. Indeed, he didn't get one day in jail but got off with a $15,000 fine—nothing to trouble a wealthy man. The New York Times for 8-31-74 quoted members of special Watergate prosecutor Leon Jaworski's staff as being "incensed at a sentence they considered too lenient. 'It's unbelievable,' one member of the staff said. . . ."

And here is the Wall Street Journal for 4-11-74 reporting: "A well-organized system of bribes and kickbacks uncovered at Grumman Corp. probably will be exposed soon at numerous other defense contractors through the U. S., according to federal investigators. . . ." In Newsday, Long Island, New York, the issue of 7-14-74, we find the story of the conviction of two of the men involved, and here are the sentences: ". . . two weeks in jail and a $5,000 fine for Neile H. Coe, 51, of Greenwich, Conn., and one week and a $500 fine for Joseph G. Mitchell, 42, of Bogota, N. J. . . . Coe and Mitchell are to report tomorrow to start serving time in a federal halfway house in Manhattan, where security is minimal and rehabilitation is emphasized. Each is to remain on probation for the balance of two years. The case involved several hundred thousand dollars in kickbacks for several million dollars' worth of government contracts to print technical military equipment manuals. . . ."

Is there a connection between the "kid-glove" treatment of the law-breaking described above by affluent businessmen and politicians, and the situation described by Clare Boothe Luce in a special article for the New York Times, 8-31-74? We will give our answer (it will occasion no surprise) after the following quotes from a justifiably angry Mrs. Luce: "Government and Federal Bureau of Investigation reports show that between 1969 and 1971 crimes of violence (murder, rape, robbery and aggravated assault) went up 80 per cent. In 1971, 5,955,200 crimes were reported to the police. Only 19 per cent resulted in arrests. *Of those arrested, only 5 per cent were convicted, and sentenced. Of those who went to jail, a large percentage, which included murderers, rapists and child-molesters, were released long before they had served out their sentences.*" (Our emphasis—SF.)

More from Mrs. Luce: "Authorities on crime further aver that at least twice as many crimes are committed as are reported. They estimate that *only one-half of 1 per cent of all the crimes committed result in convictions and punishment*. . . . Crime pays in America. It pays so well, in fact, that it has now become Big Business. Efficiently organized by pros whose prime qualifications are the willingness to commit murder, the crime syndicates annually rake in billions from a wide variety of illegal activities. How many crooked lawyers and corrupt cops work, brief in hand, and hand on holster, with the 'Godfathers' is not a much-mooted question by our bar associations and city governments. They simply prefer not to go into it too deeply. . . ." (Our emphasis —SF)

More shattering statistics from the New York Times for 9-19-74. This account should be read with care. "Calvin Jackson, who is said by the police to have 'implicated himself' in the murder of at least nine women, was arrested in Manhattan 10 months ago on felonious robbery and burglary that *could have sent him to prison for 15 years,* an examination of court records disclosed yesterday. Instead, the 26-year-old former convict *was sent to jail for 30 days* after the felony charges against him and two others were reduced to misdemeanors. He had pleaded guilty in plea bargaining in Criminal Court to the lesser charges. . . . Mr. Jackson's experience is not different from that of thousands of others who yearly pass through the city's court system. In 1973, the year of Mr. Jackson's last arrest, *there were 31,098 felony* arrests in Manhattan, according to the crime analysis unit of the Police Department. Of these, only *545* cases went to trial on the original felony charges. . . . Four out of every five of the 31,098 felony arrests were subject to plea-bargaining and were disposed of at the very outset of the court process. . . ." (Our emphasis —SF)

Who can doubt that the weak-as-water punishment of law-breaking by businessmen and politicians helps produce the shameful failure of true punishment for convicted felons who have produced the crime wave of which Attorney General Saxbe said, in a quotation given on a previous page. ". . . If we go on as we are, there is every possibility that crime will inundate us. . . ."

A Summing-Up

Crime and Corruption on all levels of our society and throughout our political structure is costing very probably a minimum of $130 billion per year in direct fashion, to which must be added the further losses in lowered productivity in every sector of our economy by the shattering of morale of Americans as we have just described.

If nothing is done to roll back the mountain-high, and still growing, tide of Corruption—and no one can deny its existence or extent—then nothing can be done to halt the advance of Inflation.

The fountainhead of civilian crime and Corruption is corruption in government on all levels, since government sets the standards. When our elected officials steal, whether openly or covertly, whether in direct violation of laws or by walking a thin line between legality and illegality, the ordinary citizen, and particularly our young people, conclude that there is nothing wrong with breaking the law, and the door swings open to the rising tide of criminal behavior which now threatens to engulf our values, our way of life.

The trend throughout the country to force "Full Disclosure" legislation on State Legislatures and local political units may well move into the national level, to Congress and the Administration in Washington, making the financial life of each politician an open book, setting forth a clear basis for prosecution with harsher penalties than now exist if relevant information is misstated or withheld, and thereby probably quickly eliminating a large percentage of Corruption merely by the existence of such disclosure requirements.

Such trends, along with other possible means of fighting Corruption should be watched carefully by readers from this point on. A strong attack on Corruption should be counted a most bullish sign for our society, for our economy, and for a resurgent stock market. A failure to make progress, on the other hand, should be a warning sign of much worse to come in all those same categories.

Our Second Guidepost:

Public Employment Policies: Eliminate unemployment, eliminate budget deficits, and meet vital national needs all at the same time—or face endless Inflation.

Budget deficits and heightened money supplies are always represented as "trade-offs" against unemployment. Our society is pictured as doomed to suffer one or the other. Inflation or Unemployment—that's our choice.

It is easy to call this idea nonsense, and prove it, but one must also recognize why, and by whom, this theory is projected, and for what purpose.

In the "feeling good" part of "ballooning the money supply," business is booming, profits are rising, and unemployment and wages are high too. Expansion is the order of the day as business builds new plants and expands inventories. But something else is happening too, precisely because of this boom; another expansion, an expansion of *Debt*. We surely pictured that very clearly in preceding chapters, and it is a completely inevitable part of the cycle as over-optimism and a substantial degree of misjudgment by entrepreneurs accompanies the higher reaches of the boom (exactly as it does in the stock market at a bull market peak.)

What happens, then, when the disease of runaway prices, of Inflation, comes into the picture—also the inevitable accompaniment of this "boom via money injection"? Gradually, a situation develops where there isn't enough money any more to keep the boom going, and as Inflation bites, businesses cut back their expansion plans and find carrying Inventory painful. The Consumer feels the bite of Inflation and must cut back on his buying. It all begins to add up to a slowdown. (Yes, a cycle has two directions, *down* as well as up!)

But what about all those businessmen who expanded unwisely—beyond prudence, by piling on Debt? Deep troubles face them if earnings cannot keep growing to handle interest payments and maturing debt.

Another question enters here. Exactly who is it that has the largest influence in our political structure from the municipality, all the way up to Washington? Frankness dictates that we recognize that for the short-term at least, it isn't the "man in the street." Indeed, at the local level the lawyer-businessman-builder-banker all merge into one image and, in truth, they very often are one and the same, with people in "politics" and "business" often being indistinguishable.

Yes, in recent decades labor unions have become powerful too, and certain citizens groups, from time to time, exert influence, but in comparison with the power of *money,* which is the first characteristic of the political amalgam we have described, none of these have ranked as high in the politics of the post-World War II era.

This political combination, so recognizable at the local level, seems to become less recognizable when Washington becomes its home, and our public servants speak from the floor of the House of Representatives, and the floor of the Senate, and from the offices in the White House. They almost all seem to be just—statesmen. But it only seems that way for many of them. It's necessary to recognize a goodly number of them as being still largely what they were at the local level, the lawyer-businessman-builder-banker, all merged into one image.

Thus it is that when the businessman-builder-banker hurts at home, many politicians in Washington feel it as if it is their own pain—it is—and what would be more normal than to try to assuage that pain. What is the logical relief for the pain of lowered profits, and the fears of unmanageable Debt? More money, of course. Budget deficits and the encouragement of debt *built* the Money Supply, produced the boom and made debt and expansion a wild, exhilarating party. So if the party threatens to end, with vast headaches and much pain—back to more deficits, and call on "Easy Money" to re-fuel the boom.

The only problem with the above solution is that it is so visibly, crassly selfish. The vast majority of citizens cannot protect themselves against Inflation, while the better-off can, so that the solution could never be expressed with anything even near candor, and it never is. Instead, the sobs begin to reach heavenward about the "unemployed." Do you realize, it is said, that if we keep these ruinously high interest rates, and all this talk about a "balanced budget," the Unemployment Rate will reach 6%, 7%, 8%, and there will be suffering and distress?

In truth, few of these gentlemen are all that concerned about the suffering of the unemployed. It's just a much more cosmetic, much more acceptable argument for more Inflation—the Inflation which will ease the pain of the overextended businessman-builder-banker back home.

The above, of course, is recognizable as the "One-Way Keynesianism" which we described at length in our chapters on Inflation, and the large and powerful unions and many political "liberals" are as vociferous in their support of its temporarily pleasure-inducing Money injections as are the representatives of some segments of the business world.

The Proven Failure of Keynesianism

It is a most important quotation—we must repeat it once again because it is so meaningful—from White's "Fiat Money Inflation In France," published in 1876: "Out of the speculating and gambling of the inflation grew luxury, and, out of this, corruption . . . It was first felt in business operations, but soon began to be seen in the legislative body. Bribery of legislators followed as a matter of course . . . Even worse than this was the breaking down of the morals of the country at large . . ."

An all-too accurate description of our country in the past few decades.

The reader should ask himself whether he is satisfied with the United States as it is, its growing crime and corruption, its disaffected youth, its flawed natural beauty? If his answer is—No—and we are certain at this time in our history that few will answer otherwise—then the reader doesn't want Inflation, because the Inflation with all its concomitant effects played the major role in producing all of that deterioration.

And if you don't want Inflation, then you don't want endless budget deficits and you don't want perpetual Easy Money.

Business failures? That's what the private enterprise system is all about. If you expand unwisely and go into debt beyond your limit to support it without a hectic boom, then you go bust, and the efficient producers remain and the inefficient producers depart, leaving a healthier economy for the longer-term, to take care of society's truer needs.

Does this mean we have to accept the suffering of the unemployed—that the "trade-off" is ineluctable—more Inflation or more Unemployment? There is an important distinction here, an *all*-important distinction. While we should not assuage the pain of the overextended entrepreneur—we *cannot* do it without producing all the ills we have been describing—we *can* very much do something about the pain of the unemployed worker. We can give him another job while he is waiting to be reabsorbed back into the mainstream of private employment.

Enter—Public Employment Policies

There are some critics of "Public Employment Policies" who will say that in order to create jobs, you either have to take somebody else's job away (which leaves you at "Square One"), or pay for the additional jobs through budget deficits, adding to the Inflation.

What these critics overlook is the fact that when one takes away the scare tactic of "Boo! Unemployment will grow!" from the "More Inflation" group, we win so many gains in the anti-Inflation fight that we must come out far ahead even if we accept the above premises—which, by the way, we don't.

Remember that if the country gives in to the siren call of "Let's ease money" and "Let's boost government spending" to counter a rise in unemployment, *you feed the inflationary psychology* which itself is responsible for so much of the Inflation—a self-fulfilling prophecy with a vengeance. To state it another way, most economists know that one of the chief ingredients of an Inflationary spiral is the *expectation* that tomorrow prices will be higher, everything will cost more. So, for the consumer, why not buy today, and for industry, why not expand plants and inventory today? And corollary to this is the over-and-over repeated assurance to oneself that "The government will never permit a large-scale business slowdown." Add these together and you have a most powerful stimulus to Inflation. Take it away and you have made great progress against Inflation. Hence, the great contribution of Public Employment Policies.

Where Public Service Jobs Should Be Directed

For decades, the issue of Public Need versus Private Need has sharpened. The late Governor of Illinois and Presidential candidate, Adlai Stevenson, spoke and wrote about "Private affluence amidst public squalor" back in the early 1960's, and what he has referred to has since become worse, much worse. We have enjoyed an ever growing stream of new consumer goods, new consumer services, and new styles of living—houses, cars, appliances, vacations, big-business "sports," motels, fast-food chains, shorter work weeks, growing pensions, numerous other "fringe benefits"—and the list could go on for a long time adding up to what would seem to be the greatest wave of prosperity seen any time, anywhere, for much of the western world plus Japan.

But along with this—to speak of only one evil at this time, and a major one— has come the degradation of our natural surroundings. There are less and less cities where the water from the tap is fit to drink, and the bottled water industry has grown apace. Fewer and fewer beaches are open for swimming and recreation—and many of those that are open need constant chemical analysis to determine whether the bounds of possible disease have been overstepped. The air quality in most metropolitan areas has degenerated to the point where in many areas one must be ready for an "alert" if a period of air stagnation sets in, and sound scientific opinion holds out the possibility that breathing the air of many metropolitan areas may represent the equivalent of smoking a pack of cigarettes a day whether you are a smoker or not. There is no question that the crippling lung disease, emphysema, has had a sharp upsurge in the past few decades, with polluted air the unquestioned culprit, and other respiratory and heart damage are laid at the door of air pollution with substantial scientific backing.

Hectic, pell-mell industrial growth to pour on the consumer goods, calling heavily on the automobile and the truck, has replaced the green countryside which used to be a short distance from every American city, with endless miles of concrete, asphalt, road signs, gasoline stations and fast-food stands. Meanwhile, almost all cities have themselves decayed, losing their previous proud status as purveyors of civilization (the long-term human price for losing our cities must be left to future historians and sociologists to measure and evaluate) becoming filled with decay and ugliness, spawning the virus of crime.

Unfortunately, no one can argue that what we have just described is exaggerated. It has happened, and it is getting even worse. Our private affluence has been measured in terms of consumer goods, to be enjoyed privately; our public squalor has been measured in terms of the loss of the quality of life, to be felt by all of us as a community. Our losses in this area have been severe.

How, then, can there be any question as to the type of government-financed jobs towards which the unemployed should be directed? That direction should be towards reinstating the balance between private needs and public needs by major emphasis on the latter. Such an approach should, in our view, follow the following criteria:

(1) Programs to put the unemployed to work for the benefit of public needs must be carefully planned long *before* the call to find jobs becomes insistent. "Leaf-raking" and "make work" programs are the result of doing nothing until the emergency is upon us. Our economic structure is now so much larger than a few decades ago, with the number of employable people so much greater, and public needs so huge, that adequate planning must precede by a considerable length of time the actual implementation of the specific programs. Once under way, of course, planning is a continuous and ongoing procedure.

(2) Each work program should be of a nature that can expand and contract easily as the need to absorb unemployed from private industry similarly expands and contracts.

(3) The incentive for the now publicly-employed worker to leave the government-supplied job and return to private employment must remain strong by means of setting the income levels of public employment sufficiently below that generally obtaining in private employment when an upswing in the private sector creates employment opportunities.

(4) The work programs should not enter into competition with private industry, but should operate in areas where private industry is not doing the job, for whatever reason.

Let's consider one possible example of such work programs which would fill the above requirements, and it will quickly be appreciated that *many* similar programs are available.

There are now 16 cities, according to the U.S. News & World Report for 8-5-74, where the majority of students and, therefore, probably the majority of citizens, are black. These include, with the highest percentage at the top of the list, Washington, Atlanta, New Orleans, Newark, Richmond, Gary, Baltimore, St. Louis, Philadelphia, Oakland, Birmingham, Memphis, Cleveland, Chicago, Kansas City, Mo., and Louisville. Other cities have very high percentages of black citizens in large areas, even though the structure of the metropolitan areas keep the over-all percentage below the 50% mark. These certainly include New York, Los Angeles, Detroit, Boston and many others.

What is typical of many of the black areas in most of our cities? They are filled with large pockets of housing blight where landlords have abandoned their buildings since prospective rental income had no hope of exceeding taxes, repair and maintenance, to produce a profit to the landlord. Thus, acre after acre of such inner-city areas are boarded-up, festering sores.

In the New York Times for 2-26-74, in a page-one article, we find the following: "Roger Starr, the city's top housing official, fears that housing abandonment—which has been ravaging New York's slum neighborhoods since the middle nineteen-sixties—may become even worse. Mr. Starr, the new Housing and Development Administrator under Mayor Beame, estimated that each year landlords were walking away from buildings containing a total of 10,000 apartments, with tenants subsequently fleeing from most as the ownerless buildings plunge into ultimate decay. . . .

". . . Urban experts . . . speak of the massive population shifts since World War II in which millions of poverty-stricken blacks and Hispanics, many from rural areas, surged to the cities and replaced middle-class whites involved in their own exodus to the suburbs. The change-over generated fiscal and social strains that overwhelmed many cities, and large-scale neighborhood decay leading to abandonment was one consequence, they say.

"George Sternlieb and Robert W. Burchell of the Center for Urban Policy Research at Rutgers University, find that abandonment appears to reflect 'the extensive phenomenon' of the 'disinvestment of private capital in core cities.' Whatever the case, the stark results—at times entire blocks resembling bombed-out war ruins—are hardly captured by the dry treatises of the urbanologists. . . ."

We have no shortage of articles such as one from the New York Times, 1-15-73, headed: "The South Bronx: A Jungle Stalked by Fear, Seized by Rage," with one picture captioned: "Packs of wild dogs, such as this group on Fox Street, pick through the rubble and roam the streets." More recent news articles are similar to this one from the New York Times for 9-2-74: "Suspicious Fires Up in Slums Here; Buildings Looted."

Recall that the previous government programs under HUD (Housing & Urban Development) called for subsidized housing to attempt to meet these problems, where the familiar teams of mortgage bankers, wealthy investors, and construction unions feasted on the taxpayer-billions spread out before them in riskless loan guarantee bonanzas, all the benefits sharp-penciled tax experts could find for their clients investing in "housing," and ever onward-and-upward construction wage scales for the unions (why should builders fight wage increases when the taxpayer so often pays them?).

These housing programs helped to saddle all of us with a goodly portion of the tens of billions of dollars of government-guaranteed mortgage commitments which this writer is certain will haunt future generations, helped to corrupt many public officials and public employees, and enriched many "smart investors," but as for their ability to noticeably hold back the destruction of the central cities and provide decent housing, we would rate the accomplishments of the program as less than zero, because the quotient of corruption and Inflation they produced far outstripped any positive contribution. We have described many of these elements in previous chapters.

Enter, A New Approach

Suppose, now, that the huge needs of the inner cities were married to the "Public Employment" goals we have outlined? Since, as previously stated, there has been an unquestioned "disinvestment of private capital in core cities," government would not be competing with private industry by taking up vital housing needs and neighborhood rescue in a new manner.

First, long-term, definitive and carefully-detailed plans would be set up to train hundreds of thousands of workers in construction skills, as they entered these programs. Areas of greatest housing needs in American city slum areas would be targeted, and enough professional guidance secured from the private sector, as needed, to build new neighborhoods from the ground up. Bulldozers and wrecking crews could level the frightful eyesores now disfiguring our once great cities, and new dwellings, parks, community centers, schools and other needed structures could replace them.

A few great advantages are immediately apparent to such a course of action as we have described, and readers should remember that what we are describing is a *general approach* to areas of "Public Employment" which could be applied to many other types of public needs with similar characteristics.

First, many economists agree that a good part of our unemployment is *structural* in nature. Thus, the June 1972 issue of the Morgan Guaranty Survey: ". . . a basic problem—so-called structural unemployment will remain. The labor force will contain a large number of people who lack the education and occupational skills that are needed in today's job markets. Here, the remedy is an effective manpower training program. . . ."

Gabriel Hauge, chairman of the board of the Manufacturers Hanover Trust Co., and one of the country's wisest economists, in this writer's opinion, had the following to say in an address to the National Association of Business Economists on 9-14-73: ". . . It is widely recognized that the hard core of our unemployment is structural rather than a function of the broad economic aggregates. It consists of those in the labor force who do not have the skills to be employable except at times of extreme labor shortage and, therefore, of rising inflation pressure. . . ."

The unemployment rate for blacks has typically been about twice that for whites in recent years, over-all teen-age unemployment about five times the adult rate, and *black* teen-age unemployment rising to far higher levels.

Since a good part of construction work is, in its nature, simple labor requiring only moderate amounts of training, a "Restore The Cities" program could not only provide jobs for hundreds of thousands of unemployed from the private sector, but also absorb a goodly percentage of the "structural unemployment," helping to sharply cut back the prevalence of drugs, delinquency and crime in the ghetto areas.

How would such a program satisfy the three requirements previously outlined?

These blighted areas are present in every large city in the country, widely dispersed geographically. Building plans could be readied far in advance of the need to call upon them to absorb growing unemployment. Since the needs of the central cities are so huge, these programs could play major roles in any needed area, capable of absorbing any number of unemployed, and providing this employment in the same general geographic area. As previously pointed out, with private capital having fled the depressed urban areas, government-planned community rebuilding would not be taking away jobs or profits that normally would be flowing to the private sector.

Thus, all the stipulations previously set forth would be satisfied by such programs. As communities were rebuilt, immediate benefits would be felt, not only in the "core" city, but in the city as a whole, with the beneficial effects radiating out quickly to the entire metropolitan area. Particularly in the "structural unemployment" which hits minority youth hardest in the poverty-stricken areas, training, income and the satisfactions of having jobs would be available to these young people, with an anticipated reduction in drug use and other anti-social behavior.

The steps we have described above could be utilized with any important public need. To return to another quotation from that speech made by Gabriel Hauge, Chairman of Manufacturers Hanover Trust: "Specifically, why should Government—Federal, state and local—not accept the role of 'employer of last resort?' Many jobs that need doing require little skill but, in our technologically advanced system, cannot be justified economically in the private sector. Such jobs as helping to keep our cities clean, to preserve and to develop our national forest, protect the ecological quality of our continent and many more. . . ."

Editor Malcolm Forbes had the following to say in the 8-1-74 issue of Forbes Magazine: "Revive The PWA/WPA/CCC! Remember them? The FDR programs to put many of the Depression's unemployed millions to work? These 'works' made Our Fathers sulfuric and supplied half the nation's comedians and cartoonists with punchlines about shovel-and-rake-leaners. But they sizably aided in solving the most gutting cancer of that awful early-Thirties era. And, in retrospect, at nominal cost great and lasting good things were done in the arts, in the woods, on the roads, to the streams, in the cities and on the farms of our Land. If unemployment becomes greater, it's a pattern we'd do wisely to repeat—infinitely preferable to, as economist Albert Sommers says, 'massively inflating the economy.' "

Business Week lines up with the same general philosophy in an editorial in its 12-19-72 issue: "But if broad-gauge economic policies cannot provide jobs for a significant fraction of the labor force, what is to happen to these people? In the long run, it may be cheaper, less inflationary, and more civilized to create government jobs for them instead of forcing them onto public charity or into the underworld."

Representative Henry S. Reuss (Democrat, Wisconsin), one of the leading economic thinkers in Congress, wrote a lengthy article for the New York Times Magazine on 7-7-74 which contained the following: "But while job training and placement are vital parts of the fight against unemployment, there must be a job at the end of the road. The fastest and cheapest way to assure jobs is simply to create them through public-service employment. Except for a small budget request this year, Mr. Nixon has dismissed the valuable functions which public-service employment can provide as 'leaf-raking projects' and 'dead-end jobs.'

" 'Dead-end?' The need for the social services which these jobs would provide is greater all the time. Teachers are beaten up in schoolyards for lack of police protection; passengers shake their teeth out in AMTRAK trains because the roadbeds need smoothing out; the water and air we drink and breathe are dirtier every day for lack of pollution-control workers; millions of young mothers are prevented from working because adequate day-care centers just do not exist; health care has become more expensive and time-consuming for want of paramedical personnel. . . ."

Dr. Arthur F. Burns, chairman of the Federal Reserve Board, has come out in favor of having a public service employment program in readiness, as has William Fellner, of the President's Council of Economic Advisers.

Social and community needs are so vast that additional large-scale programs could be thoroughly planned and "in-place," ready to absorb any number of unemployed who have fallen out of the private sector. Remarkable progress is being made in developing more efficient sewage treatment plants, and in building new types of solid-waste disposal plants which produce electricity at the same time they dispose of garbage. "Recycling" plants in conjunction with all waste disposal systems can reclaim valuable raw materials.

But all these vital community needs have been held back by lack of adequate funding. The needs here are without bounds, and geographically spread all across the country. Tying them into Public Employment programs, managed by companies with the necessary expertise, will be as value-producing as the tasks of rebuilding central cities. And if we begin to think of a list of community work programs which can restore our country to environmental health, it is quite obvious that the list would be a long one, and *all* productive of great social value as well as creating the necessary jobs when called upon to do so.

Milton Friedman's Objections To Public Employment Programs

In a Newsweek column, 9-2-74, Milton Friedman spells out some criticisms of Public Employment Programs in what we consider to be a short-sighted manner, and when we understand *why* they are short-sighted, we come to a much better appreciation of the truly large contributions these programs can make. Dr. Friedman first states: "It would, in the first instance, provide jobs for the unemployed, which seems all to the good. But where would the funds come from to pay their wages? If the funds came from reducing other government expenditures, new government employees would simply replace other government employees with no gain in total employment and very likely a loss in efficiency. If the funds came from imposing higher taxes, the taxpayers would have less to spend, which would reduce the number of persons they employ directly or indirectly. New government employees would simply replace persons employed in the private sector. 'Make work' would replace employment that met the private demands of taxpayers."

Let us immediately say that there are two lines of action which must precede the successful institution of Public Employment Policies, without which they will not work to any satisfactory degree.

(1) Political Corruption *must* be sharply reduced. Many programs set up on Federal, State or local levels heretofore, to accomplish many worthwhile ends, have suffered from widespread corruption with a good part of the funds provided misused, as we have described with the housing program, for example. On the local level, our files are replete with examples of blatant corruption. If the move for "Open Government" makes

progress, then Public Employment Programs will make progress. Without one you just cannot succeed with the other.

(2) Substantial funds will, in truth, be needed to plan, initiate, and carry forward such "public need" programs as we have described. They should be funded, in large part, by sharply reducing the billions of dollars in subsidies for special interest groups now traded back and forth in Washington. How many taxpayers realize that one of the most costly games in Washington today, and the most corrupting, is, "You vote for my favored interest's subsidy and I'll vote for yours?" Indeed, the most positive contribution an American President could make for our country would be to forcefully announce: "All right, Senators and Representatives and the Special Interests you represent: At the count of three, I want everybody's hand out of the Treasury's pocket!"

Both (1) and (2) are linked with the major problem of Corruption—remember, Corruption IS The Inflation—and if we do not make major inroads against corruption, starting in Washington because that is where we can make the fastest progress in giving guidance to the whole country, then literally none of our problems are soluble. And if we do make substantial progress, much more than enough money will be available for funding Public Employment programs. One need only recall the very realistic estimates we made on previous pages about the potential size of the bill for corruption on the Washington level.

But it is in the area of straight economics that Dr. Friedman is most in error. If he will recall that inflationary expectations are the chief propelling power behind the rising Cost of Living, as everyone rushes to invest and buy today in the confident expectation that tomorrow the price will be higher, then he surely must agree that government refusing any longer to prop up an overblown economy will do wonders towards sharply diminishing inflationary pressures.

Government *cannot* do the above without being prepared to absorb the higher numbers of unemployed which will come from calling a halt to our inflationary spiral. But the costs of underwriting Public Employment Programs will be much more than made up by the sharp gains we make against a truly ruinous inflation.

If we begin to move decisively on two fronts, hitting Corruption hard and cooling off inflationary expectations with Public Employment Programs as our necessary backstop, then our country will once again begin to make *great* forward strides.

But a *third* front must also be opened with vigor, and we come to that now.

The Third Vital Guidepost

The Automobile Culture: Bring it back to reasonable proportions, or find all other problems insoluble.

Historical Note

In 1933, two Americans, Karl Twitchell and Lloyd N. Hamilton, arrived at the port of Jiddah on the Red Sea, in Saudi Arabia, to ask for oil concessions for the Standard Oil Company of California. It was granted and, thus, Aramco was born.

Six years later, the Damman Number 7 well gushed oil, and much more world history was made than anyone could realize at the time.

A Parable

In the limitless sands of Arabia, sometime in the late-1930's, there gathered the most important desert sheiks. In their flowing robes they stood about and talked animatedly about a new event for Arabia, the discovery of oil. Everyone sensed that something important had happened, but no one knew quite what it would mean. There then stood up one sheik obviously recognized as a leader, and gestured for silence.

As a hush came over the gathering, a curtain was pulled aside and there entered, walking with deliberate steps, a man who was obviously of great age, and who seemed to tower over the entire assemblage, not merely with his tall and spare frame, but with a strange and indefinable personal force that seemed to fill the entire ceremonial tent.

The hush gave way to murmurs. "Greetings To The Wise One," said a Sheik.

"You honor us with your presence, Wise One," said another.

The Wise One held up a hand until there was again silence, and then he spoke.

"I have heard of the talk among you about this new discovery of wealth in our sands of Arabia, about the oil. And you are saying that you will charge a good price, and that finally some riches will come to our people. But you will not do this because The Great One above has had much planned for our people for very long. At this time you will allow the oil to be taken as if it were merely grains of sand. The oil will be cheap—very cheap."

Again there were murmurs—murmurs of amazement—and the words of The Wise One continued.

"Everything is written. Nothing happens by chance. Seventy-five years ago, on a small farm in the State of Michigan, in America, there was born one who was called Henry Ford. No one knew, how could they, that the Will of The Great One Above had been served. That this infant, this Henry Ford, was to be the instrument by which our people would one future day take up again their strides towards glory. When this Henry Ford would be in but his early twenties, the hands of two men of Germany, Gottlieb Daimler and Karl Benz would be guided by The Great One Above to conceive the first vehicle to get its power from gasoline. At 30 years of age, Henry Ford would build his first automobile, powered by such an engine, and in 1903 the Ford Motor Company would come into existence. Henry Ford would believe that it was Detroit businessmen who gave him the $28,000 he needed to begin."

The Wise One paused, and the assemblage knew without being told that the mention of the birth of the Ford Motor Company called for a moment of respectful silence in thanks to The Great One. The Wise One continued.

"Henry Ford, knowing not at all where his idea came from, believed that every family should own an automobile. There came a vehicle called The Model T which was destined to multiply to fifteen million in number by the time the event called The Great Depression came. By that time, also, another star would have appeared in the firmament. It was called General Motors."

Another pause as The Wise One looked into the distance. General Motors was not a name to be taken lightly.

"After the Great Depression, some ten years later, will come a Great War. The automobile manufacturers will use The Great War to build up their plants with government need for cars, trucks and tanks. When The Great War will end, the peoples of the western world will be afflicted with a great thirst, a thirst for automobiles. It will become a frenzy, dictated by unknown forces. No one will know where the force would come from, but it will work its way. In America, in five years after The Great War, by 1950, there will be 40 million automobiles, one to every four inhabitants of that rich land. And but ten years later there will be 63 million automobiles, one to every three inhabitants. When the year 1970 comes, the numbers of automobiles and trucks will be *one hundred million . . .*"

The voice of The Wise One rose in some excitement with this magic figure, and it was matched by sounds of wonder among the sheiks.

"But patience, there are many marvels to precede this magic figure," continued The Wise One, as he again held up his hands for silence. "The wonders worked by The Great One will move to the halls of the Congress of the United States. There will be a man named George Fallon. He will be a member of the Democratic Party of America from the State of Maryland and in 1956 he will think that he himself has conceived the idea of taxing every gallon of gasoline used on American highways for one purpose only—to build more highways for more automobiles. A magical concept will come into being; something called The Highway Trust Fund, to hold all these dollars for more highways, and more highways only."

The Wise One seemed to grow even taller as he held both his

hands upright, in prophecy: "The highways will produce more cars. And the more cars will produce more highways, and it will never stop. And you will soon see how from this our greatness will evolve, ordained from above."

The Wise One paused, in reverie, perhaps contemplating the magnificence of what he was seeing in the future, and then went on.

"Another magic set of numbers will spring from the head of Representative George Fallon and others who will work with him. *Many* others working with him in the Halls of Congress who will have at their side, encouraging their thoughts, the builders of roads, the builders of houses, the owners of land, the makers of gasoline, of steel, of rubber, of glass, and many others —all of whom will see before them dazzling profits to come. That set of magic numbers will be 90-10."

The Wise One paused to observe the mystification on the faces of the Sheiks in front of him, who could not imagine what 90-10 might mean.

"The magic numbers 90-10 will be contained in something called The Federal Highway Act of 1956 which will be introduced by Representative George Fallon of Maryland. In this Federal Highway Act of 1956—surely a great work ordained in a far higher place than Washington D.C.—the States will pay only *10c* of each $1 spent for highways and the Federal Government will pay *90c*. The new highways will begin multiplying under the two magic formulations from on high of The Highway Trust Fund and 90-10 and the eyes of many greed-filled local politicians and businessmen will open wide. Their hearts will quicken as many schemes for profit will tumble over one another, so many schemes will there be, and so irresistible.

"In tens of thousands of new miles of highway, costing billions of dollars each year, flowing from the magical combination of the Highway Trust Fund and 90-10, the highways will move out from the cities into the countryside, followed by numbers of city dwellers who will suddenly see a mirage of a house with a white picket fence and children playing on a lawn. And they will not know from whence the mirage came. And The Great One Above will cause more ideas to spring forth in Washington —ideas about 'stimulating' housing with easy credit guaranteed by the government, and 'stimulating' the buying of cars and much else by the same easy credit. The word 'stimulate' will be on every politician's lips, and they will not stop to wonder how the word had suddenly appeared, thinking only of all the favors they could do for grateful road builders, home builders and land developers back home. Corruption will begin, grow and then flow like the waters from a well and Look Magazine will devote an entire issue to telling the story of this corruption springing from the billions of dollars from 90-10. The story will be told in endless detail—but no one will pay any attention.

"With easy credit for new homes, and all the money desired for new Highways, the trickle of urban dwellers leaving the cities will become a larger stream, and then a flood. As the cities begin to empty of middle class people who pay taxes, the balance will begin to move towards minority peoples who take their place in the city's dwellings. These minority peoples, formerly bowed down by discrimination, still will not be able to fully earn their own way. Instead of paying taxes to support the city, many will themselves need support of every kind. The cities will begin to deteriorate, further pushing the middle class people into the countryside, now called 'suburbia'—a magical word whose origin we should well realize. As the urban centers become more and more bereft of taxpayers, and more and more filled with people needing support, the deterioration will continue to quicken, which will continue to quicken the flow to the suburbs, which will quicken the city's deterioration further.

"More Highways—More Cars—More Highways—On and On" magic formula will thus be joined by "More Suburban Flow —More Urban Deterioration—More Suburban Flow—On and On" magic formula, and much homage do we owe The Great One Above for these magic formulas for the foundations of our future greatness will thus be set in place by them, as you shall soon see."

In the slight pause that followed, one Sheik chose of speak, but with great deference. "If I may be permitted to ask, Wise One, what, in the meantime, will have been happening with our oil?"

"Happening?" said The Wise One. "What will be happening with our oil? The giant oil companies of the West will be filled with joy. They will not believe their good fortune, for everywhere in our sand that they will place a well, and even in the nearby waters, oil will spout in an endless stream. Our oil will indeed become as plentiful as the grains of sand in the desert."

There was great animation among the sheiks at this splendid prospect to come. "And we will be very rich" they all said, almost as one.

"Not yet," said The Wise One. "In the eyes of The Great One Above it will not yet be time. The oil will still be as cheap as those same grains of sand. The wondrous things I have yet to recount to you will require cheap oil, very cheap oil. Keep your peace, yet, and listen."

The Wise One continued. "As the new Highways begin to multiply, pushing out from the city in every direction like the spokes of a wheel, the ribbons of concrete will run alongside the ribbons of steel on which are running the railroads. The automobiles on the Highways will begin to take passengers away from the railroads, and the trucks on the Highways will begin to take freight business away from those same railroads. The Highway Trust Fund and 90-10 will make the ribbons of concrete cheap for the automobile and the truck, but the railroads will still pay heavily for their ribbons of steel. The ribbons of concrete will multiply and flourish. The ribbons of steel will begin to disappear, year-by-year. As the ribbons of steel decline, the tens of millions of Americans who will by then dwell in suburbia will find more and more that they have only one means of transportation left—the automobile."

The Wise One ceased his speaking to fix the Sheiks with a burning look. "Oh, my brethren, can you comprehend what this will mean for oil? In America alone, from the 1955 number of 56,000,000 cars—the year before the magic of The Highway Trust Fund and 90-10—we will go to 67,000,000 automobiles and trucks by 1960, then to 82,000,000 by 1965, and by 1972 there will be *One Hundred and Eighteen Million*. Americans will put Ninety Five Billion Dollars into their cars alone and will be traveling One Trillion Miles each year by car. Eighty-Two of each One Hundred Americans will go to his work by automobile, and Fifty-Six out of each One Hundred cars will carry only the one American. One out of Six Americans will depend upon the automobile for his livelihood, in building and caring for the automobile and all its needs. Automobiles will become a national frenzy, and no one will question where this frenzy might have come from, but only know that the love affair between a man and his car must come above all else.

"The highways will engulf the countryside in concrete and asphalt and rip through the cities, destroying whole neighborhoods as the cities try without success to accommodate more and more cars. And always the answer will be: If there are too many cars for the highways, build more highways.

"The fumes from the cars will make the air unhealthy to breathe, and the noise and confusion will be everywhere, while the cities and the countryside together sink into ugliness. The cars will become bigger and heavier, and great death and maiming will be the lot of Americans. In 1955, 38,000 will die in that one year alone on the highways in car accidents. In the one year of 1960, 49,000 will die, and 56,000 in the year of 1972. In that year of 1972 not only will 56,000 Americans be killed by automobile accidents, but two million more Americans will be disabled by automobile accidents, and the losses from it all in that one year will be Seventeen Billion Dollars.

"Each morning, in every suburbia surrounding every city in the nation, motorists will enter their cars by the tens of millions, and these cars will move like snails in endless streams to their jobs. In the evening, they will again enter those cars, and will creep with agonizing slowness to their homes, arriving exhausted and dispirited.

"Yet, the American will continue to love his car above all else and be willing to pay the price in each detail that we have described. And, speaking of price, it is time, my brethren, to tell you of the remarkable change in our fortunes which will begin in that year of 1973."

Each of the sheiks strained forward, intent upon missing not a single word.

"For all these years, the rest of the developed nations will have been following the precise path of America, and together the appetite of their cars and trucks for oil will mount at an incredible rate. When Mr. Fallon shall conceive the magic of The Highway Trust Fund and 90-10 in 1956, only 15 million barrels of oil will be used each day. But by 1960 this will have become 19 million barrels, by 1965, 27 million barrels and by 1973, the demand for oil will be *45 million barrels of oil each day*.

"With all other means of transportation abandoned or weak, with each country dependent upon the automobile for the magic word of the 1970's—'growth'—the whole economy, the entire way of life will, with no possibility of return, be inescapably tied to the automobile . . . to Oil."

The assembled Sheiks knew without being told. They rose as one and proclaimed together: "And THEN we shall raise the price of our oil!"

The Wise one permitted himself a small smile. "Yes, my

brethren. And *then* we shall raise the price. For 35 years we shall have permitted our oil to be taken at very low prices while cheap oil allows the automobile to change the face of society, alter its every way and become such an overwhelming part of The New Life of Highways and Suburbia and economic 'Growth' that there will be no escape. Suddenly, it will be found that most of the world's oil is right here where we are standing, my brethren, and that the world cannot live without this oil. We will be able to charge any price we choose and we will become very, very rich—so rich that you, my brethren, cannot even imagine it—so rich that all the rest of the world will work for us that we may give them the oil for their beloved automobiles."

The Wise One raised his eyes and his arms heavenward in grateful thanks, and the assembled Sheiks followed him in this gesture. Wondrous were the ways of The Great One!

From Parable To Iron Reality

The stock market is such a picture of devastation, as we write, and our country, indeed the world, faced by so many grim problems, that we chose to begin this part of the discussion on the all-important "Automobile Culture" in a lighter vein, although each and every fact in it corresponded with reality.

To see *how* much reality is involved, consider the fact that in October 1973, before the oil embargo, crude oil in the Persian Gulf sold for about $2 a barrel. By March, 1974 the price had quadrupled to *$8* a barrel. In that same month, in the New York Times Magazine for 3-24-74, Edward R. F. Sheehan described a conversation he had with Saudi Arabia's Minister of Petroleum and Mineral Resources, Sheik Ahmed Zaki al-Yamani, in which Mr. Sheehan said he asked the Sheik "What price would you consider reasonable?" The article went on: " 'We can get any price we want,' Sheik Zaki said with a sigh. 'There were proposals at Teheran that we raise the posted price to $23 a barrel. If we made it that high, we'd earn $100 billion in a year. The world would soon run out of Eurodollars . . .' "

Receipts by the "OPEC" countries (Organization of Petroleum Exporting Countries) consisting of Saudi Arabia, Kuwait, Abu Dhabi, Qatar, Iraq, Iran, Algeria and Libya, with the three smaller participants, Nigeria, Indonesia and Venezuela, ran as follows in approximate figures for the years shown:

1970	$ 8 billion
1971	$12 billion
1972	$15 billion
1973	$23 billion
1974	$85 billion (estimated)

Illustrating the stranglehold by these oil producing nations on Western Europe plus Japan (we will shortly consider the special responsibility devolving on the United States because of its

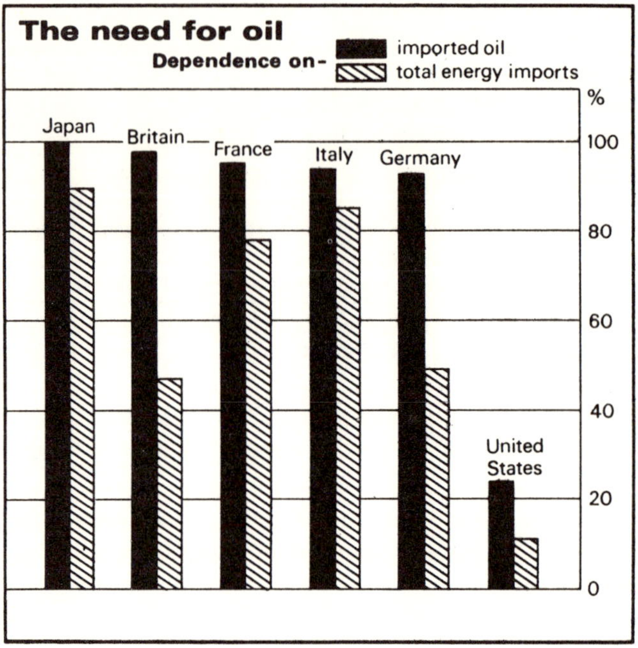

relative independence of foreign energy) consider the chart shown, courtesy of Euromoney Magazine for March 1974. Every country named is almost totally dependent upon oil imports, except the United States.

Now let's turn to an analysis by a top world organization as reported in New York's Newsday, for 8-5-74:

"The Arab oil-producing bloc could have more than $1 trillion to invest in the United States and other countries by 1985, according to a confidential study by the World Bank. That is 10 times the total $100 billion book value of current U.S. investments overseas and 100 times the value of all the gold now held by the U.S. government.

"Specifically, that report states: 'The accumulated reserves of all OPEC countries could rise to $650 billion in 1980 and about $1,200 billion ($1.2 trillion) by 1985 . . .' Although accounting for only 10.8 per cent of the total world population in 1972, the World Bank notes that the organization's countries had 78 per cent of the world's proven oil reserves, 62 per cent of oil production and about 85 per cent of the world trade in oil—giving them economic leverage far beyond their size . . ."

Looking at these figures we can hardly call "alarmist" a headline in U. S. News & World Report for 7-29-74 as follows: "Will Western Allies Go Broke Trying To Pay For Oil?" In the body of the article was such foreboding as: "British Prime Minister Harold Wilson reports that the importing nations are finding the impact more severe than 'any event in their histories short of involvement in war.' " And "Italy seemed to be heading towards bankruptcy, with its trade deficit in the first four months of 1974 running at an annual rate of 13 billion dollars, about half of it resulting from spending for oil. Fear was widespread that the nation's economy would collapse despite introduction of austerity measures . . ."

Of course, there is not only this incredible shift in world money assets to consider, but also the ruinous Inflation and the imperiled economies of the western world. How close a link is there between these developments and the Federal Highway Act of 1956?

As close a link as anyone could imagine, in this writer's opinion, and let us look first at the chart of growing world demand for oil, shown courtesy of The Money Manager 2-11-74.

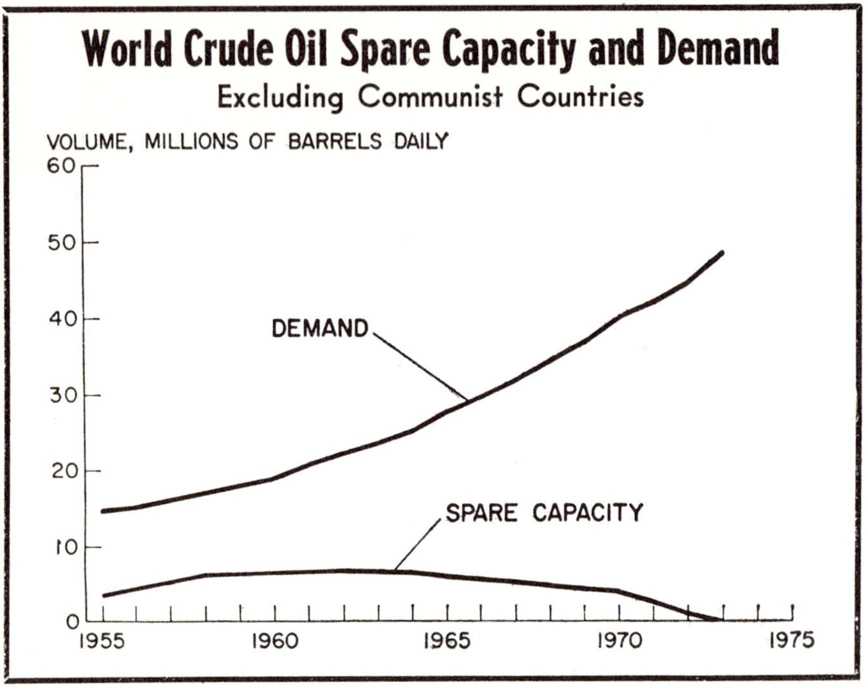

Where did this enormous better-than-tripling demand in just 18 years come from? There can be no question that it came mostly from the shift to suburban living based on the automobile. Did the dominance of the automobile arise via a conscious plan, or did it happen accidentally? The answer to that question, we believe, is not all the way over to the "conscious plan" part of the equation, but it certainly isn't *far* from it. When the Federal Highway Act of 1956 and 90-10 came into effect and the first highways began to be built under its provisons, it undoubtedly took some time for the extent of the bonanza to completely enter the consciousness of all those who would benefit, and that list was long and included many of the most powerful groups in the country. At the top of the list of those who benefited would have to be the manufacturers of automobiles, trucks and buses.

Just note the growth in the number of cars and trucks on the road from 56,000,000 in 1955 to 118,000,000 in 1972. Right alongside would be the oil companies selling gasoline and oil products to those cars and trucks.

The political power would come into the picture when one considered the enormous "pork barrel" made available to State political machines who had 90% Federal money to work with. The opportunities for profits on a magnificent scale were endless. Knowledge of where the highways would go could enable the buying up of land at cheap prices and sale at high prices. And not only for the highway and the interchanges themselves, but land for housing developments and shopping centers. Letting the contracts for actual highway construction was hardly of smaller dimensions. The over-all potential here can best be appreciated when we realize that between 1956 and 1970 alone *$196 billion* was spent on highway construction, including both Federal and State expenditures.

Also right at the head of the line—it's difficult to know who benefited most in dollar terms—would be the mortgage bankers, housing developers, builders, and construction unions as the almost limitless demand for new housing, shopping centers, theatres, motels, fast food restaurants and all other elements of the new "Automobile Culture" burgeoned.

The trucking associations and the influential trucking unions grew mightily as the magnificent superhighways spread out across the nation, and we will soon have some figures on this to discuss.

The manufacturers of steel and iron, rubber, plastic, glass and other metals developed large markets from auto production. Insurance companies, service station associations and a long list of additional beneficiaries would be added if it were useful to take the time to enumerate them.

But this is hardly necessary, for we have already specified a line-up of economic power so immense that there has been nothing to equal it in the history of our country. Nothing even comes close.

In our previous section on Corruption we pointed out the following: "Exactly who is it that has the largest influence in our political structure from the municipality, all the way up to Washington? Frankness dictates that we recognize that for the short-term at least, it isn't the 'man in the street.' Indeed, at the local level the lawyer-businessman-builder-banker all merge into one image and, in truth, they very often are one and the same, with people in 'politics' and 'business' often being indistinguishable." We then went on from the local level to paint a larger picture. "This political combination so recognizable at the local level, seems to become less recognizable when Washington becomes its home, and our public servants speak from the floor of the House of Representatives, and the floor of the Senate, and from the offices in the White House. They almost all seem to be just—statesmen. But it only seems that way for many of them. It's necessary to recognize a goodly number of them as being still largely what they were at the local level, the lawyer-businessman-builder-banker, all merged into one image."

Economic power and political power were indeed largely one, contributing enormous thrust to the growth of "Suburbia" and the "Automobile Culture," productive as they were of the greatest stream of potential profits seen in modern times, by any economic measuring tools.

Can we conclude that Greed and its bedfellow Corruption played a large part in the growing predominance of the automobile? In the opinion of this writer we most assuredly can, and one of the clearest evidences of this is the manner in which public transportation and a competing mode of transportation, the railroad, were all left to wither on the vine in what this writer can only conclude was a deliberate policy on both Federal and State levels, with the aim of *enhancing* the flow of profits from the "Automobile Culture." Let's look at a few supporting statistics here. We previously reported that between 1956 and 1970, a total of $196 billion was spent on highway construction including both Federal and State expenditures. As against this, only *$33 billion* was spent in the same time period for all other forms of transportation, including the U. S. Coast Guard. Even this doesn't tell the real story of how little was made available for public transportation and the railroads—both competitors with the automobile and the truck.

William B. Johnson in Business Week for 12-15-73 had some statistics which cast a brilliant light indeed on what the above expenditures of $196 billion on highway construction really meant. Wrote Mr. Johnson: "As a nation we are spending some $28.2 billion of public monies in 1973 for support of transportation in one form or another. *More than 86% will have been spent for highways, 10% for air, 3.7% for waterways, but less than one-tenth of 1% for rail.*" (Our emphasis—SF)

There was another type of political favoritism for the "Automobile Culture" which about *doubled* the $196 billion spent for highway building, and we devoted a good deal of time on it in previous pages. This involved *housing* and here we need only put two facts together. First Fact: Total Mortgage Debt outstanding went from $130 billion in 1955 to $564 billion in 1972. Second Fact: Government Agencies have guaranteed somewhere near $200 billion in mortgages for housing, without which shunting of financial burden to future generations the housing boom could never have developed such proportions.

So the pattern is clear. Provide taxpayers' money to build the highways from the city to the suburbs and then encourage home buying by government underwriting of home mortgages and other benefits. Add the two together and the middle class citizen leaves the city, buys a home in suburbia and then, of course, buys a car to get around because *that is the only form of transportation available.*

This was spelled out in so many words by an illuminating series of articles by Robert A. Caro in the New Yorker Magazine beginning 7-22-74, on Robert Moses, whom Mr. Caro called ". . . America's greatest road builder." What was described for New York State was true of most of the rest of the nation. Said Mr. Caro:

"To build his highways, Moses threw out of their homes tens of thousands of people. He tore out the hearts of a score of neighborhoods—communities the size of small cities themselves, communities that had been friendly places to live in, vital parts of the city which made New York a home to its people.

"By building his highways, Moses flooded the city with cars. By systematically starving the subways and the surburban-commuter railroads, he swelled that flood to city-destroying dimensions. By making sure that the vast suburbs, rural and empty when he came to power, were filled on a development pattern relying primarily on roads instead of mass transportation, he insured that that flood would continue for generations, if not for centuries."

Two charts, used courtesy of U. S. News & World Report, tell the story better than mere words, one from the issue of 3-13-72 telling of the decline in public transportation, or mass transit, and the other from the issue of 3-4-74 telling of the similar decline in Rail commuter traffic.

MORE CARS . . . LESS PUBLIC TRANSIT

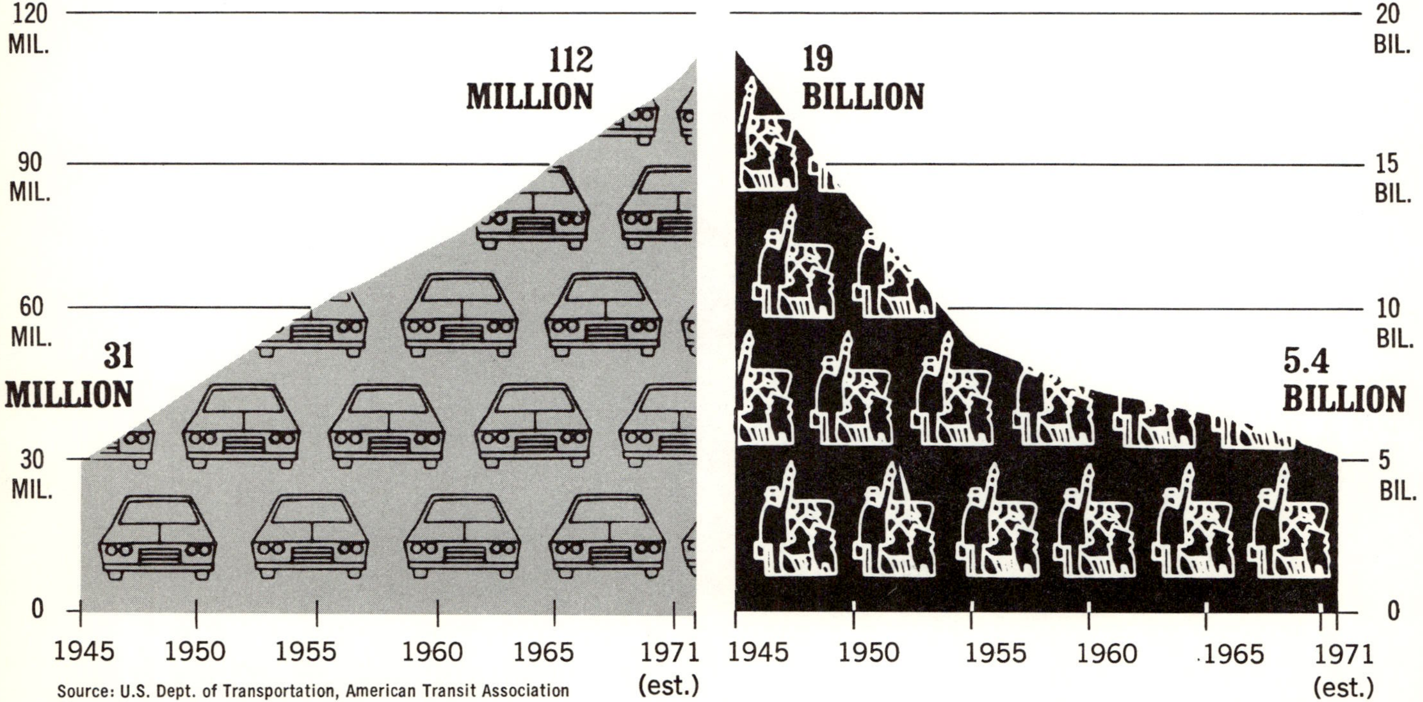

Source: U.S. Dept. of Transportation, American Transit Association

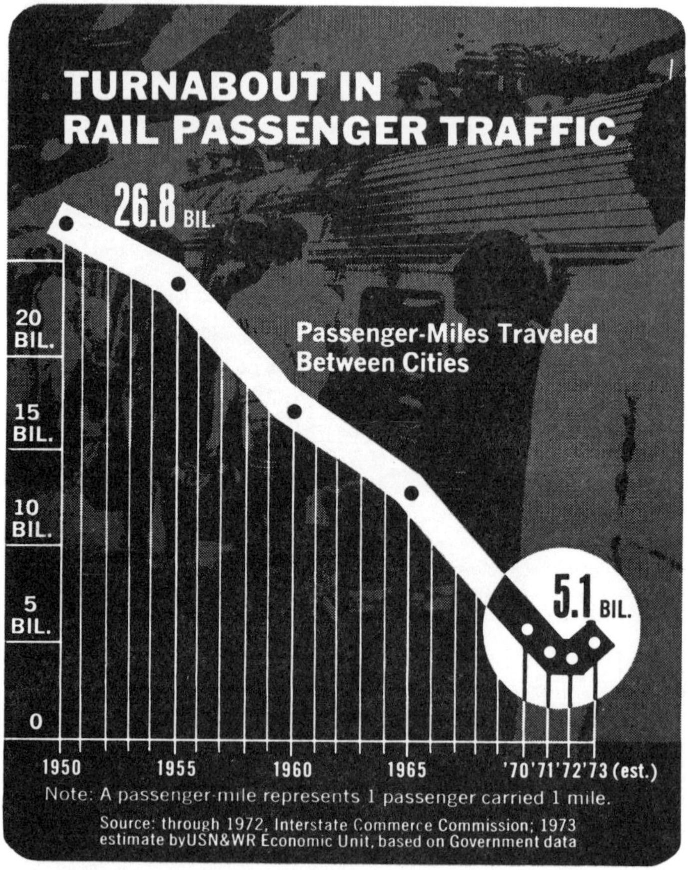

Of course, trucks too were cutting deeply into railroad freight business at the same time, particularly in the higher-profit type of carriage, hurting the railroads much more severely than a mere examination of relative "ton-miles" statistics would indicate.

1974—Suburbia is Supreme, The Car is Supreme

Already by mid-1971 the pattern had been set for the United States and the "Automobile Culture" sat firmly astride the entire country. A Fortune Magazine Editorial for July 1971 said ". . . More than 80 per cent of all passengers and freight, measured in dollars, rolls on rubber tires, and almost half of the volume is produced by private cars. The U. S. boasts a motor vehicle for every 1.9 people, and the ratio of cars to population is still on the rise. Our society hasn't yet really digested the meaning of those numbers, much less come to practical terms with their consequences . . ."

The Automobile Culture—The Energy Wastrel

One does not have to be a scientist or an economist to draw very relevant conclusions from the two following different pictures:

(1) A line-up of 500 automobiles with an average of 1.6 persons in each car, and

(2) A railroad commuter train carrying 800 people.

Which is going to use less energy? The train, of course. Indeed the accepted estimate is that a train will use about *one-sixth* the energy required by the automobile to move the same number of people, and there is something near the same great energy advantage for railroads in moving freight, as against the truck.

But many observers only see half the point in such a comparison. The true dimensions of energy-wasting by The Automobile Culture are far, far larger. It is true, to start with, that in 1970 automobiles in America used 66 billion gallons of gasoline, which was equal to 30 per cent of total petroleum consumption in the country. But those automobiles had to be *produced* and *stored* and *serviced.* It has been estimated that to manufacture an automobile uses up 150 million Btu (British thermal units) of energy, which is itself equivalent to 1,100 gallons of gasoline. It has then also been estimated that to ship the car to the dealer, and for the dealer to prepare the car and then sell it (itself a large industry in this country) uses up as much energy as it took to produce the car.

In order to get the gasoline to run the cars, oil fields must be discovered, drilling undertaken, and resulting oil transported to refineries, and finished products transported once again to sales outlets and sold.

Highways must be built and maintained for automobiles to run on, kept clear of snow in the winter in the colder parts of the nation, and policed.

The ramifications of paying for our automobiles in terms of energy—*all* that we have itemized above takes huge amounts of energy—are large indeed and if the reader stops for a moment to think of service stations, garages, insurance agents and the like he will find it hard to finally come to an end of such a list. Thus it is that when we see estimates that about 25 per cent of total United States energy consumption is consumed by the private automobile, directly and indirectly, we have the feeling that even this figure is still not high enough.

For example, when two million people are disabled in one year from automobile accidents, they must be disentangled from the twisted metal of their automobiles, transported to hospitals or other medical facilities and treated, many for a long time. How much energy is consumed in this? (And you can't measure human tragedies in terms of energy, but we are treating energy in cold, mechanical terms.)

Is this writer to be accused of becoming macabre if he should mention the energy used by hearses followed by lines of automobiles carrying the mourners while they bury the 56,000 Americans killed in automobile accidents in 1972 alone?

Does air pollution have an energy cost? The United States Public Health Service estimated when there were 90,000,000 vehicles (there are now 118 million) that these 90 million vehicles annually poured out the following emissions into our air:

66,000,000 tons of carbon monoxide

1,000,000 tons of sulphur oxides

6,000,000 tons of nitrogen oxides

12,000,000 tons of hydrocarbons

1,000,000 tons of dustlike matter

Every one of the above pollutants results in dirt and disease on a truly incredible scale.

What is the energy bill for the continual clean-up from the sheer dirt of these pollutants? How many times has the reader wiped something out of doors and come up with a black dust cloth? It is your air pollution made visible, the same, by the way, that goes on your lungs, and much of it from the automobile.

What is the energy bill for treating lung cancer, emphysema and heart disease which medical scientists all agree are involved in major ways with automobile-produced air pollution?

If the reader is a "typical" American, he loves cars, as does this writer. The automobile is an incredible instrument for personal pleasure. Else, how could it have changed western civilization! But we are also responsible human beings who can finally see evils when they have grown so large that one can no longer shunt them aside.

The Solution Is at Our Fingertips

The growth of the Automobile Culture and its companion-in-arms, Suburbia, could never have reached their heights of overweening power if public transportation and the railroads had not been continually undercut by those in political power who were looking for the unprecedented profits we previously described.

If much of America now finds itself completely dependent upon the automobile, but also finds itself in this year of 1974 unable to any longer pay the energy bill for that dependence, then there is only one path to take: as quickly as possible—a "crash" program is already years overdue—create the public transportation which was denied and starved by the highway builders for the past twenty years. And as fast as public transportation becomes available, bring the private automobile down to a level of use where its demands on wealth, on energy, on life and on health are on a much more rational basis.

The Automobile and the Central City

No one questions that many motorists enjoy driving to their jobs, or on shopping expeditions by private automobile. But when the energy cost becomes prohibitive and the whole economic situation of the country becomes adversely affected, then such privileges can be put aside if alternative means of transportation are provided. This is an idea which is spreading quite rapidly. The New York Times 7-29-73: "Rome, July 28—All private vehicles were barred today in a large area of central Rome in the first step toward a gradual closing to traffic of the noisy and polluted city center. . . ." New York Times, 6-29-73: "Ban on Cars in Main London Shopping Street Is Big Hit." Business Week, 5-26-73: "In what may be a preview of things to come in major U.S. cities, Milan, Italy, recently closed off eight square blocks of its downtown business and shopping district to automobile traffic. The restriction is part of a widespread attack against the air pollution and traffic congestion that are strangling cities around the world. . . ." New York Times, 11-15-73: "The Netherlands Takes a Car-Less Sunday in Stride; Amsterdam, the Netherlands—The people roller-skated, bicycled, strolled six abreast or trotted on horseback through the streets of their cities today. They rowed in their canals, held sitdown picnics in the middle of empty superhighways and went to soccer games in 19th century coaches drawn by mane-tossing steeds. . . ." New York City, Tokyo and other cities have experimented with similar plans for banning cars from central cities for specific periods as harbingers of things to come.

In the United States, with air pollution from automobiles in the cities, particularly carbon monoxide, defying most means of control, strict regulations are being formulated which this writer feels are quite inevitable in their coming. Reported Newsweek for 6-25-73: "For nearly three years, Environmental Protection Agency staffers in Washington and officials in more than a score of major cities had refined the details. Their goal: a series of stringent anti-pollution measures, including traffic controls, designed to meet the requirements of the Federal Clean Air Act passed by an enthusiastic Congress in 1969. Last week, the EPA finally published its proposals, and it was immediately clear that, sooner or later, the impact of Federal law is going to produce some major changes in the habits and life-style of millions of city-dwellers.

"In announcing the proposals, acting EPA administrator Robert Fri said that they conceivably could result in an absolute ban on private automobiles in some cities, a $5-a-day tax on off-street parking in central Boston, strict limitations on gasoline sales in areas like Los Angeles and northern New Jersey and much greater use of car pooling and mass transportation just about everywhere. . . . Said Fri: 'We are basically attacking the problem by asking people to change their habits—their long-standing and intimate relationship with private automobiles. This is a fundamental change, but it is the only one that will fundamentally work.' "

How Do People Get Around With Automobiles?

A quick answer to that would be: Very well! If it were not for the lack of good, alternate means of public transportation, not too many would find good things to say about the congestion, fumes and frustration of driving and parking in most central cities. On the island of Freeport, in the Bahamas, most people are very poor and do not own automobiles. Yet, they must get to work, mostly in the hotels spread around the island, and they have to get to and from the central shopping areas. This is accomplished with great efficiency by numbers of mini-buses continually making round-trips throughout these areas. In the case of any central city imaginable, suppose these mini-buses would be running on every third street, east-west and north-south, or whatever "grid" was appropriate. To get anywhere at all you would simply take one mini-bus to the cross street needed, and then take a mini-bus on that street to your destination. For those who wanted a more personal (but much more expenive) ride, taxis would be available. Can one imagine the savings if such means of transportation eliminated all private cars in a central city? Savings in fuel, in lives, in sharply-lessened dirt and disease from pollution, in traffic policemen, in street maintenance and repair. And in addition to the savings, can one imagine the restored beauty of city living without the noise and confusion of the continual traffic jams?

Other straws in the wind—here is an article from The Wall Street Journal for 2-12-74: "Seattle's Free Buses Revitalize Downtown Area; They Save Gas, Cut Traffic and Spread Goodwill; Seattle—The other day a visitor from California climbed aboard a bus here and was baffled when the driver clamped his hand tightly over the fare box and refused to take her money. 'It's a free ride,' the driver explained. After a moment, the woman stammered: 'But nothing's free.'

"Perhaps not many things are free anymore, but bus rides in downtown Seattle are, and they have been since last September. The free transportation, or 'Magic Carpet Service,' as it's called, is a one-year experiment subsidized by the city that, because of its popularity, promises to become permanent.

"Transit officials say eliminating fares has almost doubled the number of downtown riders to about 11,000 a day. Merchants are ecstatic because they say it's stimulating business. And city officials, although they haven't any firm statistics to support their contention, believe the free service has fulfilled one of its main goals: it has eased traffic in crowded downtown streets and thereby reduced air pollution. And, although the plan came into being before the energy crunch set in, it apparently has yielded the additional dividend of helping hold down gasoline consumption.

"An urban mass-transportation expert at the U.S. Department of Transportation calls the service 'a forward-looking program that has been extremely successful.' He says other cities will probably copy it in some form."

The New York Times, 6-11-74: "Justices Back a High Tax to Cut Downtown Parking; Washington—Cities may levy a high tax on private downtown parking lots and garages in an effort to reduce urban congestion and divert commuters to public transportation, the Supreme Court ruled today. The decision specifically involved Pittsburgh, but it was expected to encourage other major cities to restrict the daily influx of cars into crowded areas by forcing parking fees up through the imposition of new taxes. . . ."

Getting Around Suburbia Without the Automobile

For the commuter from suburbia to the central city, subsidized and improved commuter railroads and high-speed express buses along highway lanes set aside exclusively for their use are already pointing the way to "can't miss" alternatives to the private automobile where travel to the central city is concerned. *Intra*-suburban transportation has developed a shining hope, already quite well proven, in what is called the "Dial-a-Bus" concept. Here is how an excellent article in Business Week for 10-13-73 described this important development:

"Dial-a-Bus, an infant transportation concept that attempts to combine the convenience of private automobiles with the low seat-mile costs of buses, is showing signs of catching on. Born in the U.S. five years ago with a federal research grant to the Massachusetts Institute of Technology, Dial-a-Bus—or Dial-a-Ride, Telebus, or some other label signifying door-to-door bus transportation—is now in service in more than 30 U.S. communities, plus others in Canada, Britain and Sweden.

"Last week a Rochester (N.Y.) Dial-a-Bus conference that had been expected to attract 150 participants actually drew 333. Users and prospective users swapped success stories and predicted that their baby would be the future saviour of public transit.

"MIT Professor Daniel Roos, father of the concept and chairman of the conference, says that from three to five new systems are being started every month. The first system was launched in 1971 in Regina, Sask. Each subsequent one has been a success, and none has yet been abandoned. . . .

"The objective is to get people where they want to go by public transit without putting them to the inconvenience of walking to a bus stop, waiting for a bus, possibly transferring to another bus, and then walking to the destination. With Dial-a-Bus, the patron phones a control center that tells him when to expect a bus at his door, and then dispatches an 18-seat to 25-seat bus to pick him up along with other passengers. Once aboard, the rider is carried to his exact destination. . . ."

A picture accompanies this article showing a clean, comfortable, uncrowded mini-bus, with the heading "Dial-a-Bus went over so big in Ann Arbor (Mich.) that residents voted to subsidize it."

Another article, ten months later, illustrates the fast development of this concept. The New York Times, 8-22-74, headlined: "A California County Will Give Dial-A-Ride Its Widest Use Yet; San Jose, Calif.—One day next month, Mrs. Sydney Tyler expects to pick up a telephone in her San Jose home and call 287-4200. She will be among the first customers for one of the nation's most ambitious efforts yet to entice motorists out of their automobiles. It will be, by far, the largest and most elaborate example of a fast-growing concept in mass transportation called Dial-A-Ride.

"In a project being watched by leaders in other low-density, auto-oriented communities across the nation, 1.2 million residents of Santa Clara County will be offered direct door-to-door bus service between their homes and any other point within an urban area covering 240 square miles, most of the county. . . ."

Refuse to Scale Down the Automobile Culture?

This writer has no doubt that many readers have been shaking their heads while reading all the foregoing and saying something like: "Americans aren't about to give up their automobiles," or, "Our whole economy is built around the 'Automobile Culture.' Take it away and there will be collapse." They have large support in many places in this type of reaction! In many places, from many different types of individuals, where we have projected the ideas just discussed in the preceding pages, most reactions have been negative, the reasons typically built around the two just mentioned of the unwillingness to change, and feared severe economic reactions. As we write, the President of General Motors has declared his faith in the American love for the automobile, saying that our country is built on high mobility via the personal automobile and it isn't going to change. Some might find the words "high mobility" les than descriptive in the midst, say, of the morning and evening traffic tie-ups, but even apart from the obvious bias of a General Motors executive, here also is Denis Healey, British Chancellor of the Exchequer, saying, as reported in The Money Manager, 10-7-74: ". . . If we were to limit our imports of oil to what we can pay for year to year by exports we would create bankruptcy and unemployment on an unprecedented scale. We must accept deficits on our balance of payments of a magnitude hitherto unthinkable and we must finance those deficits by borrowing."

Borrow from whom? The U.S. News & World Report, in its issue of 10-14-74, totaled up the 1973 bill for oil imports by the United States, Japan, West Germany, France, Britain and Italy, and came up with a figure of $28.1 billion. In *1974,* the estimated bill for oil imports will be *$85* billion, according to the same article, with the United States alone footing the largest percentage with $25 billion. And, in 1975, the estimated bill for oil imports will be *$120* billion, and in 1980, *$170* billion.

Match these figures against the most recent estimates we have that the official reserves of the *entire world* are now about $165 billion! A few years of importing oil at current price levels and there *are* no reserves. It will have all moved to the OPEC countries, with the great bulk going to the relatively small Arab countries who simply cannot use anywhere near that amount of money in their own economies—not even a noticeable percentage of such amounts.

This brings us to the fantasies now making the rounds that these funds will be "recycled." Recycling these currencies by the oil producing countries could be accomplished by them in only two ways: (1) Buying property and other assets such as stock interests in companies, and (2) Lending the money back to the countries who bought the oil, or being really "Good Samaritans" and lending money to the LDC nations (Less Developed Countries).

This writer doesn't take much comfort in the thought of getting back those oil currencies through purchase of western assets. We happen to be writing these words in our Los Angeles office and today's Los Angeles Times has an 8-column page 1 streamer: "Kuwait Buying SS Catalina." This huge steamer which carries summer passengers to Catalina Island on a famous run is virtually a California landmark, but the sheikdom of Kuwait is reportedly ready to put $5 million on the table and take possession. A few months prior to that, the same sheikdom took a few oil dollars out of its purse (a mere $17.4 million) and bought a whole island off Charleston, South Carolina. Also recently, Arab purchase of a good part of London's famous "City," some of the most famous real estate in the world, was in negotiation.

As for purchasing interests in Western companies through stock purchases, Iran recently purchased a 25% interest in a division of Germany's Krupp Works with little noticeable drain on her remaining wealth, and Senator Metzenbaum has taken an interest in what might happen in our own country (we applaud his diligence) and has reminded Americans that, as reported in the New York Times, 7-20-74: ". . . it would cost the oil states only about 75 per cent of their excess dollar earnings *in a single year* to acquire a controlling interest in eleven giant American corporations including A.T.&T., Boeing, General Motors, I.B.M., I.T.T., U.S. Steel and Xerox. . . ." (our emphasis—SF)

Some observers wave away thoughts of such possibilities as being "unrealistic," even "hysterical fears" as the current head of the Securities & Exchange Commission was reported to say, but the plain arithmetic of the inevitable pile-up of the world's wealth in the hands of the oil producing countries has to be matched by equally plain arithmetic demonstrating why this wealth cannot buy up a good deal of the property and productive power of the West, rather than falling back on a "Don't worry—it isn't going to happen" type of response We ourselves take a *very* serious view of such potential, particularly in view of the fact that a world-wide economic slump following on the heels of disasters which have already overtaken most securities markets could put innumerable assets on the bargain counter to be picked up for a proverbial "song." To the extent that this happens because the West clings passionately to its right to take two or three hours each day to get to and from work in mile-long lines of bumper-to-bumper traffic, one might find some humor in the situation. (We're listening, but somehow we don't hear any laughter.)

Now to the fantasy that the oil producing countries will "recycle" their new wealth back to the countries from whence it came. Firstly, the countries that need it most are poor credit risks—Italy is at the head of the line here, with India probably next—and we would rate the chances of the oil producing countries generously taking such risks as being quite close to zero. An alternative has been suggested in quite a few quarters (it's the current favorite) that the recycling should be via some form of U.S. Treasury-guaranteed bonds to be sold to Saudi Arabia, Kuwait, etc., whereupon the *United States* would take those funds and lend them to the poor credit risks. With one-half our fiscal stability eroded, this would take care of the other half!

The fact is that the meaning of the "arithmetic" of the transfer of wealth from the developed countries to the oil producing nations is stark and cold and could be highly destructive. Heavy trade deficits for all our important trading partners cannot have any other result than but to send world trade tumbling down a toboggan slide with severe economic repercussions. World-wide depression must be counted a real possibility if we do not seek real answers to our overblown "Automobile Culture."

Fortunately, the answers are far easier to come by than one might imagine from hearing the "stone-walling" that erupts when one mentions touching a single automobile "right." What would happen, for example, if we reduced automobile driving by, say, 10 per cent. There would quickly be a glut of oil in the world markets and the price of oil would start to come down. Six million barrels of oil daily are being used by automobiles in the United States alone. If every major city in the western world plus Japan banned the automobile from the central city, how much oil would be saved? We don't have the answer to that question, but the scale of oil saving would be huge.

Donald E. Weeden, a prominent and very astute investment banker, and a respected thinker on broad societal problems, testified before the Federal Energy Commission in the Fall of 1974 and made many cogent points which we consider to be of great value. Said Mr. Weeden to the Federal Energy Commision:

". . . You have scheduled something like 43 days of public testimony with literally hundreds of witnesses. When it is all done, I sincerely hope the Federal Energy Administration will have the courage and integrity to march into the Oval Office and report in plain language to our new President that there is little prospect of the United States becoming independent in energy as in peace or prosperity. . . .

"It may not massage bureaucratic egos and it may sound like rank heresy to those experienced in empire building, but my first suggestion is that you downplay the Project Independence slogan and rename your agency the Federal Energy Conservation Administration, with the emphasis on conservation. That is where the true priorities lie. . . ." (EXACTLY RIGHT — SF)

"Privately, you might adopt Mohammed Ali's motto: 'float like a butterfly, sting like a bee.' Before the present session on Congress ends, float over to Capitol Hill with a well reasoned bill imposing steep, progressive luxury taxes on automobiles based on weight and horsepower. . . .

"Motor vehicles are the worst wasters of energy. You know it and I know it. Ergo, that is where you should focus your attack. That is what you should be preaching to every other agency of government and to the American people. . . .

"I am talking about basic strategies already mapped out to reduce the staggering numbers of private cars caught in traffic jams each morning as workers, one to a car, struggle to get to and from work. The Federal Energy Administration will prove its mettle when it has the guts to enter the Highway Fund fight and help reverse the foolish policies which give us highways we do not want and deny us the mass transit we need."

When you begin to look for solutions based on sound principles of *conservation,* those solutions are remarkably easy to find. The pleasures of automobile driving for recreation are best assured by sharply reducing the role of the automobile as private transportation to and from work, in the central cities, and in a considerable amount of suburban travel which can be handled by such systems as "Dial-A-Bus," which are capable of much greater development from their current rudimentary forms.

Having thus sharply cut down on the most energy-wasteful aspects of our "Automobile Culture," we will be giving very visible leadership to the rest of the world. They will quite inevitably follow our lead and the resulting *huge* savings in oil consumption will very quickly reduce the problem of the oil producing countries to *much* more manageable proportions.

Readers, in our opinion, should henceforth be watching with utmost care what steps are being taken to refashion "The Automobile Culture" in this country to a more reasonable design. If good progress is made, better things are in store for our way of life, for the world we must inevitably lead, for the longer-term health of our economy — and as a consequence of *all* the foregoing factors, for the future sharp betterment of the stock market.

If entrenched political and economic power (we do not underestimate their strength and determination) prevent much movement in these directions, then multiplied troubles lie directly ahead in every category we have mentioned.

A Summing-Up

The Greatest Stock Market Opportunities in Forty Years

We alerted the reader in the "Author's Foreword" to the fact that this book on "Fortune Building In The 70's" was going to be one-third stock market and two-thirds Economics, completely justified by the fact that as "Economics" had helped this writer anticipate these dark days of late-1974 by at least two years, the historic profit *opportunities* which are now littering the stock market floor will be followed to greatest advantage by the reader *only with the full knowledge of those same Economics* as they tell their continuing story in the days directly ahead.

Let us now describe the scope of the opportunities in Warrants which are opening up, and we will relate it to current market expectations after we once again go through the basic "arithmetic" of a Warrant opportunity as it relates to the superlative high-leverage opportunities now in process of completion and ready-to-go state.

The largest Warrant profit in market history occurred with the Tri-Continental Warrant, and while through the 1950's and 1960's it seemed doubtful to this writer that we would ever again see a profit opportunity of such scope, the multiplication in the number of Warrants to the highest peak in market history, combined with the most severe market bust since the legendary 1929-1932 decline, has brought a duplicate of such action much closer to reality; and even if we get only part of the way towards such a result, we cannot imagine any reader who would be made unhappy by such a short-fall! Let's look at the instructive arimetic of the Tri-Continental Warrant.

In 1942, at the bottom of a discouraged market, after a long decline, Tri-Continental common (a well-known, closed-end investment trust) was selling on the New York Stock Exchange for 75¢. Since each Tri-Continental Warrant was the right to buy 1.27 shares of common for $17.76 per share, or $22.55 for the 1.27 shares, the price of 17.76 seemed so far away from the 75¢ market price for the common that the Warrants were considered almost worthless by demoralized investors and were selling on the then New York Curb Exchange (now called the American Stock Exchange) for but 1/32nd or 3-1/8¢ per Warrant). If that seems like a ridiculous price for anything to sell at, we can point out that as we write there are dozens of Warrants selling for a few pennies and many more dozens approaching that low estate.

Now, every bear market in history has had an end, and been followed by a bull market, but this writer has 30 years of professional market experience in knowing that in the thoughts of the great mass of panicky investors at such lows, a bear market will never cease going lower and lower, and this is where the high leverage for a Warrant originates—in the "throwaway" price of Warrants at market bottoms, because the emotional reaction of the investor is that there just isn't ever going to be a higher market again.

Of course, those investors in 1942 were completely wrong, just as the ever-lower-and-lower thinking of today will be proved wrong at the proper time, and from 1942 on, Tri-Continental common commenced a steady upwards climb that reached a climax in 1969 with the common stock at an adjusted high of *72-3/4*. (Quite a difference from 75¢!)

Now let's look at the remarkable Warrant "arithmetic" which reflects the "leverage" always to be found from bear market lows to bull market highs, and to appreciate it fully we will assume two $500 investment going into Tri-Continental common at 75¢ per share, and the other $500 investment going into Tri-Continental Warrants at 3-1/8¢ per Warrant.

At 75¢ per share, $500 will buy 666 shares of Tri-Continental common. When Tri-Continental common reached a high of 72-3/4 in 1969, the 666 shares were worth 72-3/4 x 666 or $48,451.

At 3-1/8¢ per Warrant, $500 will buy 16,000 Tri-Continental Warrants. Remember now that each Warrant represented the right to buy 1.27 shares of common stock at $17.76 per share, or $22.55 for the 1.27 shares. Those 1.27 shares of common, when the common touched 72-3/4, were worth 1.27 x 72.75 or $92.39. The right to buy $92.39 worth of common for only $22.55 msut be worth a minimum of 92.39 minus 22.55 or 69.84.

The actual high for the Warrants on the American Stock Exchange in 1969 was 75-3/4, including a small premium over actual exercise value. The fact that the Warrant sold at a higher price (75-3/4) than the common (72-3/4) reflected the fact that each Warrant was the right to buy 1.27 shares of common.

Now, 16,000 Tri-Continental Warrants at 75-3/4 are worth $1,212,000, and let us re-state the leveraged action of the Tri-Continental Warrant compared with that of Tri-Continental common stock, from the 1942 low to the 1969 high.

$500 invested in Tri-Continental common had appreciated to $48,451

$500 invested in Tri-Continental *Warrants* had appreciated to $1,212,000

Tri-Continental Warrants had advanced 20 times faster than Tri-Continental common.

It will be recalled that R.K.O. Warrants, from the 1942 low to the 1946 high, also moved ahead about 20 times as fast, as the common, causing a $500 investment to appreciate to $104,000 in those four years.

The Many Different Levels of Warrant Profit Opportunities

In previous pages we described a Tenneco Warrant moving ahead 5 times as fast as its common stock in just a few months, and how the Tenneco Warrant was actually less speculative than its common stock, promising to show much greater profit on an upside move than its common stock, dollar for dollar invested, but actually providing less risk than the common stock on the downside! This conclusion always surprises many investors, habituated to consider Warrants only as radical investments, sheer speculations. But go over the simple Warrant "arithmetic" in that Tenneco example and you will see that these conclusions are indisputable.

As it was with Tenneco Warrants in the 1970's, so it was with Hilton Hotels Warrants in the mid-1960's (5-1/4 to 105), United Air Lines Warrants in the early 1960's (4-1/4 to 126), General Tire & Rubber Warrants in the 1950's (4-1/2 to 205) and many more examples could be given of leveraged Warrant profits from bear market lows to bull market highs and, indeed, at *any* level of the market cycle, since individual Warrant opportunities can now arise at any time because of the sheer increase in the number of Warrants trading.

The last point is the most important! At the times of the Warrant examples cited in the 1960's and 1950's there were only a few dozen really important Warrants trading, while today there are about 350 Warrants trading with a greater number than ever representing long-term "Calls" on top companies. Combine this with a stock market decline more pervasive and destructive than any since the 1929-1932 debacle and you have a scale of Warrant opportunity which exceeds anything seen thus far in stock market history.

Much will depend on the actual bottom reached by the general stock market, and as we write these words (mid-October, 1974) our technical studies do not as yet indicate a definitive bottom, but with so much destruction already wrought, a bottom could begin forming at any time.

In the Publisher's Foreword, excerpts from our advices given in the pages of the investment service of which we are Editor (The R.H.M. Warrant & Stock Survey + Stocks Under 10) were given, up to 6-21-74. Let us bring these up-to-date with two additional excerpts which will give our evaluation of the market and the economy up to 10-4-74.

New York Stock Exchange

New York Stock Exchange's Composite Index

WEEK ENDED OCT. 4, 1974

Chart Courtesy of The New York Times

14 8-2-74: ". . . Very importantly—probably the *most* important thing we were trying to get across to subscribers for more than two years now—we have been pointing out each step of the way that an additional leg in the market decline could see *sharp* additional losses in already decimated stock and Warrants. For how low is low when emotion takes over? And that is exactly what has happened in the past few weeks. We said just a few issues ago that many low-priced stocks and low-price Warrants could drop by another 25% to 50% with another intermediate downturn in the general market, and that is exactly what happened . . . Here were *Amerada Hess-La. Land Warrants* selling early June at 6.25, now 3.25, down an additional 48% in about six weeks. Here were *Carrier Warrants* in that same week selling at 1.87, now 1, down an additional 46%. Here were *Chrysler Warrants,* again in that same week, selling at 4.62, now 3.00, down an additional 35% in the same six weeks, and there are so many more examples. Low-price stocks? There is such widespread carnage here that there is no point in giving any examples . . . Meanwhile, what has happened to all those investors who looked upon the early-June rally as a heaven-sent opportunity to take positions at 'low' prices? They are locked in to the extent that they have committed their capital, while the same opportunities are probably available 25% to 50% lower! It all adds up to the necessity to continue to watch and wait and to *study* developing opportunities, *not* jump into them . . ."

New York Stock Exchange

New York Stock Exchange's Composite Index

WEEK ENDED OCT. 4, 1974

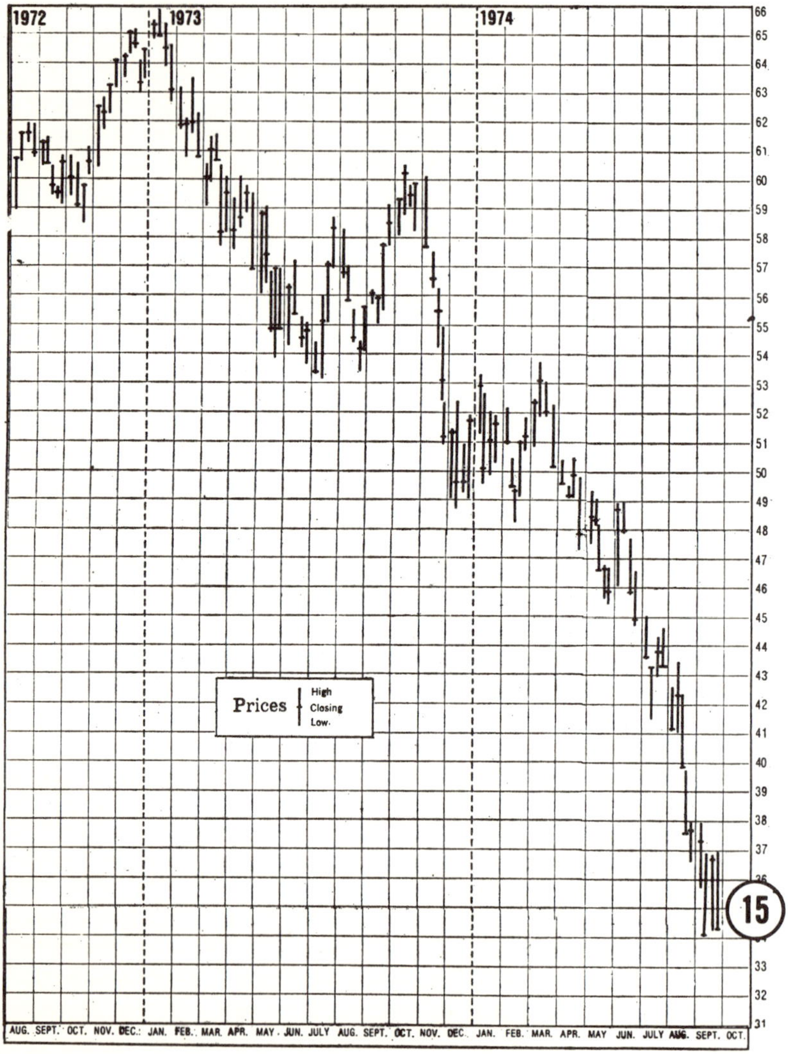

15 **10-4-74:** ". . . What emphasizes the need for continued patience in awaiting proper timing for commitments—*none* are recommended at this time in this Survey—is the "dropping the other shoe" character of today's economy, with its as yet difficult-to-define consequences. There are soft spots in the economy already, but most of the economy is still running along at a good clip, trying to make believe that nothing has really changed. What will happen, in our view, is the onset of a heightened pace of bankruptcy and liquidation to drive home the real severity of our problems. For those companies with unmanageable interest burdens on a debt which can also become unmanageable in early maturities, selling off of assets and inventories will quicken, and what we must then await is any signs of a "domino effect" in an economy suffering severely from a "liquidity problem" which was thoroughly visible more than two years ago. Indeed, we described its development in these pages in rather full detail, first in our "Money Watch" essays in 1972, and again in early-1974 in a statistic-filled series of essays, but it has come to the attention of newspapers, television and periodicals mostly in just the past few months because *now* is when the crunch is beginning to really take hold.

"So we face two question marks at this stage: (1) Will a deflationary spiral gather strength at this point, with gathering liquidations and bankruptcies, and (2) will the stock market soon prove to have *over-discounted* these developments? Not only must subscribers *wait* for the answers instead of trying to guess what the answers will be, but with most technical indicators pointing to more stormy weather for the general stock market, continuing to keep available cash in safe havens (short-term, high-grade credit instruments) is just as valid a policy as it has been for the past two years. When the profit opportunities begin, with a turn in the general market, they will be with us for *years to come,* in our opinion, in a steady stream. But the necessity for proper timing is now more crucial than ever because the last downside whirls of a bear market can be *particularly* devastating."

The Continuing Decline in Warrant Prices

It is useful at this time to update the plunge in many individual Warrants by taking the lists on pages 26-27 and giving the most recent lows since those pages were written:

Avco Warrants	18.00 to 56¢
Carrier Corp. Warrants	13.00 to 75¢
Cott Corp. Warrants	4.00 to 31¢
Continental Ill & Rlty Warrants	14.00 to 31¢
Holiday Inns Warrants	31.00 to 31¢
Instrument Systems Warrants	3⅛ to 10¢
International Tel & Tel Warrants	12.00 to 25¢
Jones & Laughlin Warrants	3.00 to 13¢
LCA Warrants	18.00 to 50¢
Loew's Warrants	39.00 to 2¼
National Industries Warrants	16⅜ to 50¢
Ozark Airlines Warrants	7.00 to 38¢
Rollins International Warrants	6¾ to 13¢
Starr Broadcasting Warrants	20.00 to 25¢
Triangle Pacific Warrants	8.00 to 25¢
United Brands Warrants	56.00 to 43¢
Zayre Warrants	12.00 to 25¢

Only one Warrant—that of Loew's—is selling at $1 or better in this updated list where there were many before, and more of the Warrants have sold below 50¢ and below 25¢ as well, with *much* company in this throughout the Warrant list.

Thus it is that "The Greatest Stock Market Opportunities In Forty Years" have been created by the destructive 1973-1974 market decline thus far, and since our technical studies do not as yet indicate that a market bottom has been definitely reached, the creation of "penny Warrants" particularly can broaden and deepen in ensuing additional market declines, or even during a sideways base-building period. The potential for more R.K.O. Warrant-type moves ($500 to $104,000) has increased sharply. The possibilities of even such historic profit moves as occurred with Tri-Continental Warrants ($500 to a startling $1,212,000) have certainly moved closer to reality. And such leveraged profit moves as we have described for Tenneco Warrants, General Tire & Rubber Warrants, United Airlines Warrants and Hilton Hotels Warrants from previous market cycles have every possibility of being duplicated many times over as a later market resurgence takes place.

Timing remains of crucial importance, but that the opportunities have been created cannot be doubted.

Additional Author's Note Regarding the Warrants Sector

The scale of potential Warrant profit opportunities is so large after the disastrous market plunge in the past two years that we have confined ourselves in this book to pinpointing *the main target area* for Warrant investment, which is in high-leverage low-price Warrants. There are a number of approaches to Warrants which are additionally valuable, such as Short-Term Trading with Warrants, and "Hedging" with Warrants, involving being Long common and Short Warrants, or the *reverse,* to produce profits with very small risk if carried out correctly. And there are some technical factors you should be aware of with Warrants, such as the ability, with some of them, to use senior securities of the same company at full face value in exercising Warrants, thus producing a valuable lowering of the effective exercise rate.

We did not wish to take away from the full impact of the *major* attraction of Warrants in today's market by going into these subjects in this book. Instead, we discuss all these points, and give all the relevant information, in a special supplement which the publishers have agreed to send to you, the reader, at no additional charge, simply on request. Included also will be a full statistical presentation of all Warrants actively trading in today's market, and this writer's Ratings on each Warrant in terms of leverage potential and relative reward and risk. A fuller description of this supplement, including the address of the publisher, will be found in the "Author's Foreword" at the beginning of this book.

The "Cornucopia" of Low-Price Stock Opportunities

In thirty years of professional stock market involvement as analyst, writer and trader, we have never seen such an array of undervalued low-price stocks as exists in today's market. The reason that such came about is in one sense typical of all bear markets—the tendency to sweep *all* stocks onto the market floor indiscriminately, without regard to intrinsic assets and present and potential earning power. The result is that we find value-filled, promise-filled stocks selling at very low prices right alongside similiarly-priced stocks which do not even deserve *those* low prices!

But the emotional disarray of investors became so pronounced in 1974 that these "typical" tendencies became even more accentuated with the result that some of the finest companies in America today find their stocks selling in the "low-price" category! From former levels of 40, 50 and even higher, hundreds of such stocks are now selling around the high-leverage $10 area, with many of them having sold down to the $5 level and even lower in some cases.

With analysis of "Fundamentals" giving us the ability to select the most value-filled of these opportunities (as you will recall from previous chapters), and with the "Four-Step Trading Technique" enabling us to add the all-important virtue of proper *timing,* the reader should be able to benefit for quite a number of years from a continuous flow of such low-price stock opportunities when the stock market concludes its decline, creates a sideways base, and then commences a new bull market which itself could prove to be one of the strongest seen in market history (more about this below). In the additional material to be sent to the reader at no charge by the publisher, at your request, we will be including an updated list of the 50 low-price stocks which we regard as having the greatest promise, and additional analysis as described in the "Author's Foreword."

As with Warrants, so with Low-Price Stocks, the 1973-1974 market disaster has created "The Greatest Stock Market Opportunities in Forty Years" and the reader should use every effort to benefit from the unique "Fortune Building" character of those opportunities.

A Final Word to the Reader—WATCH Our Three Guideposts

The three "Guideposts" we outlined in previous chapters presented quite clear alternatives for national policy in each case. We presented our reasons for believing that the course of the actions our nation will henceforth take in each of the three areas will substantially determine whether we are headed for lengthy and deep economic recession plus mounting world disorder—and further plunging securities markets; or whether we will, surprisingly quickly, right the economic ship of state, enjoy immediate large political and societal dividends, give firm leadership thereby to all of our allies in the non-Communist world suffering from "carbon copy" problems—and in doing so create the basis for a new bull market of quite probably historic proportions.

If you wish to capsulize our current crisis—and it is indeed a deep and threatening crisis—imagine a family across the street where the children, instead of carrying the day's garbage to the trash container, tossed it at will across the neighbors' lawns, created a din night and day, tore up the family's belongings and generally vandalized the neighborhood, without any restraint whatever from their parents. Aghast at such permissiveness, how long would it be before you would call in the authorities?

The above is no fantasy. It is a quick word picture of our own society since the end of World War II. In the past thirty years we have managed to sadly mutilate and distort our currency, our national habits of "work and save," the air we breathe, the water we drink, our cities, our countryside, our morality, our public safety. Readers, of course, are fully entitled to disagree with us, and to regard this picture as totally overdrawn. They can, indeed, point to "Gross National Product," and to an indisputable fact that as a whole we have more "things" (cars, houses, television sets, etc.) per capita than ever before in our history—and so do the British, the French, the Italians, the Germans, the Japanese and others in the non-Communist world.

We could, and we do, in the first instance ask the reader to look beyond "things" to the less-easily-defined "quality of life." Think about those two categories and weigh them against one another, and consider the surprising and indisputable fact that as our "affluence" mounted, so did crime, environmental degradation, the disaffection of our youth, disrespect for the police officer, the judge, government itself, the law, our basic institutions.

But there is a "second instance," too, and it is in the nature of a grim joke played upon us by history. To attain those rising statistics of "Affluence" to which "hell-bent for election" politicians could point to demonstrate what they "have done for the people," we had to fuel the engine of growth with—*Debt*. Ever larger and larger doses of Debt.

These policies and their perils were evident right from their start to those who cared to look.

In 1949 we wrote a study on a then little-known section of the stock market entitled "The Speculative Merits of Common Stock Warrants," and we already then devoted a few pages to statistics on the rise in Debt, which had the following conclusion: "Pump priming and deficit financing are permanently enthroned. The conclusion is inevitable. We are in a long-term *irreversible* trend of currency depreciation. . . ." (original emphasis)

When we became Editor of The R.H.M. Warrant & Stock Survey in 1952 we followed, in the pages of that Survey, the remarkable increase in the rate of new Debt, year-by-year, which did indeed produce the great bull market 1949-1966, reflecting the dizzying heights of Gross National Product which we were scaling. But in the late-1960's our warnings became rather shrill (we regularly inflicted reams of statistics on our subscribers) and in our Survey issue of July 7, 1972 we undertook a full analysis with the heading: "The Credit Inflation Time Bomb . . ." and opened with the short, sharp paragraph: "America is hooked on debt. Like the addict, a greater increase in net debt is needed each year now to produce a dollar's worth of GNP growth (the 'kick' for the debt addict)." We followed with a voluminous analysis of government debt, corporate debt, consumer credit, mortgage debt, etc., and one of our "warnings" was as follows:

"We said before that, like the addict, a greater and greater increase in annual net debt is now needed to produce a dollar increase in 'Gross National Product.' In the early-1950's, each $1 increase in net debt produced about $1 increase in GNP. This 1-for-1 ratio quickly disappeared and the ratio crept up, in a quite dangerous manner, so that by 1970, the one-year increase in debt was $117 billion, but GNP was up only $45 billion. It had taken a *$2.60* increase in debt to produce a *$1.00* increase in GNP.

"In 1971 the floodgates were really opened on 'easy money' to 'stimulate the economy' and since net debt is expected to hit $2,200 billion by the end of 1972, the ratio of a rise in net debt for each advance in GNP could well leap to new highs. The trend is clearly in the direction of ever higher ratios of debt increases to GNP increase.

"How long can we keep this up?"

For our own subscribers, our answer to this question had already been given in the preceding Survey issue of 6-30-72 when we advised that ". . . Subscribers should err on the side of pessimism rather than optimism and reduce their holdings all along the line. . . ."

But the "grim joke played upon us by history" which we referred to a few paragraphs back had to do with the truly *remarkable* unawareness of what had been developing for decades with crystal clarity—for those who cared to look, of course.

This could hardly be better emphasized than by looking at a recent complete issue devoted to "Debt" by that excellent magazine "Business Week," which did indeed report on "Money" and "Debt" and its associated phenomena on many occasions in the past few decades but, somehow, never saw the whole picture in anywhere near its true dimensions or significance.

This is made clear by the "Publisher's memo" preceding the text of that special issue dated 10-12-74, which read as follows:

". . . This week's Special Issue on the Debt Economy . . . was born months ago because Senior Editor Gordon Williams is nuts about gadgets. One evening, while waiting around for an overdue piece of copy to come in, Williams whiled away the time by experimenting with his latest toy—a brand-new pocket calculator. Looking for something to calculate, he began flipping through a copy of the Federal Reserve Bulletin, and he was struck by the size of the numbers reporting various forms of debt.

"The calculator lit up with a shocking total: The nation is a cool $2.5-trillion in debt. . . . 'Since World War II,' Williams ponts out, 'the key debt indicators grew three times as fast as the key economic indicators.' "

What is "shocking" about a $2.5-trillion total in 1974 when it was $2.2-trillion in 1972?

The fact is that few indeed bothered to "add up the total" as an extraordinary wave of economic "permissiveness" spread across the nation in the decades following the 1945 end of World War II.

It is our considered opinion (we have given these points *much* thought over a *long* period of time) that three factors converged to produce a historic boom, those three factors being:

(1) The awesome attraction of the private automobile for the individual. A true psychological-study-in-depth is yet to be accomplished for this 20th-Century phenomenon.

(2) The discovery by politicians of the election-winning benefits of One-Way Keynesianism, as explained in a previous chapter, leading to a "Balloon-the-Money-Supply" party which reached its peak 1970-1973.

(3) The extraordinary profits which flowed from the development of "The Automobile Culture" for road builders, land spec-

ulators, the construction industry, the oil industry, the trucking industry, etc.—and all their politician "friends."

Profits there were indeed, and "growth" as measured by all kinds of statistics.

But the party is now over and in addition to the "bill" we were paying all along—our ever-growing loss as a *community* in the quality of our lives (how many would dispute that today?) harsh economic reality is presenting us with another "bill"—one for $2.5 trillion in *Debt*. We were running the entire party on borrowed money.

And So We Come To Our Three Guideposts

Although it was more logical to explain our "Three Guideposts" in the order in which we presented them in this book, in these concluding paragraphs we find it necessary to reverse their order for better emphasis.

(1) We don't really have a choice: we *must* bring our "Automobile Culture" back to reasonable proportions;

(2) That "Automobile Culture" is so large a part of our economy now that reducing its proportions must increase unemployment. To meet this problem, and also to reduce the insidious factor of "Inflationary Expectations" as described elsewhere in this book, we must without delay push forward on "Public Employment Policies" which can, properly handled, deliver all manner of benefits to our entire society;

(3) It is completely clear that with crime and corruption adding several hundred billions of dollars each year to our "Cost of Living," we must face up to the fact that:

Corruption IS The Inflation

The quickest path to attacking this threat to our very existence as a nation, and to our ability to lead a world headed for even more apocalyptic struggles, is to fight Corruption right at the top —there isn't *time* to start anywhere else. The corruption in our political system is the true fountainhead of all other corruption and crime in our society, and the strongest weapon we have to fight it is "Full Disclosure" from the President and his Administration, through the Congress down through State and local political systems.

"Full Disclosure" cleaned up most of Wall Street's bad practices after the debacle of the 1930's and we have no doubt whatever that the mere *introduction* of comprehensive "Full Disclosure" requirements for all elected officials would at one stroke eliminate fully one-half of all corruption instantly. The remainder must be dealt with by much harsher penalties than obtain today.

The Future of the Stock Market

It is this writer's opinion that we are going to make surprisingly rapid progress in each of the three areas outlined above. Americans are not stupid! And they are not lacking in the energy to *move* when understanding of where the difficulties come from have crystallized. Thus, we expect the foundation of a new bull market to form in the near future.

The destruction of market values in 1973-1974 has, in our opinion, produced "The Greatest Stock Market Opportunities In Forty Years" and we have done our best to fully detail for readers how those "Opportunities In Warrants" should be approached, and how the "Four-Step Trading Technique" with low-price stocks can produce market profits for years to come once the tide of the market definitively turns.

1975 approaches as we write these concluding words, and we see an America facing many challenges which we have more confidence than we have had in quite a number of years we will be able to surmount because *the eyes* of many more Americans are now open!

If we do face our difficulties squarely, and take the appropriate actions, the title of this book—Fortune Building In the 70's—will be proved appropriate in every respect.